Up Close *with* Lee Kuan Yew

Up Close
with
Lee
Kuan
Yew

Insights from
colleagues
and friends

 **Marshall Cavendish**
Editions

Cover image of Lee Kuan Yew by Bob Lee (www.thefatfarmer.com)
Mr Lee's red box: Courtesy of Ministry of Communications and Information, Singapore
Photos on pages 174–186: Courtesy of Ho Meng Kit, Robert Kuok, Kwa Kim Li,
Liew Mun Leong, Ng Kok Song, Andrew Tan, Wee Cho Yaw, Philip Yeo, Yeong Yoon Ying

Minister Heng Swee Keat's essay on pages 257–262 was originally written for this book but
first published on his Facebook account and then reported in the media on 24 March 2015
upon the demise of Mr Lee Kuan Yew.

Published by Marshall Cavendish Editions
An imprint of Marshall Cavendish International,
1 New Industrial Road, Singapore 536196

Other Marshall Cavendish Offices
Marshall Cavendish Corporation. 99 White Plains Road, Tarrytown NY 10591-9001, USA
• Marshall Cavendish International (Thailand) Co Ltd. 253 Asoke, 12th Flr, Sukhumvit 21
Road, Klongtoey Nua, Wattana, Bangkok 10110, Thailand • Marshall Cavendish (Malaysia)
Sdn Bhd, Times Subang, Lot 46, Subang Hi-Tech Industrial Park, Batu Tiga, 40000 Shah
Alam, Selangor Darul Ehsan, Malaysia

Marshall Cavendish is a trademark of Times Publishing Limited

Library Board Singapore Cataloguing in Publication Data
Up close with Lee Kuan Yew : insights from colleagues and friends. – Singapore : Marshall
Cavendish Editions, [2015]
pages cm

ISBN : 978-981-4677-79-0 (paperback)
ISBN : 978-981-4721-58-5 (hardback)

1. Lee, Kuan Yew, 1923-2015 - Anecdotes. 2. Prime Ministers – Singapore – Anecdotes.
DS610.73.L45
959.5705092 -- dc23   OCN918875316

Printed in Singapore by Markono Print Media Pte Ltd

CONTENTS

FOREWORD 7

Robert Kuok 13 | Yong Pung How 21
Othman Wok 31 | Puan Noor Aishah 37
S.R. Nathan 41 | J.Y. Pillay 53
Lim Chin Beng 57 | Wee Cho Yaw 65
Ch'ng Jit Koon 71 | Sidek Saniff 81
Philip Yeo 93 | Jennie Chua 103
Liew Mun Leong 113 | Lim Siong Guan 129
Jagjeet Singh 133 | Ng Kok Song 141
Lam Chuan Leong 155 | Bilahari Kausikan 159
Stephen Lee 169
Photographs
Li Ka-shing 187 | Tan Guong Ching 189
Dr S. Vasoo 193 | Moses Lee 203
Ho Meng Kit 215 | Yatiman Yusof 227
Yeong Yoon Ying 235 | Alan Chan 241
Peter Seah 251 | Heng Swee Keat 257
Leo Yip 263 | Andrew Tan 269
Peter Tan 277 | Cheng Wai Keung 285
Lee Seow Hiang 291 | Chee Hong Tat 303
Anthony Tan 311 | Lim Teck Kiat 325

FOREWORD

When Mr Lee Kuan Yew passed away in the early hours of 23 March 2015, I had an essay in my computer, titled "Mr Lee's Red Box". It was already fully written — referring to Mr Lee in the present tense. After 23 March, I opened the document, changed the present tense to past tense, rewrote the last lines of the essay, and shared it with the public.

The reason I had a complete document in my computer is because Liew Mun Leong approached me in 2014 to contribute an essay for this book. Earlier that year, Mun Leong and Ong Beng Seng found themselves on the same flight one day, and enjoyed a long chat about Mr Lee. Both had known Mr Lee professionally and in different capacities for many years.

As they exchanged stories about their interactions with Mr Lee, it dawned on them that while much had been said and written about Mr Lee's accomplishments, there was no book that told the personal, more intimate side to him — from the viewpoint of the people who worked very closely with him. They wondered: Wouldn't some Singaporeans like to see Mr Lee at work and outside of work?

So they asked around amongst Mr Lee's friends and colleagues if they would be willing to share their stories. Mun Leong also raised the idea of this book with Mr Lee twice, and Mr Lee had no objections.

Mun Leong then formed a small group with Andrew Tan and Jennie Chua to put the book together. I am pleased to know that the proceeds from the sale of this book will go to a charitable cause.

Mun Leong asked me because I had worked for Mr Lee from 1997 to 2000. I spent some months reflecting on it, and managed to put all my thoughts down only in February of last year, the month before Mr Lee passed away.

We had a week of national mourning in the days following Mr Lee's passing. I spent that week talking with residents who came to community tributes, and going to thank the many who stood in line for hours to pay their respects at the lying-in-state in Parliament House. I felt a deep sense of loss, but that sense of loss was overwhelmed by a growing amazement at the strength and graciousness of fellow Singaporeans.

The day after Mr Lee's funeral, I was supposed to go on a school visit and launch the Junior Sports Academy. We had scheduled these quite some time ago. The thoughtful officers at the Ministry of Education asked me if we should postpone things. After some discussion, I decided to go ahead, as Mr Lee would have wanted things to return to normal as soon as possible.

That was a difficult day. Some of the teachers were emotionally drained. The members of the media who came for the launch were exhausted from the week before. But, I think, we were all buoyed by the children's bright laughter as they played games during their Physical Education class. Their laughter reminded us to keep looking and moving forward.

I later discussed with Mun Leong if I should write another reflection. He felt that the red box story should be a part of this book and suggested I write a foreword to set out the background to this book.

While this was taking place, something happened as a result of the essay.

If you are familiar with the red box story, you may recall that, late one night, after he had been at Mrs Lee's wake, Mr Lee went for a walk along the Singapore River, like he and Mrs Lee had done together when she was alive. In fact, during that period, Mr Lee took many long, late-night walks by himself. He was deep in grief. He could not sleep. The night before Mrs Lee's funeral, at the Singapore River, he saw some trash on the river and he asked his security officers to take a photo of it. In my essay, I guessed that there was probably a note about the trash in the red box the next day, for immediate follow-up. But I couldn't be sure as I was not working for Mr Lee at the time.

A few days after the essay came out, a colleague sent me an email with two photos attached. Some officers at the Ministry of the Environment and Water Resources, after reading the red box story, went to check their records to see if they had ever received any instructions about the trash floating on the Singapore River. They had. Mr Lee had sent over two photos. One picture was of the trash. The other photo was of himself. Mr Lee wrote: "I asked for photos to be taken of the flotsam and of my position against the UOB backdrop so you know where it was." He wanted to pinpoint the location to make it easier for the officers.

I was struck by the date of Mr Lee's email — 6 October 2010, the day of Mrs Lee's funeral. Even in his deepest grief, Mr Lee never stopped caring about Singapore.

The photos were taken late at night, and there wasn't much light. The picture of Mr Lee is blurry, not the kind we are used to seeing in news articles or on book covers. But it does the job. And that's what mattered to Mr Lee. He didn't think of himself as the subject of the picture, only as a marker to point out where work needed to be done.

"I asked for photos to be taken of the flotsam and of my position against the UOB backdrop so you know where it was." These photographs were taken on the eve of the funeral of his wife, Mdm Kwa Geok Choo.

That photo of Mr Lee is bittersweet. He was grief-stricken that he had lost his wife of over 60 years, but he sat upright and friendly, to put his trusted security officers, who remained by his side at his lowest point, at ease.

This is the side of Mr Lee that very few see.

This book shows the sides of Mr Lee that very few have seen. Among the contributors are former President of Singapore S.R. Nathan, Puan Noor Aishah who is the wife of our first President Yusof Ishak, former Chief Justice Yong Pung How, Mr Robert Kuok who was Mr Lee's classmate in Raffles College, all of Mr Lee's former principal private secretaries, as well as friends and leaders in various fields whom Mr Lee rallied to the Singapore cause. Through their recollections, we see his lifelong concern for Singapore and Singaporeans.

Underneath his stern and steely exterior, we see curiosity, discipline, dedication, consideration, and — well-known to those of us who sometimes found ourselves caught between his sweet tooth and Mrs Lee's gentle reminders that he watch his sugar intake — his weakness for ice cream. We see his humility; he sought to learn from everyone, from commanding world and business leaders to fruit sellers in a market in Taiwan to the residents of Tanjong Pagar.

We see the warmth of the man who once told Robert Kuok, "Come to think of it, finally, it's only friendship that matters."

We see a portrait too of Mrs Lee, from Mr Lee's long-serving Press Secretary YY Yeong, and several others. Mrs Lee was an irreplaceable part of Mr Lee's life — he would not have been the man he was, without her.

I thank the book committee for giving me and the other contributors a chance to share our stories about Mr Lee. I would like to thank all the contributors, not just for their time in putting their thoughts to paper, but more importantly for their friendship with Mr Lee and their service together with him to his lifelong cause: Singapore. Mr Lee valued deeply his friends and friends of Singapore. There are many others with meaningful stories to share, whom Mun Leong and his team did not have the chance to approach. I hope we can all continue to share our memories and lessons, and keep moving forward.

We dedicate this book to the late Mr Lee Kuan Yew and his generation of pioneers. We shall do our best to protect and grow this Singapore you built, and keep your pioneering spirit alive.

Heng Swee Keat
March 2016

ROBERT KUOK

Chairman, Kerry Group, Hong Kong

"Come to think of it, finally, it's only
friendship that matters.**"**
– Lee Kuan Yew

I first met Lee Kuan Yew in May 1941 in Raffles College. He was a
second-year student while I was in the first year. I had just completed
my Senior Cambridge examinations at a school in Malaysia, the English
College of Johore Bahru. Raffles College was a wonderful institution
compared with the colonial odour of my former school where some of
the teachers were really quite unpleasant. The main campus of Raffles
College was in Bukit Timah where the first rubber trees were grown
before they were transferred to the Singapore Botanic Gardens.

In college, most of my friends and I got by on shoestring budgets.
My father was supposed to be a rich man but he was not doing well as
that was the time of the Great Depression. My pocket money was so
little I could not even afford an egg daily.

Mr Lee as a college student

I did not know Kuan Yew well in school. In fact, his name did not
come to my attention until later because he was a non-resident student
and lived at home, although I had heard he was brilliant but somewhat
aggressive and pugnacious.

He was a striking figure. I was like him physically, but smaller in
build. He was about two inches taller than me and also heavier. I had

sharp features but his were sharper. He had a compelling and fierce set of eyes, certainly not the eyes of a meek person. He was about three weeks older than me.

One day a friend suggested that I meet Kuan Yew. I was told never to get into an argument with him because he always had to win. To that I replied, "Why would I want to meet him then?"

I was eventually introduced to Kuan Yew. He came across as having a very sharp mind and very strong views on every subject that was being discussed. I think even then he had a clear vision of where he was going. I thought he was also slightly disdainful of people unless he thought you were as smart as him or a very interesting person.

I never had any arguments with Kuan Yew. He was more standoffish than warm but you could sense it was not snobbery. It was because the man had something going on in his mind all the time, probably superior to anything going on in your mind. He just felt there was no point mixing unnecessarily or engaging in small talk.

Among the people at Raffles College was Eddie Barker,[1] who was rather aloof but a gentleman. He was very good-looking, a Gregory Peck type. There was also Maurice Baker,[2] a lovely man and very intellectual. Lee Kuan Yew was certainly among the top ten students at the college, but Kwa Geok Choo, whom he later married, was either No.1 or No.2. Such was the talk among the students.

My dorm was the only one of six dormitories which had a much-used corridor linking College Hall with the cafeteria. I would constantly hear the clickety-clack of women's shoes outside. The most famous pair of sounds belonged to Geok Choo and her friend, Chua Swee Sim, who was the second daughter of Chua Cheng Liat, the founder of the Cycle & Carriage Company. Geok Choo was the taller of the two, and she was the daughter of one of the general managers of OCBC Bank.[3]

Mr Lee during the war

During the war years of 1942–45, I heard Kuan Yew was doing a bit of black-marketing in Singapore, selling second-hand goods such as batteries and retreaded tyres. It was black-marketing because the Japanese Administration had put a tight clamp on almost all activities. We all had to survive.

I was offered a job by Mitsubishi Corp when they decided to open an office in Johore Bahru. I accepted the position and when it opened on 1 August 1942, I was their first local employee. Three years later, on 15 August 1945, Emperor Hirohito announced Japan's surrender. The next morning, the Japanese managers, eyes all swollen and red, some sniffing into their handkerchiefs, came to the office. They said they would soon have to report to concentration camps and the office would be closed.

One evening after the end of the war, I was invited by a Medical College student to a garden party thrown by a rich and famous elderly widow, Mrs Lee Choon Guan,[4] and asked to bring my girlfriend, Joyce Cheah. This was at the end of 1945 or very early in 1946, after three and a half years of occupation by the Japanese Armed Forces, and so everything was still in a broken-down state. We were all drinking orange juice, beer, at most. I remember Kuan Yew was there and he saw this pretty girl, Joyce, and came around to meet her. He said hello to me but was more struck by Joyce's beauty and intelligence. I said to myself, "Eh! Eh!" But it was all harmless.

Later I learnt that Kuan Yew had boarded a troopship and travelled to England to study. He eventually settled at Cambridge University from where he graduated with flying colours.

A forthright man

Kuan Yew achieved a lot and became Prime Minister of Singapore in 1959. He was definitely ruthless. I was close to the action because my brother William, a senior figure in the Malayan Communist Party, felt the heat, although he never directly clashed with him.

Sometime in the late 1960s, something interesting happened which went on for three or four years. Every few months, Kuan Yew would send for me. I would get into my car (the car number would have been earlier supplied to his secretary) and drive up a neat palm-lined driveway to Sri Temasek where he had his office in the Istana grounds. His secretary would greet me and take me to a room where I would sit down, and Kuan Yew would come in shortly. Each time, he wanted my insights into what was going on in Malaysia. He was very forthright and said, "I have an embassy but sometimes I still can't get at the heart of the truth." He would ask questions and I would answer. If I knew the answers and felt they would do no harm to Malaysia, the country of my birth, I would give them. We chatted amiably. I never misguided him. If I felt I could not give him an answer, I told him so.

Mr Lee's frugal ways

One day, the request was to stay for lunch. I wasn't aware that Kuan Yew was so extremely conscious of healthy living until I had lunch with him that day. First, they served soup, not quite four spoons. The soup came with a piece of bread and butter, and I soon realised the bread was very valuable indeed! After the soup came a small piece of fish; after that, a very thin slice of steak. Everything could be eaten in three mouthfuls. And then they brought out the coffee and tea. But I thought I had just had my starters! He was very frugal as well as health-conscious. I certainly respected him for that.

Mr Lee and Singapore's separation from Malaysia

I was one of the first to know about the decision to kick Singapore out of Malaysia. I was living in Queen Astrid Park at the time.

One night in early August 1965, at about 10.30 p.m., there was a banging on my house gate. "Robert! Robert! It's Jamal, open up!" "*Celaka*,[5] what time is it?" I called out. Jamal was the Malaysian High Commissioner to Singapore. He said he had an important message: Razak[6] would be arriving in Singapore from Kuala Lumpur by an Air Force plane at around 6 a.m. and he wanted to go straight to the Bukit Timah Golf Course for a quick round of golf — and he wanted me to play with him.

After tee off, Razak, who was then Deputy Prime Minister of Malaysia, told Jamal to walk ahead as he had something to say to me. He then related to me what had happened the night before at an UMNO[7] leadership meeting in Kuala Lumpur that had gone on till almost midnight. Some extremists in the UMNO leadership were lobbying for the arrest of Singapore's leaders, from Kuan Yew all the way down, but he and other moderate leaders managed to swing the meeting around. He said that arresting them was not a solution as one couldn't keep them in jail forever and they would become political superheroes the day they were released. So they decided the best recourse was to kick Singapore out of the Federation. "I've come to deliver the message to Kuan Yew." I was shocked even though we all saw it coming in some form or shape.

At 4.30 p.m. on Monday, 9 August 1965, Kuan Yew appeared on television and emotionally broke the news to the people of Singapore.[8] It was a very sad and heartbreaking scene.

My reaction at the time was that Kuan Yew, through his brilliant mind and oratorical skills, had riled many UMNO Malays, including

Prime Minister Tunku Abdul Rahman, because in any debate, you could never match Kuan Yew. At that time, I felt he should have been softer or more diplomatic. But now, I realise that it was a blessing in disguise. The timing was just perfect.

Kuan Yew had a very smart and courageous team around him and they immediately carried out brilliant plans and schemes, quite a few of them provided by some of the best advisors in the world. These included the famous Dutch economist Albert Winsemius[9] as well as colonels, majors and captains from the Israeli Defence Force to build up and train the Singapore army.[10] Singapore leaders had also established strong friendships with Taiwan's leaders and the Sultan of Brunei.

What we saw happening in Singapore over the next 15 to 20 years was truly amazing. In any other scenario, the continuing animosity between the extremists in UMNO and the political skills of Singapore's leaders would have led to horrendous consequences.

Mr Lee and our friendship

After I moved to Hong Kong, I sort of became Kuan Yew's second port of call. Run Run Shaw was No.1; my wife Pauline and I, No.2. He liked Pauline and found her simple and earthy ways agreeable.

He and Geok Choo would often come over for dinner. I would get a caterer and offer good food. I would get instructions, of course, that he could not eat this or that. The conversation would be light with interesting anecdotes, and I would like to believe they had pleasant evenings dining at our home.

Kuan Yew and I seldom engaged in super warm or super friendly talk. But sometime in 2007 or 2008, he said a very funny thing that touched my heart. We were walking down from his hotel to the car to go to dinner. Pauline was with Geok Choo in front. He turned to me and said, "Come to think of it, finally, it's only friendship that matters." In other words, everything is gone but the only thing left is friendship. I thought, my God! I am seeing the human side of him!

On their last few visits to Hong Kong, Kuan Yew became increasingly warm towards me. He and Geok Choo would stay in our hotel. She was already unwell and because of her vision problem we pasted coloured paper on the walls of their room so that she wouldn't bump into them. A few years later, I found myself walking with Kuan Yew to make sure he wouldn't bump into the corridor walls.

Kuan Yew visited me a few times after Geok Choo passed away in October 2010. One thing about him I would say is that he stayed true to one woman his whole life, and that is quite remarkable for a man of those times. He led an exemplary life, a disciplined life. He never womanised or drank to excess. He smoked for a short time, but that was it.

Mr Lee and his legacy

About five years ago, in 2010, he wrote me a letter asking for my candid views. He wanted to know why he always found Hong Kong full of business activity and people with strong enterprising spirit. Whenever he visited Hong Kong, he always asked to be taken to some government unit or a home industry where something new was always being invented and he would be totally amazed by what he saw. He asked me to write to him and tell him frankly my views.

So I called up my niece, Kay,[11] and asked if I should talk so straight that I hit him in the solar plexus. She said it sounded like that was what he wanted. So I wrote back to him and told him that he had straightjacketed too many of his people in his zeal and impatience to build up Singapore quickly. There was genius in them, but they could not move. I told him to take a pair of scissors and cut them loose.

Kuan Yew had a super gung-ho style. He was like such a powerful elephant that when he stomped on the ground, all the plants were crushed. But in so doing, he created the miracle called Singapore. Also, because of his great zeal and dedication, Singapore was his obsession, and his attitude and behaviour flowed from that — *You harm Singapore, I smash you.*

My assessment of Singapore as an outsider is that no one could have achieved what Lee Kuan Yew had achieved for Singapore and for the people of Singapore. Singapore, compared to China, is like a drop of water to a bucket of water. But that does not mean the drop of water is not important.

Notes

[1] Edmund William Barker was a Singapore politician who served in the Cabinet from 1964 to 1988. He is considered as one of the Old Guard leaders. He held various appointments, including Minister for Law and Minister for National Development.

[2] Maurice Baker was one of Singapore's first-generation diplomats. He was Singapore's Ambassador to India, Nepal, Malaysia and the Philippines.

[3] OCBC Bank was then known as the Oversea-Chinese Banking Corporation Limited.

[4] Mrs Lee Choon Guan founded the Chinese Women's Association in 1915. She was honoured as a Member of the Order of the British Empire (MBE) for her charitable achievements and for her contributions to the British Red Cross during the First World War.

[5] Malay equivalent word for "damn it".

[6] Tun Abdul Razak bin Hussein. He was the second Prime Minister of Malaysia from 1970 to 1976.

[7] United Malays National Organisation.

[8] The independence proclamation was announced over the radio at 10 a.m.

[9] Albert Winsemius was an economic advisor to the Singapore government for almost 25 years.

[10] Then Defence Minister Goh Keng Swee contacted Mordechai Kidron, the former Israeli Ambassador to Thailand, to ask for assistance in creating Singapore's army. In October 1965, a military delegation from Singapore arrived in Israel.

[11] Kay Kuok is currently Executive Chairman of Shangri-la Hotel, Singapore; Managing Director of Shangri-la Hotels (M) Berhad; and Director of Allgreen Properties Limited. She is also the Chairman of the Board of National Healthcare Group, President of the Singapore Hotel Association, and Director of the Wildlife Reserves Singapore Conservation Fund.

YONG PUNG HOW

Chief Justice of Singapore, 1990–2006

❝I don't like this. It's rubbish. I want
to know exactly what each person said.**❞**
— Lee Kuan Yew

The first time I met Lee Kuan Yew was in Cambridge in 1946. It was the end of my first term at university. I had actually been admitted before the war and was ready to leave, but there were no boats as many had sunk on the journey out. I was stuck and stayed back in Malaya. At the end of the war, I jumped at the opportunity to head out to England, just in time for the opening of the first term.

Kuan Yew had already spent almost one term at the London School of Economics (LSE), which was popular with overseas students in those days. But he was not happy in London because he had been well looked after at home. Those were very grimy days in London; I think he had to wear plastic collars and had trouble getting his shirts clean. He was very unhappy with the living conditions, but not with his studies. He had a fabulous mind. Sometime in October that year, he had made up his mind that if this was what studying in England was like, then he was going to be very unhappy. So he went to his Dean who said, "Look, you are unhappy because of this place. There's nothing wrong with you. Why don't you go to Cambridge? I graduated from Cambridge and it's a lovely town in the middle of the country."

Persuaded by the Dean, he went over to Cambridge to look around. But one term had gone by and there was no vacancy for him as the war had just ended and people were going back to school. He knew a few students at Cambridge from his Raffles College days. One of them was Cecil Wong.[1] Cecil had gone to Fitzwilliam House and he persuaded the university authorities to take Kuan Yew in. He was admitted to Fitzwilliam and attended lectures but was still unhappy and started looking around for a better college. Fitzwilliam then was not a proper college but a non-collegiate body.[2]

He moved around the colleges. Eventually he got to mine, Downing College. I was reading when he walked to my room, knocked on my door, and introduced himself. He gave his name as Harry and asked if there was a place for him in my college. I said I would find out. I remember him telling me that the law subjects taught at LSE were slightly different from Cambridge's. I said to him that if he could persuade someone to let him attend lectures at Cambridge, he should come. It's not so far away from London and he could buy a motorcycle, which he eventually did. At that time, Cambridge was an informal place; I suppose they didn't have proper student records then and it was possible for him to attend lectures like any other student.

He also asked if he could stay with me, but that was not possible as I was sharing the room with another student. So he said he would go back to Cecil and sleep on the floor. He stayed with Cecil for most of the first year until he found his own lodgings. In Cambridge, he had a ramshackle bicycle to get around.

Mr Lee at Cambridge

Even in those days, Kuan Yew had the gift of persuading people. He knew how to get help. We used to meet during lectures and I would lend him my lecture notes and essays. He seemed to know the content better than me. My first impression of him was that he was very bright and quick. I was passably bright, I guess. My tutor would tell us these were all the questions likely to be asked at exams. He met with his own tutors at Fitzwilliam and he also had my notes for at least the first term. He seemed to be very complimentary of them.[3]

Very early on, he impressed everyone. All the lecturers and tutors knew this chap was very bright. They would ask if anyone had any views and up would go the hand of a man called Harry Lee. He had lots of ideas and would often argue with the professors. I was quite shaken by this at first. He asked difficult questions which I thought was a bit audacious. But after a while, I thought he was very good.

I recall Professor Percy Winfield's[4] lectures. Whenever this great man gave a lecture, Harry Lee was one of the few persons who asked anything worthwhile. Once or twice, Professor Winfield even said, "Mr Lee, can you please come to my room after the lecture to discuss that point you wrote to me about?"

In the final year, Kuan Yew was top of the class. He not only got a First, he got a First Class with special distinction. In the class list, his name was there — HKY Lee — and against his name was an asterisk with an explanation at the bottom of the page: It indicated a mark of distinction for work of special merit. That was known as a Starred First and it was very rare. I was told that all the teachers grabbed him and took him to their college rooms, brought out champagne and forced him to drink. He drank it all up and people said they saw him climbing down the stairs, red in the face, and getting into a taxi to go back to his room. He was a star, no question about it.

At that time, he had a very good friend who was President of the Cambridge Union, Percy Cradock.[5] Percy later became Ambassador to the People's Republic of China and brought Margaret Thatcher out to meet Deng Xiaoping. He would stop in Singapore to visit Kuan Yew on his way to China. Percy had diabetes and I heard later from Kuan Yew that his legs had to be amputated. Whenever Kuan Yew was in London, Percy would make a special trip from his home in the north of England just to meet him. When Percy died of diabetes in January 2010, Kuan Yew wrote an obituary which appeared in the *Times*.[6]

Mr and Mrs Lee

Kuan Yew and I did quite well in our first year at Cambridge. His girlfriend, Ms Kwa Geok Choo, came to Cambridge the following year as a Queen's scholar.[7] She managed to get into Girton College.[8] Later, I recall, she told me that they had gotten married at Stratford-upon-Avon. On the way there, he had gone to a shop and bought her a ring.

I didn't know her well, but I thought she was a very nice young lady and I liked her. I met her a few times with Kuan Yew and we talked over some coffee. In fact, I liked her more than I liked him! She was very kind. And she was a Queen's scholar! I heard from other people that if Harry had stayed back in Singapore, it would have been a tough fight between the two for the Queen's Scholarship.

In our third year, she invited Kuan Yew and me to visit her at Girton, about an hour or so from Cambridge city centre by bicycle. She had managed to get some rice and prepared a wonderful meal for us — it was heaven-sent! Kuan Yew's mother was well known in Singapore for her cooking and Geok Choo had learnt how to cook from her, so you can imagine how much we enjoyed the food.

Each time she cooked, she would refuse to let us help. She would buy the ingredients herself even though it was not easy for her to go into town on her own. Occasionally, she would ask us to get meat and eggs. My landlady worked on a farm, so my job was to get an egg or two from her; I would put them in the basket of my bicycle and cycle to Girton. Kuan Yew would go to the butcher and coax him for some chicken or pork.

Mr Lee's kindness

In my second year, I was preoccupied with my studies and so was Kuan Yew. In fact, I nearly failed my second-year exams because I had fallen ill with the flu due to the cold winter. I was put in the sick room where there was only one nurse who tended to me. Every day she would pat me on the face, tell me I was still alive and bring me some lunch. I was sick for about six weeks and missed many lectures that year — and they were difficult subjects like Constitutional Law and Advanced Roman Law. But I somehow squeezed through them.

When I got a little better, I recuperated in my rented lodgings on the other side of Cambridge (I was only allowed to live in the college accommodation for one year). I was still unwell and could hardly get up. In those days, we had no electrical heating, just a coal stove which was good for boiling water. We had to collect our own coal. Once in a while, my landlady's husband, Mr Chapman, would bring me some coal to start a bit of a fire so that I could have hot water to drink. A doctor and a college nurse came by regularly to check on me and give me medicines.

One day, I woke up and found the stove lit. I wondered how that happened. I got out of bed and learnt from Mr Chapman that my friend, Harry Lee, had brought a bucket of coal, carrying it across the common. He added, "Your friend Mr Lee must be very strong because he must have carried it 200 or 300 yards." The bucket was full and Kuan Yew had come through the snow on foot because he couldn't very well carry it on a bicycle. It must have been more than half a mile from his lodgings. I will never forget this kindness of his.

Perhaps few people would describe him as kind and humane. But he certainly was very kind to me.

Mr Lee's hospitality

After graduating, I went back to Kuala Lumpur where my father[9] had a small law firm[10] and was working for Tan Cheng Lock.[11]

I travelled to Singapore a few times, hoping to get some lead work. I would meet up with Kuan Yew and he would take me out for lunch at a chicken rice stall in Middle Road. On my first visit, he asked where I was staying. I told him I was at the hotel next to the railway station. He said, "Oh, it's a terrible place! I have a spare room in the house." So I stayed with him a few times at Oxley Road. I think I slept in what would eventually become his daughter Wei Ling's room because she wasn't born then. He was very kind to me. The first time I went to his home, his mother, whom I had already heard was a very famous cook, insisted I stay for dinner. She cooked everything. I think I nearly burst myself that night.

When Kuan Yew won the elections in 1959 and became Prime Minister, I would meet him at his office at City Hall and we would go for lunch. Those were good times.

One of his favourite fruits was pomelo. Once, while enjoying some pomelo at his office, he told me it was from Ipoh, specially brought in by Malayan Airways pilots. At the end of that visit, he called his secretary to ask how many of the fruit were left and asked her to put two in my car.

The last time I saw Kuan Yew was in late December 2014, at a dinner, together with a group of his friends. They always included me in these dinners which were held every two months; they considered me to be his oldest friend, I guess, at least in age. Someone would organise a dinner for him. They would give the excuse that the poor chap was lonely, but actually all they wanted were his views. He knew everything!

Mr Lee as a co-worker and boss

There were a couple of occasions after graduation where Kuan Yew and I worked together on some legal cases. In one case, the richest man in Penang had insulted Dr Lim Chong Yew, a prominent politician and medical doctor. We worked on the case together for a short while until it was settled. We also did a few other small cases together. At that time he was famous as a lawyer.

Clearly, he was brilliant. He was the most brilliant man I have ever met. If he was on a legal case, he would work through every detail and angle. When he set up the People's Action Party, he was absolutely thorough, in the same way he responded to questions at university or analysed cases. When we studied our cases, he always made sure he covered everything.

The very first time he came to Kuala Lumpur was in the early 1950s. We went for dinner at a restaurant in an amusement park in Bukit Bintang. We walked into a room that was empty but this newspaper chap, who was part of a wedding reception in the next room, noticed him and recognised him as Lee Kuan Yew from Singapore. He came up to Kuan Yew and asked him some questions, and soon half of the wedding guests trooped over. I think Kuan Yew never ever liked any of this attention.

In 1982, when I was vice-chairman of OCBC Bank, I was seconded to the government to help restructure the Monetary Authority of Singapore. Eventually, I was appointed to head the Government of Singapore Investment Corporation.[12] But I had to leave after a while.

What happened was that there had been a question asked in Parliament which was filed but not published. The issue was about Singapore money being transferred to a Malaysian. Dr Goh Keng Swee asked me, "Are you a Malaysian?" Indeed I was. So I was sent to see Lim Siong Guan, who was then principal private secretary to Kuan Yew, who then said I should become a Singapore citizen. He would put up a paper with three names — Lee Kuan Yew, Hon Sui Sen and Goh Keng Swee — and also get them to sign it. I remember going to Empress Place to get this done. There was a nice lady there who gave me a book. I held it, took an oath, and so I became a citizen.

I then worked for Lim Kim San.[13] I was in a room next to Dr Goh, who was at the Ministry of Education at the time; Kim San's office was across from Dr Goh's. I was actually on loan to Kim San because he was short of staff. He wanted someone to write letters for him — he said lawyers always wrote good letters — but he looked at me and said to Dr Goh, "I just don't like this bloody chap." Dr Goh dismissed it and told me Kim San was just in a bad mood that day.

The next time I saw Kim San, he was in a good mood and had forgotten we had ever met. I wrote simple letters for him; they were for his constituents or people requesting help from him, promising them that things would be done but that it would take time and we would do our best in the meantime. Kim San was very nice to me after that.

I had learnt to write very short letters, and the minutes I wrote while at the Government of Singapore Investment Corporation were also short. When I first gave the minutes to Kuan Yew, its new chairman, he said, "I don't like this. It's rubbish. I want to know exactly what each person said." He wanted more details.

In 1989, Kuan Yew was looking for a new Chief Justice and he said my name had been put up by several judges. He said, "Think about it," and told me to make a decision quickly.

I replied, "Can I think about it?"

He said, "That was what I said. But I hope your answer will be yes because you have done nothing for Singapore!" He practically scolded me, bringing up the fact that I had declined his offer to be a Supreme Court judge in 1972.

He said there was no time to waste. I asked him what I was supposed to do. He said, "Become Chief Justice! Just clean up the whole thing, you know what to do."

I said, "Fair enough. But if the job is too much for me, will you release me?"

There was no answer. The next thing I knew, he was telling people he had found a person and my name was published in the papers. So that was how I became Singapore's second Chief Justice.

Notes

1 Cecil Wong attended Raffles College and read law at Cambridge University. After graduating, he went to LSE where he studied accountancy. He returned to Singapore after six years in London to helm his father's accountancy business. His father, Mr Evan Wong, set up one of Singapore's first accounting firms, Evan Wong & Company, in 1926. Cecil Wong is an independent director for locally listed Pan United and Venture Corporation, as well as two other privately owned businesses.

2 Fitzwilliam College is one of the constituent colleges of the University of Cambridge. The college traces its origins back to 1869. It was a non-collegiate body for poorer students where the fees were much lower. Fitzwilliam attained collegiate status in 1966.

3 Lee Kuan Yew, *The Singapore Story: Memoirs of Lee Kuan Yew*, Prentice Hall 1st Edition, 1998. Lee Kuan Yew mentioned that Yong Pung How's notes were "in a neat hand, comprehensive and a good synopsis of the ground I had missed."

4 Sir Percy Winfield was Professor of English Law from 1928 to 1943. He was the author of *The Chief Sources of English Legal History*.

[5] Sir Percy Cradock was British Ambassador to the People's Republic of China from 1978 to 1983. He played a significant role in the Sino-British negotiations which led up to the signing of the Sino-British Joint Declaration 1984 on the return of Hong Kong.

[6] "Lives Remembered: Sir Percy Cradock", *The Times*, 6 February 2010.

[7] The Queen's Scholarships was a British colonial government scheme which enabled two promising students each year to enroll at a British university. From 1885, this scheme provided most Singaporeans and Malayans with their only opportunity for tertiary education before Raffles College opened in 1929. The scholarship ceased after 1910 but was revived in 1923. From 1931, the government of the Federated Malay States offered two Queen's Scholarships annually, reserving one for Malays, until the scheme was abolished in 1959.

[8] Girton College was England's first residential college for women. Established in 1869, it obtained full college status in 1948 and marked the official admittance of women to Cambridge University. Kwa Geok Choo had been awarded the Queen's Scholarship but the colonial office could not find her a place. Lee Kuan Yew convinced Miss Kathleen Butler, the mistress of Girton, to accept Kwa Geok Choo into the university.

[9] Yong Shook Lin was a lawyer in Kuala Lumpur and also a member of the Federal Legislative Council, serving in its Executive Council both before and after the war.

[10] Shook Lin & Bok was founded in 1936 in Malaya by Yong Shook Lin and Tan Teow Bok. In 1964, Shook Lin & Bok was established in Singapore in an effort to create a pan-Asian law firm.

[11] Tan Cheng Lock was a Chinese Malaysian businessman who founded the Malaysian Chinese Association, which advocated for the Malaysian Chinese population.

[12] Government of Singapore Investment Corporation is a sovereign wealth fund established by the Government of Singapore to manage Singapore's foreign reserves. It was later renamed GIC Private Limited.

[13] Lim Kim San was the first chairman of the Housing and Development Board, a position he assumed in 1960. Under his leadership, Singapore's public housing programme took off successfully. He also held other government appointments in the 1960s and 1970s, as Minister for Finance, Minister for Interior and Defence, Minister for Environment, Minister for Communications and Minister for National Development. He was Member of Parliament for Cairnhill constituency from 1963 to 1980. From 1981 to 1982, he was Deputy Managing Director of the Monetary Authority of Singapore.

OTHMAN WOK

Minister for Social Affairs, 1963–1977

"He was from Telok Kurau Primary School and was very familiar with the Malay community.**"**

– Othman Wok

I first met Mr Lee in 1952 at the *Utusan Melayu* office where I was news editor of the Malay language newspaper.[1] He had come to offer a story to us, as a representative of the Singapore Post and Telegraph Uniformed Staff Union. Postal workers had gone on strike for better salaries, working conditions and uniforms, interrupting postal services for a couple of days. Then they went on to arbitration. Mr Lee was their legal advisor and spokesman, and he managed to get them some of their demands. He had come to tell us about the results of the negotiation as most of the postal service staff were Malay.

I noticed straightaway that he was a great leader. He had a strong personality and came across as very honest and sincere. He was also impressive and charming, and generally pleasant, as long as you were honest and sincere with him.

Mr Lee and the Malay community

In 1959, I campaigned in Kampong Kembangan but we lost to the Singapore branch of the Malaysian political party, UMNO (United Malays National Organisation). It was hard work to win the constituency back from UMNO. Mr Lee accepted the loss and encouraged me to do my best.

The People's Action Party (PAP) had a branch there where we held Meet-the-People sessions. At first, very few people turned up and most of those who did came to seek help for citizenship and employment matters. Very few Malays attended the sessions but that changed when the incumbent legislative member for Kembangan did not look after the constituency well. The Malays started coming to see me for help to improve the village, to get rid of mosquitoes and to clear the drains. They also asked for a community centre. I got them all that and that is how we won over the Malays there eventually.[2]

When Mr Lee became Prime Minister, the first thing he did was to call in members of the PAP to form the Malay Affairs Bureau to discuss the best way to help the Malay community move forward faster to be on par with the rest of the community. One of the suggestions was to give free education to Malay students from the primary to tertiary levels so that Malay parents would not have to worry about school fees. That was his first move to help the Malay community in Singapore upgrade themselves through education. The Malay Affairs Bureau always gave its perspective on how things would affect the Malay community as a whole in Singapore. Mr Lee listened to us and we guided him so as to maintain a multiracial Singapore.

Mr Lee was well-liked by the Malay community. He mixed well with the Malay boys in school. He was from Telok Kurau Primary School and was very familiar with the Malay community. He could speak Malay very well and he had lots of Malay friends, besides the party members.

One day in 1963, Mr Lee told me he wanted me to become a Cabinet minister. I was very surprised but took up the offer to work with others like Rahim Ishak[3] and Ya'acob Mohamed[4] to help bring people together. We had all wanted to establish a multiracial society in

Singapore because we knew that without this, it would not be easy for Singapore to survive.

On 13 July 1964, then UMNO Secretary-General Syed Jaafar Albar[5] gave a communally charged speech at the Pasir Panjang New Star Theatre in Singapore, where the audience was made up mostly of UMNO people, not only from Singapore but also from across the causeway. They were very emotional and were shouting "Kill Lee Kuan Yew! Kill Othman Wok, the traitor!" I was frightened, but I have always believed in multiracialism and I will stand up for it come what may.

Mr Lee's reaction at the time? He knew it was all big talk. How can you just kill the Prime Minister of Singapore?

A few days before Malaysian Prime Minister Tunku Abdul Rahman decided to ask Singapore to leave Malaysia on 9 August 1965, Mr S. Rajaratnam, who was our Minister for Culture, called me. It was a Friday night, on the 6th, I think. He said, "Come to my house tomorrow, Saturday. Drive your own car and don't tell anyone you're going back to KL."

I asked, "Why? Have they arrested PM?"

He said, "No, just drive up."

So we drove up to Kuala Lumpur and went straight to our Singapore house. There, I saw Mr Lee. He had a piece of paper and showed it to Mr Rajaratnam. It was a letter from Tunku saying that it was decided that Singapore should opt out of Malaysia.

Mr Lee then showed me the letter and called me into a room. He was a bit uncertain about what my response would be, being a Malay. He asked me what I thought. I said, "I am a Cabinet minister. I am a PAP man. I am a Singaporean. So I agree." Then I asked him what he was going to do about the communists in Singapore. He said, "Don't you worry. I will handle them."

I had never known Mr Lee to be an emotional man so I was quite surprised to see him cry on television when he announced the news to the public. I think the next time I saw him cry was at his 75th birthday celebrations[6] when he was speaking about me and how I was loyal to the party. I felt a bit embarrassed.

Mr Lee as a colleague and friend

We had a close working relationship. He was a great leader and always very serious when it came to work. He seldom joked but he was very friendly and always willing to help others as long as you were sincere and honest with him. That was why he was very popular with the Malay community. They felt they could trust him.

I never had arguments with him. I respected him very much. When he discussed something, he always did so thoroughly, stating his reasons clearly and asking for our opinions. He would listen to us. There were times he changed his mind but he would always give reasons for his decisions. Usually, though, after explaining to us, we would always agree with him. We knew that what he proposed was for the good of Singapore.

Notes

1   Othman Wok joined *Utusan Melayu* as a clerk. In 1946, he was offered a reporter position. He pursued his diploma in journalism in London on a Colonial Development Scholarship in 1950. When he returned in 1951, he was promoted to news editor, and later became the newspaper's deputy editor in 1957. He resigned in 1963 when he was elected Assemblyman for Pasir Panjang Constituency following victory in the 1963 general elections.

2   Othman Wok represented Pasir Panjang from 1963 to 1977. He was also the Minister for Home Affairs in 1963 and the Minister for Social Affairs from November 1963 to 1977. He was Ambassador to Indonesia from 1977 to 1980.

³ Abdul Rahim Ishak (1925–2001) was the youngest brother of Yusof Ishak, Singapore's first Head of State and President. In 1959, Rahim Ishak entered politics and his first appointment was Political Secretary, Ministry of Culture. In 1963, he contested as a PAP candidate in Siglap and won. He remained the Member of Parliament for Siglap until 1984. He also served in the Education and Foreign Affairs ministries. He was Ambassador to Indonesia from 1974 to 1977. In 1981, he was appointed as the High Commissioner to New Zealand. He retired in 1987.

⁴ Haji Ya'acob bin Mohamed (1925–89) was a former politician and diplomat. He was a member of UMNO before joining PAP in 1958. In 1959, Haji Ya'acob won the Bukit Timah seat in the Legislative Assembly, followed by the Southern Islands seat in 1963. He also held various appointments including Parliamentary Secretary of the Ministry of National Development, and Minister of State and Senior Minister of State in the Prime Minister's Office. In 1968, he became the first Member of Parliament for the Kampong Ubi constituency, a seat he held for three terms. He was Singapore's first Ambassador to the Philippines (1969–71), High Commissioner to India (1977–84) and Ambassador to Egypt (1984–86).

⁵ Syed Jaafar Albar was a Malaysian politician. He resigned as UMNO Secretary-General in 1965 after Singapore's separation from Malaysia.

⁶ Speech by Senior Minister Lee Kuan Yew at his 75th birthday celebrations and the launch of his memoirs at the Suntec City Ballroom, 16 September 1998. Extracted from SM Lee's speech: "Othman, I remember your staunch support and loyalty during those troubled days when we were in Malaysia and tensions were most severe immediately before and following the bloody race riots in July 1964. At that time, the greatest pressures were mounted by UMNO Malay extremists who denounced PAP Malay leaders, especially you, as infidels and traitors to the Malay race. I heard it, the crowd heard it and it was designed for you. Because of the courage and leadership you showed, not a single PAP Malay leader wavered."

PUAN NOOR AISHAH

*Wife of Singapore's first President, Yusof bin Ishak,
who served from 1965–1970*

**"When he spoke in Malay his diction sounded
like one who had been schooled in Malay."**

– Puan Noor Aishah

I do not know when my husband first met Mr Lee Kuan Yew. I am
told that sometime in 1953 my husband went to consult Mr Lee as a
lawyer at Laycock & Ong. My husband was then the Editor-in-Chief
and Managing Director of *Utusan Melayu* which he had started some
years earlier. My husband went to see Mr Lee to consult him because
Samad Ismail, a sub-editor of *Utusan Melayu*, had been arrested and
interned by the British on St John's Island. This led to other meetings
between my husband and Mr Lee.

The first time I met Mr and Mrs Lee was when they visited our
house in Gombak, Kuala Lumpur. Mr and Mrs Lee and their children
were on their way to Cameron Highlands for a holiday. Whilst my
husband and Mr Lee carried on a conversation about political issues
and other matters of the day, Mrs Lee and I spoke about our respective
children. Mrs Lee was extremely kind and gentle; and I had been told
by my husband that she was a very clever lawyer. I felt very comfortable
in the company of Mrs Lee.

Some ten years later, in 1963, my husband consulted Mr E.W.
Barker of Lee & Lee to make his last will. It is significant to note that
my late husband appointed Mrs Lee as one of the trustees of his will.

Mrs Lee, however, renounced probate when my husband passed away in 1970 because she was of the view that I would be able to administer my late husband's estate with her advice and help. I am mentioning this fact to show my late husband's absolute trust in Mrs Lee.

Although Mr Lee appeared formidable and overbearing in the public eye, he was always polite, kind and gentle to me. When we attended formal dinners at the Istana, Mr Lee would normally sit next to me. He spoke freely with me on simple matters so that I would be at ease with him and take part in the conversation. At such functions, both Mr and Mrs Lee were very kind and considerate to me because they knew that I was more fluent in Malay than in English.

There are a few personal observations that I can make of Mr Lee, having observed him at close quarters. First, he had a formidable personality and loomed larger than life. Secondly, he spoke in a measured manner with a clear diction and tone. Thirdly, when he spoke in Malay his pronunciation and diction sounded like one who had been schooled in Malay or Bahasa. Fourthly, he was extremely kind and polite to my children and I despite his high office. Finally, though serious by disposition he had a unique sense of humour which he often muffled with a smile.

When my husband passed away in 1970, Mr Lee came to see me. He said that the Cabinet had been thinking of giving me a pension as I was not working and my children were still young. Mr Lee kept his word and subsequently raised the matter in Parliament for me to be given a pension for life. I am still receiving the pension to this day. I understand I am the only widow of a former President to receive such a pension.

My children and I will forever be grateful to Mr Lee for first identifying and selecting my husband from amongst so many others to be the first Yang di Pertuan Negara (Head of State) and later President of Singapore, even though he was just the managing editor of a Malay newspaper; and secondly, for reposing on my husband the trust and confidence to discharge the duties and functions of that high office. I am very pleased that my late husband did not disappoint Mr Lee in this regard. I am also eternally grateful to Mrs Lee for her warmth, kindness and advice during those years.

You may ask what is Mr Lee's legacy to Singapore. In my humble view, there are not many men in history who had transformed a little island of mudflats and tiny villages into a thriving metropolis and city-state in one generation. What is unique is that when Singapore separated from Malaysia some 50 years ago, most political commentators and pundits felt that with the pull-out of the British forces — and with neither natural resources nor hinterland to sustain its growing population — Singapore would not survive as a nation. This was compounded by the fact that Singapore had a multiracial, multicultural and multireligious population, and racial tensions, political strife and the threat of communalism and communism loomed large over Singapore's survival as a nation.

It was through the vision, genius and stewardship of Mr Lee (and a handful of his original colleagues) that we now have a thriving metropolis and city-state where 85 per cent of its population live in homes built by the government (through the Housing and Development Board) and with a standard of living that many advanced nations would be proud of. It is a city-state that is a beacon in this part of the world with an infrastructure and modern facilities like hotels, an efficient underground train network, museums, theatres and an international airport. It is above all a garden city with five million trees. In my view, Singaporeans should be grateful to Mr Lee for all this.

Finally, on a personal note, my family and I will always remember Mr Lee for what he had done for Singapore. He had dedicated his whole political life to create an honest and just society which future generations of Singaporeans will be proud of. It is my fervent hope that future leaders of Singapore will continue his good work and try to emulate his example in whatever they do.

S.R. NATHAN

President, Republic of Singapore, 1999–2011

❝I must honour what they have given me.❞
– Lee Kuan Yew

I was in his shadow. I lived and worked for him for many years. He came to me, later in life, as some sort of "revolutionary" bent on making multiracial people "unite" to make Singapore what it is today. Later on, he focused on "development" so that Singapore would continue on its path to prosperity. He was an extraordinary man for the times, indeed, most extraordinary.

My first meeting

I first saw Mr Lee in 1953, in Singapore, at the University of Malaya campus where I was a student. He was with his wife. He was curious, always looking around, paying a lot of attention to his surroundings. This was my first impression of him. He remained a keen observer throughout the years. He observed everything.

The second time I saw him was when I was secretary of the University Socialist Club. The club, which was formed in 1953, was divided into three groups: leftists, moderates and the in-betweens. I belonged to the moderates. I soon learnt that this man was only interested in the leftists. He invited them to his tea parties; he never invited the moderates. When the "Fajar"[1] case was brought up by the government and came up for hearing, the leftists of course approached him and he went to their defence. He seemed a little uncertain to me and it was only in the later years that I saw the purpose of his closeness with the left.

Development of relations

Later, as I got involved with trade union meetings, Prime Minister Lee became more familiar to me. But I was in the shadow of Devan Nair who had helped establish the National Trades Union Congress (NTUC). He and Nair met regularly and I would be there when they discussed local politics. By then, things had changed. Strikes were frequent. This man who was pro-left was now dealing with the left, and I saw the reason for his meetings with Nair. I was working at NTUC then and left in 1965.

The next year, I joined the Ministry of Foreign Affairs. It was new — the minister was new, the permanent secretary was also new, and so were the few senior officers. We were all housed in the same building at City Hall. Mr Lee's office was on the third floor and those of the Foreign Affairs ministers were on the first floor, along with the Public Utilities Board. The government was very small then. Although I had come from NTUC and was a civil servant, I think some of my colleagues in the ministry were wary of me possibly because Mr Lee was always talking to me.

Once, in the early years in the ministry, Mr Lee met with the Thai Foreign Minister. I was told to attend the meeting and take notes. At that time, I had my fears of the man. He was a daunting figure. I felt like I was being thrown into the lion's den. I went to the meeting with a lot of apprehension. But what surprised me was that he came directly to me, adjusted my necktie in a fatherly way, and said, "You're no longer in the labour movement, you must dress properly." This overwhelmed me. My impression of him changed from then on. He was no longer a dangerous man to me, but someone extremely kind and protective. At that meeting, I decided not to take notes. I just listened. Everything was in my head. I could see Mr Lee was apprehensive but I thought the conversation wouldn't be free if I took notes. So after the meeting, I went back and did the notes and sent them to him. He wrote back: Good report. From then on, he would invite me to sit in frequently to take notes. I sat in on his meetings with foreign ministers from the United Kingdom, Australia, New Zealand, India and the United Arab Emirates.

At another important meeting (it was with either the Australian or New Zealand High Commissioner), I told myself I could not afford to miss out any points and so I wrote lengthy notes. He wasn't too pleased with that. He called me and said, "You think I have nothing else to do except to read your notes?" Before I could explain myself, he told me to take it away and said there should be no notes beyond four pages. In other words, you should only write the essence of the discussion so as to keep it within four pages.

In 1971, he sent me to the Ministry of Home Affairs, where I was acting Permanent Secretary. I was at the ministry for about nine months until Dr Goh Keng Swee had me transferred to the Security and Intelligence Division (SID). I worked closely with Dr Goh at SID. While there, Mr Lee would still call me to ask questions and I had to be ready to give an answer.

One of the things I learnt from working with Dr Goh was to think ahead. You never knew what questions the Prime Minister would ask and if you didn't have an answer, you had to tell him so and ask for some time to get back to him with the answers. When I was with SID, I became even closer to Mr Lee. The relationship I had with both Mr Lee and Dr Goh was one of closeness. They would sit me at the table, and we would eat and discuss many issues, particularly about trade and politics.

In 1979, Mr Lee sent me back to the Foreign Affairs ministry. He told me he would give me two years to improve it and added that if it didn't improve, the ministry would go to the Prime Minister's Office. In other words, if it failed, my head would be chopped off. So I worked very hard, morning, noon and night. In two years, the ministry changed. He continued to call me and ask me questions. That was when our relationship really began. There was a sense of relief when one day, he acknowledged publicly that the ministry was up to his mark. In fact, I am grateful to Mr Lee for accepting me despite my lack of qualifications. I had only a diploma[2] whereas many of my colleagues had university degrees. They called me the "Maverick". He never asked for my qualifications.

I next joined Straits Times Press. How that all began was interesting. I still remember it was a Saturday when Peter Lim, the leading journalist in *The Straits Times*, rang me at home and told me he had had a long meeting with Mr Lee. I think this was in 1981. He said he had given my name to Mr Lee as a possible senior official in Straits Times Press. I kept quiet. The next day, I received a call from Mr Lee. He said he wanted me to go to Straits Times Press. I told him that I was already 55 years old and had no journalism experience. That did not matter, he said. He assured me that I could go to him if I had any problems.

The day before I joined the newspaper, I went to see Mr Lee. He told me he had now given me a porcelain jar and if I were to break it into pieces, he could put it back together but it would never be the same. I just kept quiet.

He stared at me and said, "You're keeping quiet."

I replied, "You've already told me what to do and what not to do."

He then smiled. During the six years I was with Straits Times Press, there was only one occasion when he scolded me, and that was in Fiji when somebody leaked information that damaged our security interest.

After Straits Times Press, in 1988, Mr Lee wanted me in Kuala Lumpur.[3] So there I went where I made a point of visiting various states to get to know the many personalities and state leadership. Every time he came to KL, I would be there. On one occasion, when things were not going well, I asked him what the mood was like. He replied sombrely that the Malaysian Prime Minister had his daggers set on me. I told him I had not done anything wrong but he said that I was too active. In my defence, I said I was merely doing my job. The next morning, he informed me that I was to go to Washington. I was there for several years during the Bush and Clinton administrations.[4]

On my return to Singapore in 1996, Dr Tony Tan[5] asked me to start the Institute of Defence and Strategic Studies.[6] This was part of Nanyang Technological University. The university had no political science department so I had a free hand. Of course, there were occasions when I was questioned by senior university staff.

Then one night in 1999, Mr Lee called me and asked all sorts of questions, like the age of my children and what they were doing. It was 11 p.m. and my wife was curious as to who was on the phone at such a late hour. She was somehow anxious as well. He then told me to see him the next morning.

The next day, he said, "I want you to be the presidential candidate but there's no guarantee you would be chosen. I will only throw in your name as a candidate."

I told him I needed to consult my wife. My wife and I discussed the matter and we realised we could not say no to him for all he had done over the years. He had this ability to command personal loyalty!

Mr Lee's purpose

If I were to come up with three words to describe Mr Lee, they would be: determined, uncompromising and purposeful.

Right from the days of the trade unions, I knew his purpose. I could almost feel it. That was the relationship I had with him. He was determined to do what was right for Singapore. He lived purposefully to achieve what he wanted. He had his frustrations and disappointments but he never wavered. For the labour movement, he did what he felt was necessary, admonishing workers when they were wrong and encouraging them when they were right. I learnt purpose from him and then saw it as my duty to carry out my purpose.

He had a purpose and somehow you would want to get that purpose. Whether the future generation will see his purpose in the same way I did, I am not sure.

He had one big purpose — to have Singapore recognised. The future generation may look towards the Americans, the Chinese, the Indians, but their purpose should be here, in Singapore. I always say, we are almost like the Pilgrim Fathers. We were taken by him across the sea and reached the Promised Land; indeed we had a land to build on. But in 1965, our dreams were shattered. The idea that we were discarded made us stand up for ourselves.

I think it would take another one or two generations before we can begin to see purpose again. I only hope the young will understand Mr Lee's purpose. Singapore saw a glimmer of that in his death but whether it would carry us through the next phase is something we will have to wait and see. Life is too easy and comfortable for young Singaporeans right now so it is going to be hard to find a common purpose. The world is their oyster. It's natural that the young people cannot see purpose but once they have a family, maybe they will.

What I miss most about Mr Lee is his perfectionism. Anything you sent to him, if it came back with no correction, well, you would be happy.

Mr Lee's beliefs

Mr Lee always believed in the community helping themselves, and he had a strong sense about people, their culture and their different interests. One telling example is the Mosque Building Fund.

He said, "Each Muslim will donate one dollar to the Mosque Building Fund. I want them to feel that they are building their own mosques and that they are not using the government's money. It's their mosque."

What many people don't understand is that my generation, and Mr Lee's, never thought of ourselves as Indians or Chinese or Malays. We only thought of ourselves as Malayans. That was what was common. We never thought of ourselves as Singaporeans.

Mr Lee's uncompromising ways

In 1976, Mr Lee went to Beijing. There, Chinese Premier Hua Guofeng presented him with a book, saying, "This is the correct version of the war between China and India. I hope you will find it useful."

He took it, looked at the front cover, looked at the back, and said, "Mr Prime Minister, this is your version of the war. There is another version, the Indian version. And in any case, I am from Southeast Asia. It's nothing to do with us."

Then, he handed the book back to the premier. It took extreme courage to do that in China, especially as a guest and after touring the Great Wall and all that. I remember feeling very proud of Mr Lee's convictions. I am sure many others in the entourage felt the same.

Mr Lee's influence

I saw his good moments, his angry moments but, above all, I saw the exceptional way he conducted himself in public, and I strived to emulate him during the 12 years I was President.

I noticed that on official trips overseas, Mr and Mrs Lee never asked to see any stage shows or go on sightseeing tours. There was a clear line between the official time and private time. Likewise, I did that too during my Presidency.

I remember a trip to Zambia where we were provided with bungalows. University students had been assigned to serve Mr Lee but they did not even know how to poach an egg! I went to him and asked if I should arrange for him to stay in a hotel. His reply surprised me. He said, "I must honour what they have given me."

There were many other such instances. He never wavered and always stood by his principles. He taught me how to "behave" in public.

Mr Lee and his peers

S. Rajaratnam, Goh Keng Swee, Lim Kim San and Eddie Barker — they were all his comrades in arms.

Dr Goh would say to Mr Lee, "Why don't you shut up and talk some sense?" This happened on many occasions with Dr Goh and other ministers but Mr Lee would also tell them off if they were wrong. It was a kind of banter but it expressed the personal relationship among them. Sometimes their meetings would drag on and continue into the following week. They were in the post-independence struggle together and they accepted each other as equals. There were no questions of superiority.

Mr and Mrs Lee

On his first tour to Africa, we travelled to many places across Asia and Africa, and then to Europe, including Colombo, Bombay, Kenya, Cairo, Germany, Russia, Paris and London — where we parted company. It was a long trip and that was when I got to see him most intimately.

He went everywhere with Mrs Lee. At dinner time, if he happened to see me waiting outside the restaurant, he would ask me to join them for dinner. Even as I sat there, they would continue with their conversation. He was not a prime minister, he was a man to his wife.

Mr Lee was a quick-tempered man and Mrs Lee would intervene when necessary. At times, during dinner, Mrs Lee would say, "Come on Harry, why don't you listen to them first instead of jumping to conclusions?" or she would say, "Don't be silly." Indeed, Mrs Lee was his stabilising force.

Mr Lee never chided Mrs Lee in my presence. They may disagree, but there was no victor in any arguments.

My last meeting

The last time I met him was in early 2015 when Goh Chok Tong invited us for lunch. Mr Lee didn't talk much although we all tried to engage him. It was a lunch of quiet moments.

Mr Lee's legacy

The other day, my wife and I took a drive to Punggol. We saw a lot of greenery. There are trees all around the island. The number of trees that we see today all over Singapore is a tribute to Mr Lee. I remember back in 1963, when I was living in Bukit Panjang, there was a massive clearing of trees on a hill to make way for attap houses. It all happened so fast and within three days all the trees were felled. We were in Malaysia then and had no control of the situation.

When Mr Lee passed away, young Singaporeans who had never known him or who were critical of him suddenly saw his hand in the greening of Singapore. With this realisation came the outpouring of emotions. Even the older Singaporeans who were critical of him felt a sense of loss.

However, we must remember that the legacy is not Mr Lee's alone; it is together with all his comrades. The memory may fade in time but we will remember his resolve and how we arrived here.

What I remember of Mr Lee

Looking back these 50 years, I would say that he came into our lives, saw — and at the end, transformed — our experience of Colonial Rule and the experience of Internal Self-Government. In the days leading to, and during the pain and turmoil of, Malaysia, he led us to a Revolution and a path of National Unity. He called on the people to face the needs of future Singapore, that is, multiracialism and security, followed by the road to affluence. The enormity of that task did not deter him at all. During that period there must have been frustrations and failures which he did not share with us. For Mr Lee, Singapore was a mission.

During those times he never spoke to me about what was happening or his objectives. I came to my conclusions by watching the tensions around me. I witnessed Mr Lee and his colleagues debate and argue. I learnt much then; it was to me my own Long March. What struck me was his great resolve and determination to win arguments. These were times when I felt, at the end of each argument, that he had accomplished something. At other times, there was disappointment written in his eyes. Being in his presence at such times, I even felt his pains as he addressed the many issues that befell the young nation.

These are the memories I carry with me, of the man who nurtured me in my adulthood. No doubt it was 50 years of much tension and uncertainty. But I can't ask for more of what was a privileged and invaluable experience to work with Mr Lee and see his vision at such close range. His hope was that multiracialism would survive the passage of time and the geopolitics of the region.

Notes

1   *Fajar* was the title of a monthly periodical published by the University of Malaya Socialist Club. In the "Fajar" case, the British arrested, in 1954, student members of the editorial board and charged them with sedition over the anti-colonial sentiments that were expressed in the publication.

2   Diploma in Social Studies from the University of Malaya.

3   S.R. Nathan was High Commissioner to Malaysia from 1988 to 1990.

4   He was Ambassador to the United States from 1990 to 1996.

5   Dr Tony Tan was Deputy Prime Minister from 1993 to 2005 and Minister for Defence from 1995 to 2003.

6   The Institute is now known as the S. Rajaratnam School of International Studies.

J.Y. PILLAY

Chairman of the Council of Presidential Advisors

"His principal concern was the political dimension.
Then his antennae would start vibrating.**"**

– J.Y. Pillay

The first time I saw Mr Lee Kuan Yew was in 1956. I was a student in London in my final year at the Imperial College of Science and Technology. He was a member of a Singapore parliamentary mission led by David Marshall, the Chief Minister, seeking self-government. He turned up at Malaya Hall to address students from Singapore and Malaya, arguing the case for the type of Singapore his party, the People's Action Party (PAP), aspired to: self-governing, democratic, non-aligned and socialist, if my memory serves me well. He impressed the audience with his passion, good sense, energy and humour.

I joined the Ministry of Finance in 1961, and was posted to the Economic Development Board shortly after. I had a close association in my career with Dr Goh Keng Swee, my first minister, and Mr Hon Sui Sen, my first permanent secretary.

Mr Lee and Dr Goh

I had earlier met Dr Goh in London. At that time he was working on his PhD thesis at the London School of Economics, which he completed in two years instead of the customary three.

Dr Goh has often been called the "economic architect" of Singapore. He was the economic czar when the PAP took power in 1959. He held several appointments, including Minister for Finance, Minister for Defence, Minister for Education and Deputy Prime Minister.[1] Mr Lee was the political maestro and left the running of the economy largely to Dr Goh.

Dr Goh, who passed away in 2010, was pre-eminently focused on fiscal consolidation. No deficit financing, but a willingness to invest in, and take some risk on, capacity building. Occasionally, that would lead to interesting squawking between him and Mr Lee.

For example, Mr Lee was keen on the greening of Singapore. Dr Goh thought little of a particular idea of Mr Lee to give a tax deduction of S$300 to every household that cultivated a presentable garden. In that plan, assessors from the Parks and Recreation Department would visit every house that applied for this deduction and decide whether the garden passed muster. But how does one define "presentable"? He thought it was all pie-in-the-sky. So there was some ding-donging. In the end, Dr Goh relented, but the scheme eventually fizzled out.

The episode did illustrate one point about Mr Lee: He was quite fastidious about the greening and prettifying of Singapore. He sought parks and green areas all over the island. No doubt the environment, anti-pollution, sanitation, cleaning up of waterways starting with the Singapore River, and so forth, were also his passions.

Mr Lee and Mr Hon

Mr Hon Sui Sen was Permanent Secretary in the Ministry of Finance in 1959, and became Minister for Finance in 1970, a post he held for 13 years. He was a great manager and leader of people, and sensitive to the needs and aspirations of his officers. He treated his staff with respect, and in return they were prepared to do virtually anything for him. He did not make excessive demands, and was ready to support and defend them if they made honest mistakes.

Mr Hon, who passed away in 1983, had known Mr Lee from their early days. Mr Hon had sized Mr Lee up well, and knew his strong points and foibles. Whether he liked it or not, if Mr Lee wanted something done, he would try his best to comply.

Mr Lee and his peers

Mr Lee's style was to listen closely to economic and technical discussions until some consensus arose. His principal concern was the political dimension. Then his antennae would start vibrating. But he would leave the implementation to experts like Dr Goh and Mr Hon. As an example, Mr Lee may have been the chairman of GIC (formerly Government of Singapore Investment Corporation) from 1981 to 2011, but Dr Goh was in the driving seat for the first decade and a half.

Mr Lee was able to forge a common understanding, purpose and spirit among his colleagues. They were strong-willed and had heated disputes, but he managed to cobble them together. Whether anyone else could have done it is open to debate, but the style and outcome would have diverged.

Notes

[1] Minister for Finance (1959–65, 1967–70), Minister for Defence (1965, 1970–79), Deputy Prime Minister (1973–80) and Minister for Education (1979–80).

LIM CHIN BENG

Singapore Ambassador to Japan, 1991–1997

" There's no harm in gilding the lily. **"**

– Lee Kuan Yew

The first time I met Mr Lee Kuan Yew was an important day in the history of Singapore. It was 30 May 1959, the day of Singapore's first general election under its new constitution. It was held to elect 51 members into the Legislative Assembly. I was a young administrative officer working in the Treasury at the time.

I was one of the people called upon to act as Returning Officer at the election. I was posted to supervise the voting in the Tanjong Pagar ward and had to go around the schools, which served as polling stations, to check that everything was okay. That day, at one of the schools, I saw Mr Lee striding in with four or five *samsui* women. He was escorting them to the polling station to vote. I told him that, under the law, he could not come in and canvass. His reply was that he was not canvassing but merely showing the women where to go to vote.

In 1960, I resigned from the government and joined Malayan Airways, which became known as Malaysian Airways with the formation of the Federation of Malaysia in 1963. In 1966, the airline became Malaysia Singapore Airlines (MSA). My subsequent encounters with Mr Lee were related to work and I met him again when I was with MSA. We would have discussions about the eventual formation of Singapore Airlines (SIA),[1] together with other senior civil servants.

Mr Lee, the visionary pragmatist

I remember clearly what Mr Lee said at these meetings, as well as at SIA's inaugural dinner. He said that he was creating the airline not for prestige, and that if SIA were to lose money he would not hesitate to close it immediately. At that time, there were 20 airlines flying into Singapore and it was his view that the country would not suffer without a national airline. His thinking would become the bedrock motto of SIA — to be profitable.

Mr Lee never interfered with how you ran things and left the operational side to you. It is my belief that we were more efficient than neighbouring airlines because our government did not interfere. When we bought Boeing 747s, we took a long time to decide on which engine to use. We eventually decided to go with Pratt & Whitney[2] for all the planes. One regional airline had only three 747s, each with a different engine type. Imagine the amount of spare parts they had to stock up on, as well as the extra hours of training their staff had to go through to understand the different systems!

There was one incident that sums up the man and his sense of ownership of SIA to me. He was in transit somewhere in the Middle East, probably Bahrain, on the way to Europe. One engine on the 747 failed on take-off. Luckily, the pilot successfully aborted the take-off. The VIP passengers and the pilots were put in a room to wait for news. I think the media was also there. Someone then asked the captain to explain what happened and describe the incident. The captain replied that he could not speak until he had obtained approval from his head office. At this point, Mr Lee turned towards him and said, "I give you permission." He clearly felt SIA was his baby.

Mr Lee and his attention to detail

He was very meticulous with details and would always give suggestions on what could be done better. After one of his trips, I received a note saying the flight had gone well except for the announcements made by the cabin crew. He said they could do with some improvement. "There's no harm in gilding the lily," he remarked.

When in the plane, he would often speak to the cabin crew in Mandarin, which made them very nervous. He was always interested to listen to their opinions, especially about his "Speak Mandarin" campaign and its effectiveness, and he even sought their views on policies.

On another trip, he happened to be sitting right at the front of the cabin, where the bulkhead is located. There were holes in the panel for attaching a bassinet. He noticed that the screw in one of the holes had been wrongly installed and was upside down. I received a note from him shortly after the plane touched down to have the problem rectified. He could be exacting and tough, but his comments were always useful.

Mr Lee, the kind perfectionist

One day, when I was at MSA, he called me to his office at City Hall. I was a young admin trainee at the airline at the time. His office was cold; I remember he had the temperature at exactly 68° Fahrenheit (20° Celsius).

He told me he was going to Phnom Penh to see Prince Norodom Sihanouk and wanted to know who would be piloting the plane and whether they were good and reliable. Then he asked what airplane he would be flying in. He was told it would be a Comet 4.[3] Now, the Comets 1, 2 and 3 had had problems in the past, with three of them breaking up in mid-air. The Comet 4 had no such problems although it always experienced electrical failure during rainy weather. He then asked, "Is my flight going to be delayed?" I told him I could not guarantee him anything but I would certainly do my best to make sure everything went smoothly. He said if he were to be delayed flying out of Singapore, he could excuse it. But if the plane should fail to appear in Phnom Penh, where Prince Sihanouk and his ministers would be seeing him off, somebody's head would roll.

Luckily, everything went well.

I was at Paya Lebar Airport to see that the arrangements for his arrival back to Singapore were in place. I stood discreetly behind a pillar at the other side of the tarmac where his plane was parked. The airport had no aerobridge then, so passengers had to go onto the tarmac to board or disembark from planes. Mrs Lee came down the steps first and got into the car. Mr Lee followed after her and walked around the car to get in on the other side. And then he saw me at a distance. He turned and walked all the way across the tarmac towards me to shake my hand and thank me.

On another occasion, when I was with SIA, I was at my office in the airport when I got a call saying that Mr Lee would be coming up because he had some extra time. He was at the airport to receive some VIPs but their flight had been delayed. He didn't fancy waiting in the holding area, preferring instead to visit the SIA offices.

I quickly alerted my PA about his visit, but when I opened the door he was already standing there! I took him to the boardroom and offered him a drink. He asked a few questions about the airline and before long, it was time for him to go. The lift lobby was at the end of a corridor so I started walking him out. He asked, "Where are you going?" I replied that I was seeing him out. He said there was no need and told me to go back to my office.

I told my staff not to be nervous around him. But for them, their job was their bread and butter. Mr Lee could be direct but he was not unkind.

Mr and Mrs Lee

I was Singapore's Ambassador to Japan for six and a half years, from 1991 to 1997. During that time, Mr and Mrs Lee visited me about a dozen times. Every time they returned from a visit to Japan, they would write me Thank You notes.

On one trip, I remember Mrs Lee stayed behind at the hotel to swim in the pool while we were away at a conference. The conference ended early and we headed back to the hotel. Our rooms were at the end of the corridor. Just as we got out of the lift, Mrs Lee was getting out of another; she had just finished her swim. When she saw us, she ran towards us to welcome us.

On another visit, Mr Lee said he wanted to see the earthquake recovery efforts in Kobe so I made the necessary arrangements. When we arrived at the venue for the briefing, I saw that they had put us in a room with two big round tables, with the men seated at one table and the women at the other. During the briefing, I noticed that Mr Lee was distracted and not paying attention. He was looking over constantly to check on Mrs Lee to make sure she was fine. At this point, I got up and asked her if she would prefer to sit with us. She agreed and after she moved to our table, Mr Lee was no longer distracted.

Mr Lee and his constant questioning

Mr Lee asked a lot of questions, but if you analysed them you would realise they were not irrelevant. On one visit to Tokyo, he noticed that some cars had "open book"[4] signs on them. He asked what they were for and I told him the signs indicated that the drivers were new. Before long, in 1994, new drivers in Singapore had to display a red triangle sign on the windscreen of their cars.

On another visit, we were in the car when the car phone went off. This was before mobile phones were truly commercialised. I answered the phone and after the call ended, Mr Lee asked me how many car phones there were in Tokyo. I said I didn't know the exact number but that almost every car had a phone. Then he asked how much one cost. Luckily, we had just changed ours and I remembered the amount — about 25,000 yen then. He then asked how much it would cost to speak for three minutes. I thought that would be the end of all the questioning on car phones, but a few days later I received a note from Singtel asking me the same questions and requesting official answers. Mr Lee had obviously been thinking about the viability of having car phones in Singapore.

Mr Lee's lighter side

There was a funny incident once when he invited me to lunch. For dessert, he ate fruits and was peeling his pomelo while talking about politics at the same time. He said, "Now you share with me."

I thought he wanted to hear my views, to have me share my views with him. I said, okay, and was about to talk when he offered me half his pomelo. He had wanted me to share his pomelo with him. I felt bad to have taken half his pomelo.

In the beginning, he was much tougher and maybe not so forgiving. But I saw him mellow over his many visits to Tokyo. During my time in the capital, I saw six Japanese prime ministers come and go. On one visit, Mr Lee wanted to meet with the head of the opposition party. But on the morning of the meeting, the politician called to say he could not make it because he had to go to Parliament. Now, with Mr Lee's strong sense of punctuality, changing an appointment at the last minute was a serious offence. But he just said, okay, he would see him on another day.

One time, at dinner, my wife and I ordered sukiyaki. He and Mrs Lee had ordered sashimi. He looked at me and said, "That's very unhealthy, what you are eating." Luckily, his doctor had also ordered sukiyaki.

Mr Lee liked things done a certain way and he did not like disruptions to his schedule. We had an old exercise bicycle in the embassy which we would put in his hotel room every time he visited. One day, we decided to get a new bicycle because the old one was getting a bit worn. He was not pleased. He asked for the old bicycle back. It was good that we hadn't thrown it away.

Mr Lee and Japan

He liked Japan very much because of the discipline of the people, the history of the country and the food. And he was always very interested to speak with the Japanese politicians. The politicians, too, were eager to meet him and hear his thoughts, especially on China. He was in great demand. I learnt a lot just from listening to him. It was a great privilege for me.

He and Mrs Lee used to come into Tokyo on the morning flight, arriving at about 5 p.m. There would only be time for dinner. They would stay for about three or four days and participate in the activities we planned for them. At the end of the visit, they would leave Tokyo on the morning flight as well. All flights were smoking flights then.

One day, SIA decided to make their evening return flight a non-smoking one, and Mr Lee decided they would use that flight. That meant we had to plan another full day's worth of visits for them. Towards the end, we found ourselves running out of things for them to do because the Lees were so knowledgeable about Japan and had been to just about every museum and temple!

Once I took him to an electronics store in Akihabara. At that time, GPS navigation had just come out and I showed him some GPS devices. His immediate response was that an invading force could use it to find specific locations.

Mr Lee was always thinking about the big picture, with Singapore's welfare at the heart of it.

Notes

1   The different needs of the two shareholders led to the split of MSA in 1972 into two new entities: Singapore Airlines and Malaysian Airline System.

2   Pratt & Whitney is a United Technologies Corporation company. It is a world leader in the design, manufacture and service of aircraft engines and auxiliary power units.

3   The de Havilland DH 106 Comet was the first production commercial jetliner. The Comet 1 prototype first flew on 27 July 1949. A year after entering commercial service the Comets began suffering problems, with three of them breaking up during mid-flight. The first fatal accident occurred on 3 March 1953 during take-off at Karachi, Pakistan.

4   The Beginning Driver's Sign, introduced in 1972, is a green and yellow V-shaped symbol that looks like an open book. New Japanese drivers must display this sign on the front and back of the car for one year after obtaining a standard driver's licence. It is also known as the Shoshinsha mark.

WEE CHO YAW

Chairman Emeritus, United Overseas Bank

"He had a formidable brain and was always three steps ahead of others.**"**

– Wee Cho Yaw

I first heard of Mr Lee from my father Wee Kheng Chiang who, in the early 1950s, was the chairman and managing director of the United Chinese Bank (UCB). Mr Lee had joined the law firm Laycock & Ong and saw my father occasionally for the bank's legal matters.

My father was impressed by the earnest young lawyer and spoke highly of his grasp of legal issues. The respect was apparently mutual. At the official opening of UOB Plaza in August 1995, in conjunction with the 60th anniversary of the United Overseas Bank (UOB),[1] Mr Lee, who was Senior Minister at the time, spoke fondly of my father. He said in his address: "He was a tall, slim, energetic, highly intelligent and very sociable man. When I visited at his home in Kuching in the middle '50s, he entertained me lavishly. He said the secret of his health and energy was daily swimming and champagne."

The bank's twin celebrations were held at the atrium of UOB Plaza in Raffles Place. Just as Senior Minister Lee started his address, the storm clouds that had been gathering burst into torrential rain. We immediately asked if he would prefer to continue his speech at the main branch which had been prepared with a back-up sound system. However, he chose to carry on in the partially covered atrium. Despite being under an umbrella, by the end of his ten-minute address, his trousers were damp.

His decision to speak in the rain greatly impressed my good friend from the Philippines, Washington Sycip. The founding chairman of accounting firm SGV in the Philippines commented:

> "This is what makes Singapore so successful. The leader decides to brave the rain and the rest stay to support. You will not see this in the other Asian countries."

Mr Sycip's observation reminded me of how fortunate Singapore was to have had a determined man like Lee Kuan Yew at the helm. It was only a bank's reception, but he refused to be deterred by a thunderstorm.

By the time I started working as managing director of UCB in 1960, Lee Kuan Yew was already Prime Minister of Singapore. So I never had the opportunity to consult him professionally. However, Lee & Lee was (and continues to be) one of the bank's panel of lawyers, and I would occasionally meet Mrs Lee on legal matters. Mrs Lee was not only a legal eagle with a sharp mind; I will always remember her as a gracious lady who never once used her position to ask for any special favour. On one occasion after a meeting, she mentioned that she needed to go to the branch for a banking transaction. When I offered to send a staff to facilitate, she politely declined and chose to stand in the queue instead.

Mr Lee, Nantah, and an exercise in patient persuasion

My interactions with Mr Lee only started after I joined the Singapore Chinese Chamber of Commerce & Industry (SCCCI) and the Singapore Hokkien Huay Kuan. As president of these two organisations in the late 1960s and early '70s, I had the opportunity to meet Mr Lee both socially and officially. I remember approaching him for advice prior to my leading the Chinese Chamber's first trade delegation to China in 1971. We were planning to ask the Chinese to help us break the monopoly of the European freight conferences, and I sought his views on this.

But I really got to know Mr Lee at close range over the merger of Nanyang University (NU) and University of Singapore in 1980. I had taken over the chair of the Nanyang University Council in 1970. Founded by the Chinese community as the first Chinese university to be built outside China, Nantah — as NU was popularly known — was beset with administrative and academic problems from the day it opened its doors in 1956.

The University Council did its best to improve enrolment and upgrade the institution by introducing more English courses, recruiting better staff and attracting better undergraduates. But the brighter pre-university students continued to prefer University of Singapore. In 1977, Mr Lee decided to step in. He started a series of meetings with members of parliament who had graduated from Nantah and with me and the Council members.

I had long discussions with him over the future of Nantah. Both of us agreed that something had to be done to prevent the university withering away through attrition. So we tried setting up a joint campus for business administration and accountancy students of the two universities. But this did not help lure the better students to Nantah as we had hoped. In the end, the Council had no choice but to accept Mr Lee's proposal to merge Nantah with University of Singapore.[2]

The three years preceding merger were traumatic as I found myself on the opposite side of the table to Mr Lee. As is widely acknowledged, he had a formidable brain and was always three steps ahead of others when analysing any issue or problem. I found myself in a bind. Objectively I had to agree with him that drastic action was called for, but my emotional attachment to Nantah made merger tremendously difficult to accept.

Looking back, I must say that Mr Lee was very patient throughout. He did not brow-beat us to accept merger. Instead, he persuaded with numbers and statistics because, as he had admitted publicly, he appreciated our position as leaders of the Chinese community. To ensure the public understood the whole picture, he released our exchanges to the media.

In a letter to me in March 1980, he wrote:

"You have a responsibility to that generation of the Chinese Chamber of Commerce & Industry that raised public support and funds to found NU. I have a responsibility to ensure the best education of our students, without upsetting the sentiments of the older Chinese-educated generation which remembers with pride its difficult struggle to set up Nantah."

Thirty-six years have since passed and on Nantah's beautiful old Jurong campus now sits proudly another institution of higher education, the Nanyang Technological University (NTU). A whole generation of Singaporeans has been well served by NTU. I think that generation of the Chinese community which raised funds and support to found Nantah would take comfort in that and would be very proud today.

Shortly after Mr Lee stepped down as Prime Minister in 1990, the two major Chinese organisations — SCCI and the Singapore Federation of Chinese Clan Associations (SFCCA) — jointly held a dinner to pay tribute to his long years of service. For the occasion, we produced a book carrying extracts of his speeches touching on the Chinese community.

As president of the SFCCA, I contributed a foreword to the book. I wrote then, and I still believe, that "Singapore's success story ... is primarily due to Mr Lee Kuan Yew's vision, intellectual superiority, determination to succeed and his courage to press ahead with necessary policies even when he is aware that they would be unpopular. Truly, without Mr Lee Kuan Yew, Singapore would not be what it is today."

Notes

[1] United Overseas Bank was incorporated in August 1935 as the United Chinese Bank. Its name was changed to United Overseas Bank in 1965.

[2] The National University of Singapore was formed in 1980 as a result of this merger between Nanyang University and University of Singapore.

CH'NG JIT KOON

Senior Minister of State for Community Development, 1991–1996

66 Mind you, don't hurt the feelings
of the older ones. 99

– Lee Kuan Yew

Don't ask me how many times I tried to say no to Lee Kuan Yew. And don't ask me how many times he accepted it. The number is zero. Mr Lee is one who, once he sets his mind he wants you, doesn't expect you to decline. He will use his way to convince you. You cannot say no. Because, you know, whatever he asks you to do, it is for the nation.

The first time I tried to say no to Mr Lee, he wasn't even in the room. In September 1967, I received a letter from the Prime Minister's Office (PMO), signed by the Deputy Secretary. It got to me late because it was not sent to the right address. It had been sent to Nanyang University, and they took some time to redirect it to me. The letter said, "This is urgent. When you receive this, contact the undersigned immediately."

I called up the PMO. The gentleman on the line said, "I have been waiting for your call! Quick, come over!"

So I went to City Hall. The moment the Deputy Secretary saw me, he scolded me. "Why are you still here?"

I said, "If I'm not here, where should I be?"

"Don't you know?" he said. "The United Nations General Assembly has already started. You're supposed to be there. Why are you still here?"

I told him truthfully, "Nobody told me. What am I supposed to do there?"

At this point, he said, "Wait," and turned to behind his desk to pull out a stack of papers. He found the extracts of some Cabinet meeting notes. "See? Here. PM told Cabinet he himself wants to talk to you. He didn't tell you?"

He did not. The Deputy Secretary told me the Singapore delegation would be headed by Yong Nguk Lin.[1] But as a Cabinet Minister, he would not be able to stay throughout from the opening until the end of the session. I was supposed to be with the guys who would stay for the whole General Assembly. He would leave everything to the remaining members of the delegation. And who were the other guys? If I recall, I believe they were S.R. Nathan from Ministry of Foreign Affairs and Osman Omar, a senior police officer. And the third guy — that's me.

PM Lee had already gone off to the United States. President Johnson had invited him. Singapore was just a newborn nation, a tiny little one. Yet we were invited by a superpower. It showed that the US regarded us as important. So of course PM had to go. He was accompanied by the Foreign Minister, S. Rajaratnam, and Rahim Ishak, the Minister of State for Education.

At the time, there were two great powers in the world: the United States and the Soviet Union. Rajaratnam had said before, *we are friends with everyone*. So we had to balance things. At the same time that PM went to the United States, Dr Toh Chin Chye, the DPM, led another delegation to visit the USSR.

So, with both our PM and DPM away, another delegation was needed to represent Singapore at the UN General Assembly. At the time, one of the topics being discussed in the UN was the seat of China. It was then held by the Republic of China government in Taiwan, but the People's Republic of China government in Beijing was claiming that they should be the rightful owner of the seat in the

UN. I thought maybe S.R. Nathan and Osman Omar would need someone to help read the Chinese reports in the UN papers, so I should go help. That was my ignorant thinking at the time. Later on, I learnt that everything we received was in English.

So I said to the Deputy Secretary, "How many days do I need to be there?"

"It's three months!"

I jumped. "I cannot go. Three months is too long. I'm not a civil servant, I am helping in my family's business. It is year-end. I have to help to close the company accounts."

But the gentleman explained that because both the PM and DPM were out on official trips, he had nobody to give the approval to change the members of the delegation to the UN General Assembly. He said, "Please help me to solve this problem."

Since he told me his difficulties, I said I would go back and discuss it with my colleagues in the company. Luckily, they understood that this was an important task; it was for the nation. They advised me not to decline and said they could handle the company's accounts themselves. With their consent, I immediately informed PMO. They arranged for my air ticket and the necessary papers, and I was off to New York within three days. This was the first time I flew that far a distance.

As part of his US visit, PM Lee visited New York. All of us in the UN delegation gathered to greet him. When he saw me he said, "Eh! How come you are here?"

I was stunned and didn't know what to say. He had already forgotten! Singapore was not even three years old at that time, and he was already so busy running from place to place to make sure people knew us and took us seriously that he even forgot that he wanted me to go to the UN! He expected all the rest of us to do our work too, so much so that he even forgot to tell some of us to do the work. But actually, he knew very well what you did and when you did your work. He is one who is very grateful and really puts it in his mind that you were with him through the hard times, whatever your status. Whoever helped him during the crucial years, he will always remember you.

I became MP for Tiong Bahru in 1968, and started helping Mr Lee in his Tanjong Pagar ward in 1976. Mr Lee told me that Tanjong Pagar was no longer the same as when he first became Assemblyman. In the 1950s, the people who lived there were construction workers, *sampan*[2] men, trishaw riders, Harbour Board workers, hawkers. They were very hardworking people and supported Lee Kuan Yew through the hard times. They started the Goodwill Committee after the racial riots in 1964. PM Lee never forgot what they did.

By 1976, the residents living around Duxton Road who were affected by the government's resettlement plans in the area had been given priority to relocate, to places like Kampung Silat and Bukit Purmei. Some young families from other areas were moving in to the newer housing blocks at Tanjong Pagar Plaza. PM Lee knew that the old ones would no longer be relevant to the new residents. He wanted me to find new residents to keep the grassroots organisations alive. He also told me, "Mind you, don't hurt the feelings of the older ones."

By the 1970s, things were stable and the economy was progressing well. I saw that the early residents, even if they moved away, wanted to stay close to PM Lee and support him. They still felt very proud of the old days when they fought the elections with him. I also saw that PM Lee remembered and was grateful to them. So I shared the idea to have an award recognising them as Friends of Tanjong Pagar. It's not like the PBM[3] or BBM,[4] the National Day Awards that the government gives out. This was something exclusively for Tanjong Pagar grassroots. PM Lee gave his approval and agreed to sign the award certificates personally. It meant a lot to the stalwart supporters of Tanjong Pagar.

The next time I tried to say no to PM Lee, I did it in person. It was in 1981. I had been in Parliament for about 13 years, as a backbencher. Now and then, Mr Lee would ask me something, or tell me something he wanted me to do, or I would tell him something I think he should know about. That was all our interaction. I wasn't involved in any big policies or anything like that.

One Saturday in December 1981, near mid-day, he called me to see him in his office. I went there. He asked me to sit down, then chatted with me, sharing with me his worries. This was after we lost the Anson by-election in October. He felt an urgent need to groom the younger generation of party leaders. He thought the young ones had good brains, but not the skills to reach out to the people and be accepted by them. He said he needed someone to help him. Earlier, he had people like Lim Kim San. Lim Kim San had very rich experience in the Chinese business circles and had a wide network. Now that Mr Lim was already retired, PM needed someone to help him provide a bridge between the young ministers and the people. He wanted me to help him in the PMO as his Senior Parliamentary Secretary.

It was a Saturday. He wanted me to start the next Monday.

I told him I couldn't because I had responsibilities in the family's business. But he wouldn't take my no for an answer. It was in December. I explained to him I would need to settle the company's year-end accounts, so I requested to start the following year.

"Okay. Second January," he pronounced. He was very decisive.

With that settled, he then asked me, "Now, what do you have in mind to do?"

My mind was racing. I was thinking to myself, *you just called me into your office this morning, I didn't know what for, and now straightaway you want me to tell you how I intend to get it started!*

But I managed to reply, "First, I agree with you. This group of young ministers, they have very good brains. But they are more technocrats. They don't have the experience of communicating with the masses. Once the people have the chance to see them face-to-face, to talk with them, they may accept them more."

I then reminded PM about the way he had conducted himself in the 1950s during the fight for self-government, and in the 1960s in the battle for merger, all the things he did to convince people to support him. I myself was young at the time, and I knew very little about politics. But I went to listen to him at the rallies. We were all eager to see how this man could help us get rid of British rule. This was the feel of the people then. This man would go for talks in London, and then once he landed back in Singapore, he would go straight to the *kampungs*[5] to see the people, staying until the middle of the night still talking to the villagers. That was deep in my mind. "I was very impressed by you," I told him.

So I suggested, "Why don't we organise walkabouts? I think it can work for us."

"Do you think that will work?" he asked me.

"Let us try it out first," I said.

"You go ahead," he said.

The PMO then organised ministers' walkabouts every Sunday. I made sure that each one ended with a dialogue. This was the important part when the people could talk to the ministers. We still have the walkabouts, organised by the People's Association now, but not every Sunday anymore.

In 1988, I tried to say no again, in a way. I knew Mr Lee wanted to recruit more young candidates, so I offered my seat to be replaced. I had been in politics 20 years by then. I got scolded. "Why?" he demanded.

"I have served my time. I think it's time for me to give way to a younger candidate," I replied.

"What nonsense are you talking about? I'm 11 years your senior and I'm not thinking about stopping work."

What could I say to that?

Later, when I thought about it some more, I realised that 1988 was a very important year for Mr Lee. That was the year we started testing out the GRC[6] system. Since 1976, or maybe even earlier, PM was concerned that Parliament should reflect our multiracial society. The People's Action Party (PAP) would always field a candidate in every constituency, and it would make sure that its full slate of candidates represented all the races. But the opposition could put in a Chinese guy in a constituency where the PAP candidate was not Chinese, and the opposition could win by playing on the Chinese majority. What is the end result of that? The end result is, you walk into Parliament, and every face you see is Chinese. What kind of multiracial society are we talking about then?

In 1976, PM intended to try out a pairing system. I was told to pair with N. Govindasamy in Telok Blangah. I would help him understand and address the needs of his Chinese residents in Telok Blangah, and he would help me with the non-Chinese residents in Tiong Bahru. But Govin passed away soon after the 1976 elections, so the idea never materialised. I am not sure if PM tried it out in other constituencies. I think, in all that time, he kept this question on his mind. Then he came up with the GRC. I believe that was why I had to stay on in 1988. Tiong Bahru was one of the first four GRCs.

But all this while, Mr Lee was very caring. I remember one incident very well. That election, I was moved to Bukit Merah to replace Lim Chee Onn. I was so tired after the elections that I just turned off everything — my pager and one of those big cell phones last time — and went to sleep. I woke up only to attend my first event in Bukit Merah. It was a Hungry Ghost Month dinner.

Because I was not contactable, Mr Lee, who by then was Senior Minister, couldn't reach me. Someone told him I was at a function in Bukit Merah, and he sent one of his security officers out on a motorbike to look for me. He went to every Hungry Ghost event in Bukit Merah, asking, "Is Ch'ng Jit Koon here?" When he found me, he said SM wanted to speak to me urgently.

I went to call SM from a ten-cent phone outside a provision shop. As usual, he said, "Where are you? What are you doing there?"

I explained to him I was getting to know the residents in Bukit Merah.

"I want your view," he told me. "I'm thinking of adding Bukit Merah to the Tanjong Pagar Town Council. What do you think?"

I understood why he was doing this. I was still helping him in Tanjong Pagar. If I had to look after both Tanjong Pagar and Bukit Merah from two different town councils, it would be a lot more work for me. He was trying to ease my workload.

But I had a concern. I said, "SM, thank you, that would certainly lighten my workload. But I feel it is a pity for the existing town council here." The Redhill Town Council at the time was made up of Bukit Merah, Telok Blangah and Leng Kee constituencies, and it was one of the three best-performing town councils in Singapore. Telok Blangah was already absorbed into Tanjong Pagar GRC. I felt if Bukit Merah was broken off, then Leng Kee would be left alone and have to be absorbed into another town council. My concern was that a well-performing town council would get broken up. It seemed to me quite a pity.

SM thought about this. "Do you think we should bring in Leng Kee? Do you think this would work?"

I said we should, and that is how Tanjong Pagar came to be a mega town council. It was the only town council to have one GRC and two SMCs[7] — Bukit Merah and Leng Kee. I disagreed with Mr Lee, but he listened to my reasoning and accepted my suggestion.

I finally got my way in 1996 — to an extent. I got permission to step down from Mr Goh Chok Tong, who was now the Prime Minister. In 1992, after joining Bukit Merah, I was diagnosed with cancer at around the same time as Lee Hsien Loong and Ong Teng Cheong. At the time, I was not sure if I would survive. When PM Goh came to see me in the hospital, I told him that should I survive until the end of the term, I would put in a request to be allowed to retire. PM Goh did not say yes or no. All he said was, "You don't talk about this. The first you have to do is get yourself well."

I survived. A few months before the January 1997 elections, I went to remind PM Goh of our earlier conversation when he visited me in the hospital. He agreed.

At the hustings, I still helped SM Lee run his election campaign in Tanjong Pagar. On nomination day, when he came to the nomination centre, the reporters surrounded him. They asked him, "We understand that Ch'ng Jit Koon will not be standing this time. What will he be doing now?"

"Ch'ng Jit Koon will still be around," he told them.

Later on, he asked me, "Since you still can continue, why do you insist to retire?" He thought like that. If you can still contribute, you should continue.

But his faith in me was maybe more than I deserved. The cancer made me know my limitations.

When I think of all the times I tried, and failed, to say no to Lee Kuan Yew, I find it quite funny. He had his way of making you believe in him and do your best for Singapore. I never really wanted to say no to him. I just didn't think I could do as much as he thought I could.

He had a vision for Singapore, for all of us. At the time, you may not see it. Some did not agree with him. But when you look back, from now, you see that what he had done has brought us to where we are today. You see that we were capable all along of what he saw in us. In the end, after everything, when I close the accounts of our time together, I realise he would not accept my no whenever he believed I should play a part to help move Singapore forward. And if you had good ideas, useful ideas, he would not say no to you. He would listen to your reasons, and he would say, "Go ahead."

Notes

1   Yong Nguk Lin was Minister for Health from 1963 to 1968.
2   A small flat-bottomed wooden boat propelled by oars and commonly used in Southeast Asia.
3   Pingat Bakti Masyarakat (Public Service Medal).
4   Bintang Bakti Masyarakat (Public Service Star).
5   Malay equivalent word for "village".
6   Group Representation Constituency. The GRC system was established in 1988 to ensure that the minority racial communities in Singapore will always be represented in Parliament. A group of Members of Parliament represents the interests of those residents in the constituency. Under the Parliamentary Elections Act (Chapter 218) 8A (1): "the President shall ... (b) designate every group representation constituency as (i) a constituency where at least one of the candidates in every group shall be a person belonging to the Malay community; or (ii) a constituency where at least one of the candidates in every group shall be a person belonging to the Indian or other minorities." Source: Parliamentary Elections Act (Chapter 218)
7   Single Member Constituency.

SIDEK SANIFF

Senior Minister of State for the Environment, 1997–2001

❝ No, don't waste money. Ahmad Mattar has a good overcoat. Borrow from him. **❞**

– Lee Kuan Yew

Many countries in the world have their own paternalistic leaders. Third World countries, too, have long been identified with their paternalistic leaders. These include the likes of Nelson Mandela (South Africa), Kwame Ngkrumah (Ghana), Gamal Abdel Nasser (Egypt), Mahatma Gandhi and Jawaharlal Nehru (India), Sukarno and Mohammad Hatta (Indonesia), José Rizal (Philippines), Tunku Abdul Rahman and Tun Abdul Razak (Malaysia) — and Lee Kuan Yew, our late Prime Minister, Senior Minister and Minister Mentor. They are synonymous with accolades such as Father of Independence, Father of the Nation and Father of Development.

With Mr Lee, three important characteristics must be consciously added to these accolades — belief in meritocracy, pragmatism (in his view, it wasn't necessary to be politically correct all the time), and his love for peace.

Mr Lee and education

Mr Lee believed strongly in education. As a nation that upheld meritocracy, he always urged us to concentrate on education so as to ensure that our children would go on to become trustworthy trustees of our nation.

Sometime in 1976, Mr Lee invited me to join him in the General Election that was to be held in December that year. The election was meant to introduce the second-generation leadership. I was very surprised with the invitation as just some five to six years earlier, I had criticised the government for not doing enough to ensure that Malay students had a decent grasp of English when they left school.[1] My decision to accept his offer to stand as a PAP candidate[2] created quite a stir in the Malay community.

In the early 1970s, the Singapore Malay Teachers' Union (SMTU),[3] of which I was President, had suggested a total overhaul of the education system into a single stream, national type school[4] where every subject would be taught in English; this was important to prepare our youth to take on the knowledge, technology and expertise of the modern world. In addition, Mother Tongue languages[5] and religious or faith-based learning should be added to the curriculum so as to maintain our cultural traditions. SMTU also proposed the teaching of the National Language, that is the Malay language, to all students including non-Malays, perhaps for two periods in a week. After all, Singapore is part of the Malay Archipelago.

Around the same time, in 1971, Shamsuddin Tung, editor-in-chief of *Nanyang Siang Pau*, a Chinese language newspaper, was imprisoned because he had been harping about the Chinese language, Chinese literature and Chinese culture. Thereafter, all eyes were on SMTU and me after PM Lee was quoted in the *New Nation* on Tuesday, 7 September 1971 as saying:

"Singaporeans are getting a little on the soft side. This will not do. We are all aware that a new situation is likely to develop in the region. We must nip some of these problems in the bud. Take the recent *Nanyang Siang Pau* agitation, heating up Chinese language and culture issues. We acted. By 'national type of schools', using English as the medium of instruction. Malay, compulsory as a second language. All Chinese schools were to be closed! They were both playing someone else's game. They both stopped, but only after they knew we meant business. By the time we were prepared to act against the majority, everyone else got the message."

"Jangan jadikan Singapura tempat orang-orang jujur terbujur, jangan jadikan bumi ini tempat orang-orang jujur terkubur". (Don't allow Singapore to be turned into a land where honest and sincere citizens are punished for their own convictions or beliefs.) I delivered those words at a farewell gathering organised by SMTU for two of our members, the late Mamat Samat and Wan Hussin Zohri, before they continued with their studies in the United Kingdom. Both had confided in me that should the fate of Shamsuddin Tung befall me, they would terminate their studies and return home. "Don't!" I told them. They are my true friends. I will never forget that episode in my whole life.

I had once asked Haji Ya'acob,[6] MP for Kampong Ubi, why would the Prime Minister want to invite me, a vocal critic, to join the government? Haji Ya'acob said I did not know the man well, adding, "Mr Lee had a problem if you were criticising for the sake of it. If your motivations were right and you wanted the best for the country, he would work with you."

Mr Lee was so concerned about education that he even ordered the Ministry of Education to release the results of the Primary Six national examinations by ethnicity. You see, it was much easier to hide the problem (of poor educational performance of the Malays) by lumping statistics and pretending that all was fine. But Mr Lee was not interested in what was easier or more popular. He wanted to confront the problem. If I were reluctant to do so, he said, another officer would do it. I readily accepted Mr Lee's instruction without a moment's hesitation because I believed it was the right thing to do. Ten years after we announced the results by ethnic group, Malay grades improved significantly. It is significant to note that Mr Lee himself opened the first Mendaki[7] Congress on 10 October 1982. It was an historic event for the Malay community. He had also set Mendaki a target of 12 years for any major programmes to be achieved. We made it in ten!

The late Mr Lee was a tough taskmaster indeed. Never waffle or procrastinate, he always said. But he was also very astute and advised us to be open to the views of others. Be attentive and firm. And, above all, be polite. He believed that being open and attentive, firm yet polite, made it easier for issues to be discussed, especially the most sensitive matters concerning race and religion.

Practical Mr Lee

Despite his tough demeanour, Mr Lee was polite and caring. Permit me to elaborate. My family and I were on a vacation in Malaysia when I got a note from PM's office asking me to see him when I returned.

During lunch a couple of days later, Mr Lee said that he wanted me to follow Hon Sui Sen, then Minister of Finance, to China. He then asked if I could take the cold weather which was 18° Celsius below zero at that time.

"Do you have an overcoat?" he asked.

I said that I would buy one.

"No, don't waste money," he replied.

He paused for a while and said, "Ahmad Mattar has a good overcoat. Borrow from him."[8]

"What about boots to cover your shoes for walking?" he continued.

I said I didn't have any, and this time I thought that I had sounded more convincing in saying that I would buy a pair.

"No, no, don't waste money. Borrow from Chok Tong," he said in earnest.[9] He was rather fatherly!

So I went to China in 1979 with a borrowed overcoat and a borrowed pair of boots! When I returned home from the trip, as a form of appreciation, I made sure that I sent Ahmad Mattar's overcoat for dry-cleaning. In China I managed to squeeze in some time from our hectic schedule to buy Goh Chok Tong a pair of chopsticks; hopefully it was not the cheapest in the market!

Mr Lee emphasised the need for us to be thrifty and not wasteful, even at the national level, and that it had to begin at the individual level first. He did, indeed, walk the talk.

Speaking of not being wasteful, Mr Lee disliked wasting time. He was not one to procrastinate. In late 2010, I presented him with a copy of my book of speeches and news articles entitled *The Singapore Malay Paradigm*. He sent me a personal handwritten note saying "Best Wishes" a few days later. I was touched by his gesture of appreciation and replied that the book would not have been possible without his foresight and astuteness in inviting professionals with diverse backgrounds and views to come forward and transform this tiny nation into a thriving, prosperous and harmonious city-state. He responded on that very day itself with a note in his own handwriting that said, "Sidek, thank you."

Mr Lee, the visionary

Soon after independence on 9 August 1965, Prime Minister Lee quickly despatched S. Rajaratnam on a mission to announce the city-state's new status and establish ties with the nations of the world. Singapore's first Foreign Affairs Minister visited Russia, India, China, Japan and neighbouring Southeast Asian states. He also went to the United Nations; this was instrumental in getting Singapore accepted into the world body some six weeks later, on 21 September.

Politically, Mr Lee invited like-minded Singaporeans with the interests of Singapore at heart, including those with differing views, to be involved in transforming Singapore. He believed in an all-encompassing approach for the well-being of this country, even to the extent of inviting a losing General Election candidate with the highest votes into Parliament.[10] In 1990, he went further and implemented the Nominated Member of Parliament scheme, whereby individuals with different expertise were invited into Parliament to provide a check on our ministers — to keep his ministers on their toes! Strange? But true. This was testament indeed to the values he held on to tightly — pragmatism and openness. To let a thousand buds bloom.

I had several opportunities to accompany our former PM abroad. One such occasion was to Australia in 1980. At one of the meetings, an Australian minister came forward to Lim Chee Onn and me. Looking at us he said, "Your PM has the foresight and is always looking beyond the horizon. Other PMs brought along their ministers. But he, mere MPs, like both of you. Young men, be prepared to shoulder some responsibility when you return home."[11]

Shortly after the trip, in 1980, I was made the first Parliamentary Secretary to hold portfolios with two ministries — Communications and Culture. In the same year Chee Onn, who was appointed the Secretary-

General of the National Trades Union Congress (NTUC) and Minister without Portfolio, invited me to be the Deputy Director of Political Education with the NTUC. The NTUC was in the midst of robust discussion on a new strategy of cooperation rather than confrontation, in the pursuit of industrial peace and justice to enhance future growth.

Mr Lee, a proponent of peace

Mr Lee strived for peace at home. To achieve this, he and his like-minded colleagues such as Ministers S. Rajaratnam, Goh Keng Swee and E.W. Barker put in place strong leadership in the government and civil service machinery, and a trade union movement that was able to keep pace with the rise of industrialisation. The late Mr Lee constantly impressed upon subsequent leaders of the need to stay competitive through revamping the education system, modernisation and globalisation. With his team, Mr Lee forged a sense of common understanding of, and mutual respect for, race, language, culture and religion, emphasising that the newly independent Singapore was not a Malay nation, nor a Chinese nation, nor an Indian nation.

In 1994, Mr Lee, by then Senior Minister, went to Israel and Jordan to help expedite the peace process between Arabs and Jews. He was one of the early world leaders to do so. My understanding is that he firmly believed great — and urgent — efforts were required to achieve lasting peace. While it was, and still is, crucial for the Arabs and Jews to settle their issues between themselves, it is equally important, if not more important, for the international community to be closely involved. Recent developments in the Middle East have proved how correct Mr Lee was.

I was part of the delegation to Israel and Jordan. Israel's Prime Minister Yitzhak Rabin and Jordan's King Hussein both entertained us at their respective homes. Being invited to a person's home is the epitome of Jewish and Arab hospitality, and the gesture indicated the leaders' utmost appreciation and respect for Mr Lee. Respect that was tinted in gold — and much valued by friends and foes alike.

A mentor throughout his adult life, Mr Lee even asked the journalists who covered the trip to Israel and Jordan to interview the three young ministers who accompanied him — Teo Chee Hean,[12] Lee Yock Suan[13] and I — for our views of the visit. Ms Sumiko Tan from *The Straits Times* reported the following:

"Mr Sidek Saniff, who was part of SM Lee's delegation to Israel and Jordan, made this observation after meeting Israeli Prime Minister Yitzhak Rabin and Foreign Minister Shimon Peres last week: 'There is a genuine desire among Israeli leaders to strike a comprehensive peace accord with its Palestinian and Arab neighbours. The way I saw it, Israel must have realised that in modern war, nobody wins and everybody loses. This was a lesson Iraqi leader Saddam Hussein learnt to his peril during the Gulf War. I am confident and hopeful about the progress of the peace process between Israel and its neighbours.' Mr Sidek added that 'once peace was created, there would be prosperity in the region'.

To a question from another Singaporean reporter on whether there had been any reservation among some Muslims in Singapore on why he had agreed to visit Israel, Mr Sidek remarked that his conscience was clear. He said: 'I believe that just as one is quick to respond to war, one must be equally quick, if not quicker, to respond to peace, as it is stated in Islamic teachings.'"

Mr Lee was an exemplary student, a brilliant lawyer, a loving and caring family man, a visionary, and a magnanimous leader. He was instrumental in creating a first-class system of governance in Singapore. His harrowing experiences of the Japanese Occupation emboldened him with the resolve to achieve self-government from British rule, and then merger with Malaya (under the shadow of communism). In 1965, he had to deal with Singapore's separation from Malaysia and lead a newly independent nation (with the foreseeable danger of communalism). He had to quickly oversee the urgent development of a new city-state.

When he passed away on 23 March 2015, I said at his eulogy that he was the *embodiment* of the term "statesman". Singaporeans are indeed indebted to him. The world has lost an elder statesman, a forefront crusader of democracy in the post-modern era. I also shared a Malay saying:

Pisang emas dibawa belayar
Masak sebiji diatas peti
Hutang emas boleh dibayar
Hutang budi dibawa mati.

The quatrain means that monetary debts can be paid off, but debts of good deeds cannot be repaid. A person brings such debts to his grave.

There is another Malay saying: *Harimau mati tinggalkan belang, manusia mati tinggalkan nama*. It means that a person who has done many great deeds will always be remembered.

I owe it to Mr Lee to ensure that his legacy remains intact. I shared during his funeral service that I would always cherish his advice especially on governing. He used to say, "If you want to be popular all the time, you will misgovern."

And I will heed his advice to always be pragmatic. Pragmatism is the combination of Ideal and Reality, with Perception as the mosaic of that reality. He gave me this advice: If you believe strongly in a programme or issue that people find difficulty accepting, you should proceed with it once you are clear in your mind; and then make sure you deliver it *before* the next General Election! That is what credibility is all about. People will then learn to believe in your judgement and future undertakings.

Although Mr Lee can be seen as a tough taskmaster, the all-systems-go type of leader, I noticed from early on that he was able to accomplish many things by being mindful, and steering clear, of three undesirable traits — superficiality, prevarication and procrastination. These are invaluable lessons for all leaders to take note of, and emulate.

Notes

1 Sidek Saniff was then a teacher at Maju Secondary School and President of the Singapore Malay Teachers' Union (Kesatuan Guru-Guru Melayu Singapura). He graduated with a BA (Hons) in Malay and Indonesian Studies from the University of London.

2 He went on to become Member of Parliament for Kolam Ayer.

3 The SMTU was formed in 1947 to represent Malay-language teachers. The union began as a welfare organisation in 1926, but a decision to change its status to that of a trade union was made in May 1946. One of SMTU's early causes was to campaign for a fair salary scheme for Malay teachers.

4 A single stream school where English is the medium of instruction for all subjects.

5 These are Chinese, Malay and Tamil.

6 Haji Ya'acob bin Mohamed was Member of Parliament for Kampong Ubi from 1968 to 1980.

[7] Yayasan MENDAKI (Council for the Development of Singapore Malay/Muslim Community) is a self-help group formed in 1982 dedicated to empowering the community through excellence in education, in the context of a multiracial and multireligious Singapore.

[8] Ahmad Mattar was then Minister-in-charge of Muslim Affairs.

[9] Goh Chok Tong was then Senior Minister of State for Finance.

[10] This was the Non Constituency Member of Parliament scheme introduced in 1984.

[11] Sidek Saniff was Member of Parliament for Kolam Ayer from 1976 to 1988. Lim Chee Onn was Member of Parliament for Bukit Merah from 1977 to 1991.

[12] Teo Chee Hean was then Member of Parliament for Marine Parade Group Representation Constituency.

[13] Lee Yock Suan was then Member of Parliament for Cheng San Group Representation Constituency.

PHILIP YEO

Chairman, SPRING Singapore

"He would talk while you were trying to eat.**"**
– Philip Yeo

I interacted with Mr Lee Kuan Yew over several periods. My encounters with him were different from those of people on his staff, such as his principal private secretaries who were on call 24 hours a day. They were short and focused — to get a job done.

For the most part of my career, Dr Goh Keng Swee was my boss[1] and I continued to work with him even when he retired. Dr Goh had a special relationship with Mr Lee, so whenever I needed to get anything done, he could speak to Mr Lee directly. The good thing about the two old colleagues was that they had a lot of respect for each other.

Both Mr Lee and Dr Goh knew me as impatient to get on with the job. If it were not for my scholarship bond, I would probably have left public service very early on. I stayed on largely because of Dr Goh. He was a good boss. Howe Yoon Chong and George Yeo were two others I had the opportunity to work with. And, of course, Mr Lee.

Ministry of Defence (Mindef)

I first interacted with Mr Lee in 1971 when I was Head of the Organisation and Control Department in the Logistics Division of Mindef under Dr Goh. At a briefing session for Mr Lee, he was curious and wanted to know how many parts of the M16 rifle were locally manufactured by Chartered Industries of Singapore (CIS). I replied that we still had to buy high-value parts from Colt's Manufacturing Company[2] under a 1968 agreement. In mid-1972, I was appointed Mindef Director of Finance to manage the defence budget. In August 1974, I left for two years of MBA studies at Harvard Business School, and when I returned in June 1976, I assumed the appointment of Director of Logistics. I could then push CIS engineers to locally produce all parts of the M16.

Mr Lee always asked good questions and when I answered him, I did not over-commit. We were not emotional people. We had short, effective meetings after which I would run off. It was the same when I worked with Dr Goh; our conversations were almost one-liners. We had no time for idle chit-chat. For example, on a late Friday afternoon in February 1979, Dr Goh asked me to take charge of the Air Defence build-up portfolio and then promptly went off the following Monday morning to his new post at the Ministry of Education.

Sometime later, he called me to his office for our usual ten-minute catch-up. He asked me how my SADA (Singapore Air Defence Artillery) build-up was going. I replied that we needed Airborne Early Warning capabilities to complete the air defence build-up. He knew what equipment was needed and asked how many I wanted. I replied, three. He countered, "Two is enough."

The next day, I was called to attend an unscheduled Defence Committee meeting at the Istana with Prime Minister Lee. Minister for Defence Goh Chok Tong[3] and Second Minister for Defence Yeo Ning Hong[4] were present. Dr Goh said, "Philip says we need this." Mr Lee asked what the next step was. I replied that I would be going to the Pentagon. The meeting lasted less than two minutes. No memo was needed.

In Washington, I met up with John Lehman, Secretary of the US Navy. The US Department of Defence Letter of Offer and Acceptance to Singapore was US$601 million for four Hawkeye E-2Cs and a basic integrated Logistics System package. Our project staff completed the overall programme for US$340 million. Between Mr Lee, Dr Goh and myself, we worked fast.

In 1984, Mr and Mrs Lee visited Tengah Air Base for a tour and briefings. At tea break, Mr Lee asked me who our successors would be. My team was taken aback, thinking that they were unwanted and dispensable. There was some alarm after he left, but I reassured them that Mr Lee was worried that our successors would not be as capable and might ruin the RSAF.

In late 1985, after 15 years with Mindef, I thought it was time to move on. It was my first attempt at escaping to the private sector. I went to see Dr Goh (then at Monetary Authority of Singapore) who advised me to go to Singapore Airlines (SIA). Dr Goh personally spoke to Mr Lee who called me up and requested I go to the Economic Development Board (EDB) instead. The Singapore economy was in recession and I was needed there. He added that I could go to SIA anytime, so I moved to EDB on 1 January 1986. However, to date, that agreement has not been honoured!

Economic Development Board (EDB)

Mr Lee told me he would meet any investor whom I considered important for a project; I just had to arrange the meetings, which I did. I rarely attended those meetings myself and sent my young EDB officers to take notes. I had confidence in them and Mr Lee knew that. They learnt a lot from those meetings and it was always a great experience for them.

I can promote Singapore but investors also want political assurance. If investors are not confident in Singapore's political stability and leadership, they will not invest. They were always pleased to meet Mr Lee. He was the one to help seal the investment. And unless he asked me to be present, I would not show up. He judged people quickly and he either liked them or not.

Mr Lee was always conscious of details. Following a visit to Jurong Chemical Island in January 2001, he sent a congratulatory letter to all involved, with these suggestions:

"Try to green up the island and beautify it including an imaginative use for that pier either as a restaurant, or for fishing, or as a promenade. There should be a permanent plaque on the island with photos from the book to show the conception and fulfilment of the plan, with the names and photographs of all those who played a major part in bringing this about."

In 1988, when he was still Prime Minister and I was Chairman of EDB,[5] Mr Lee called me one day to the Istana. He asked if I could bring investments to Woodlands, which was an *ulu*[6] place at the time. I countered, "Can you put an MRT station there?" I walked out of the room; he picked up the phone. I quickly got TECH (Texas Instruments, EDB, Canon and Hewlett Packard) Semiconductors to set up in Woodlands, way before the MRT was even up.

In February 1989, the Indonesian Ambassador called on me. He asked me to consider investing in Batam, Indonesia. After visiting the Indonesian island in March, I thought it was not a bad idea and when I brought Dr Goh to Batam in May, he agreed with me. However, he said I had to detail the proposal in an aide-mémoire for Mr Lee to take up with President Suharto. I had never written an official aide-mémoire before! Dr Goh drafted the aide-mémoire, gave it to me to check, and he then personally brought it to Mr Lee.

In August 1989, we had an agreement in principle. In September, President Suharto sent Dr Jusuf Habibie,[7] who was in charge of the Batam development, to Singapore to brief Dr Goh and me. In December, I flew to Jakarta with Dr Goh. We had our groundbreaking ceremony in February 1990.

I worked with a generation of no-nonsense, straight-talking leaders — people like Dr Goh, Howe Yoon Chong and, of course, Mr Lee himself. We focused on action and outcomes. I would have working lunch meetings with Dr Goh, and it was not food focused, mind you. We would discuss ideas and problems to which answers had to be derived by the end of the day. It was the same with Mr Lee. He would talk while you were trying to eat.

In 1992, Mr Lee, then Senior Minister, called me on the phone and asked me why the Chinese Executive Vice Premier Zhu Rongji was hosting a dinner for me in Beijing. "How do you know Zhu Rongji?" he enquired. I replied that I had met Mr Zhu when he visited Singapore in 1990 as mayor of Shanghai. "How do you converse with him?" he next asked. I replied that Mr Zhu spoke to me in English, as I was effectively monolingual!

In 1994, Mr Lee showed me the master plan for the proposed Suzhou Township, which would later be renamed the China-Singapore Suzhou Industrial Park (SIP). I had already been involved in the groundbreaking for the Wuxi-Singapore Industrial Park championed by Dr Goh since December 1992. There were only two of us in the room. Mr Lee put the master plan in front of me and asked me what I thought of it. Too few brown spots, I said. He was puzzled. I explained that brown spots were industrial spaces, which translated to jobs, and therefore few brown spots meant insufficient jobs. He looked up, furious. I walked out.

The next day, he summoned the Suzhou team and me to the Istana. He thundered in great displeasure. "Philip says your master plan is wrong. There are not enough industrial spaces for job creation!" They were quiet, and he angrily walked out of the meeting room. It was the shortest meeting ever.

Sometime in 1996, I received a phone call, at night, to my home from Mr Lee. Lim Swee Say, then Managing Director of EDB and Director of the Singapore Software Projects Office (SPO), had just returned from China that day. He had reported to Mr Lee that the SIP project was in serious trouble and recommended to Mr Lee that I be asked to help salvage it. At Mr Lee's request, I quickly assembled my team, with David Lim as the new CEO of SIP. I assured Mr Lee that we would get to it. He entrusted the work to us and we quickly focused on job creation in 1,000 hectares of the 7,000-hectare master plan.

The only argument I ever had with Mr Lee was over SIP. He grilled us over a breakfast meeting one morning in late 1999 as we felt there were conflicting interests and motivations in the project. Later that afternoon, he broke the news to the media that the SIP project was in trouble and that Singapore wanted out unless the Chinese made fundamental changes.[8]

In mid-1996, during a private lunch with Mr Lee, he had asked me what my main worry was at EDB. I said that in ten years' time, China would be in a position to overtake Singapore in manufacturing. I could already see it from my visits to MNCs in China where there was state-of-the-art machinery as well as unlimited labour supply and low wages.

I retired in March 1999 from the Singapore Administrative Service after nearly 29 years of public service. I signed on with EDB on a five-year contract from April 1999 to March 2004.

On hearing of my retirement, a Hong Kong friend flew to meet me in Boston in August 1999 with an inviting offer: to be the chairman of a Singapore-based holding company which owned his Hong Kong-listed entity. The terms were attractive: S$20 million and 1.6 million share options for a three-year contract.

On 11 February 2000, I was in Hong Kong to finalise the contractual details. Singapore's *Business Times* leaked the news on 12 February that I would be leaving the public service. Public clarification was sought on my decision to stay or leave EDB.

On 18 February, Mr Lee asked me to see him. He expressed his deep concern about my exit plans and personally asked me to stay. Then I would not 'abandon' the Biomedical Sciences Initiative which I had been working on with colleagues from the NUS School of Medicine: Dean Professor Tan Chorh Chuan and oncologists Professor John Wong and Dr Kong Hwai Loong. I stayed.

On 24 June 2000, George Yeo, who had just come on board as Minister for Trade and Industry, publicly launched the Singapore Genomics Programme.[9] With it was formed a Ministerial Committee for Life Sciences, chaired by then Deputy Prime Minister Tony Tan whilst I chaired the Life Sciences Executive Committee. That was the beginning of the Biomedical Sciences industry we see today.

Agency for Science, Technology and Research (A*STAR)

In February 2001, I took charge of the National Science and Technology Board and changed its name to Agency for Science, Technology and Research (A*STAR).

By December that year, we had broken ground for the construction of Biopolis Phase 1 in the 200-hectare One-North Park and had selected and sent the first batch of A*STAR BS-PhD scholars to the United Kingdom and United States. My goal was to train 1,000 PhD scholars over a ten-year period. In July 2003, we launched the groundbreaking of Fusionopolis Phase 1.

By October 2006, I felt it was time to finally move on — my third escape attempt. Mr Lee once again persuaded me to stay on, this time to be his Special Advisor for Economic Development.[10] I told him that I was happy to work for him.

In November 2006, Mr Lee hosted a Japanese dinner with A*STAR BMRC[11] directors and senior researchers at NUS Hall. Present at the dinner were Lim Chuan Poh, designated Chairman of A*STAR from April 2007; Professor Tan Chorh Chuan, President and Deputy Chairman of National University of Singapore; Peter Ong, Permanent Secretary of the Ministry of Trade and Industry; and myself. He assured the senior scientists that the change of leadership at A*STAR from April 2007 would be smooth, that I would help oversee the transition and keep him posted. He said he would be back in November 2008 to meet them to make sure that the A*STAR enterprise carries on.

When Mr Lee retired from the Cabinet in August 2011, he graciously extended an appreciation of my service as Special Advisor for Economic Development in a final letter.

Mr and Mrs Lee

Mr and Mrs Lee were always together. She took good care of Mr Lee and moderated him. She never pushed herself to the forefront. When she became ill and eventually passed away, he most sadly lost his soul mate. I have some fond memories of Mr and Mrs Lee.

In February 1988, I launched our first Asian Aerospace air show at Changi wherein I set up a Singapore Technologies pavilion. Mr Lee and Mrs Lee came to see the show. On entering the Singapore Pavilion, he asked why there were guns at our air show. Before I could respond, Mrs Lee replied drily, "So they can shoot aircraft."

In December 2006, I was with Mr and Mrs Lee when we were hosted to a private dinner in Riyadh to discuss the King Abdullah Economic City (KAEC). The next day, there was a formal presentation on the KAEC master plan by the Saudi Arabia General Investment Authority which elaborated plans for a sea front beach. Mrs Lee asked the presenter if bikinis would be allowed on the beach.

In October 2008, we travelled to Hanoi. Mr Lee had been invited to give a lecture to the Vietnamese Party leaders. Mrs Lee did not come along. Earlier in the morning, Mr Lee made an official call on the President of Vietnam who was previously the Party Secretary of Ho Chi Minh when we set up the Vietnam-Singapore Industrial Park in 1994. We then had a private lunch with our Ambassador to Vietnam. Mr Lee asked what I was having. I replied that I had ordered Vietnamese pho noodles. He was particular about his food and concerned about MSG; nevertheless he asked to try a small bowl of pho. For dessert, I suggested the restaurant's ice cream. He asked for two scoops of ice cream — one scoop of vanilla and one scoop of chocolate — as Mrs Lee was not with us.

Mr Lee, his foresight and dedication

In all that Mr Lee did, he always thought of Singapore. Many people did not, and still do not, fully understand him; but for those who worked with him, we knew his style. He was always about the public good and worried constantly about Singapore's future. The average

Singaporean may not have seen his hard work while he was still alive, but he was always investing his time for us.

Unlike some other countries, there are no framed pictures or statues of Mr Lee all over Singapore. To many he may seem like an autocrat, and yes, he was firm. But he only wanted what was best for our young nation.

Notes

[1] Dr Goh Keng Swee was Minister for Defence from 1970 to 1979 and Deputy Prime Minister from 1973 to 1980.

[2] Colt's Manufacturing Company is a United States firearms manufacturer founded in 1855. It is known for the engineering, production and marketing of firearms.

[3] Goh Chok Tong was Minister for Trade and Industry, Minister for Health and Second Minister for Defence from 1981 to 1982.

[4] Yeo Ning Hong was Minister for Defence from 1990 to 1994.

[5] Philip Yeo was Executive Chairman of the Economic Development Board (EDB) from January 1986 to January 2001. From February 2001 to March 2006, he was Co-Executive Chairman, EDB, responsible for the Biomedical Science industry cluster and concurrently Executive Chairman, Agency for Science, Technology and Research (A*STAR) from February 2001 to March 2007.

[6] Malay equivalent word meaning "rural" or "deserted".

[7] Bacharuddin Jusuf Habibie was the fourth State Minister for Research and Technology of Indonesia from 1978 to 1998.

[8] The Singapore consortium lowered its stake to 35 per cent, raising the Chinese consortium's stake to 65 per cent from 35 per cent. The development site was also reduced, from a planned 70 km^2 to just 8 km^2. The Chinese side appointed Wang Jinhua, vice-mayor of Suzhou and the former manager of the New District, as the new chief executive. In 2001, one year after Singapore lowered its stake, the park made its first profit of $3.8 million.

[9] The Singapore Genomics Programme is a national initiative to spearhead research into human genomics, with particular focus on generating data reflective of the diverse ethnic composition in the Asia-Pacific region. Press Statement by the Minister for Trade and Industry at the Life Sciences Executive Committee Meeting, 24 June 2000.

[10] Philip Yeo was Special Advisor for Economic Development (Prime Minister's Office) from 1 April 2007 to 15 August 2011.

[11] Biomedical Research Council.

JENNIE CHUA
Chief Executive, Raffles Holdings, 2003–2007

"Of course there will be ... even better!"
– Lee Kuan Yew

I was in my early twenties when I first met Mr Lee Kuan Yew. I was dating Dr Goh Keng Swee's son at the time; we were maybe engaged even. It was the 9th of August and I was with the Goh family at City Hall where we watched the National Day Parade march past, peeking from the windows onto the grounds below. I was in awe of Mr Lee but I wasn't scared as I had already had interactions with Dr Goh, himself a formidable man. So I guess any anxiety about being intimidated had already been tempered.

I never saw the two men in a social context. The early Cabinet people were friends without being pals. They knew each other's strengths and what they could bring to the table where building the new nation of Singapore was concerned. They respected each other but I don't think they were people who became buddies and went drinking together. They probably played golf but that was probably a platform for them to discuss matters of state, rather than socialising. This is my sense. I don't think they ate in each other's homes. They had Cabinet lunches together perhaps.

I had, of course, heard of Mr Lee way before then. In the first ten years of my life, my family was rich and I was brought up by "black-and-white" amahs.[1] They left our employment when we became poor but we still kept in touch. There was a temple at Balestier Road where I continued to see them. This was in the early 1960s. The Cantonese-speaking amahs always spoke about certain remarkable men — legendary Robin Hood figures in their minds — like a certain Dr Pun who would give free medical treatment. It was through these amahs, who had just returned from visits to Chinatown, that I first heard of a man called "Lei Kwon Yew".[2] They said he couldn't even speak Chinese, which meant to them that he couldn't speak Cantonese. But he had come back from overseas and wanted to fight for them. They thought of him as their hero even though they probably did not know what exactly he was fighting for. All they knew was that he was fighting against "the communists" and wanted to make Singapore strong and give them all jobs.

Mr Lee and Raffles Hotel

There is an urban legend that Raffles Hotel is standing today because of Mr Lee's intervention. The story goes that in the mid- to late 1980s, when he was Prime Minister, an old professor from his Cambridge days visited him at his office in the late afternoon.

Towards the end of their meeting, Mr Lee noticed the professor looking anxiously at his watch and remarked that he seemed to be worried about time. Wasn't his flight not till much later in the night? The professor replied that he wanted to squeeze in a visit to Raffles Hotel for a drink before he departed. This was before the hotel was restored. The professor said he wanted to see it because it was an icon of Singapore and that people from Britain and the Commonwealth regarded it as a must-see destination.

The professor's comments may have intrigued Mr Lee and set his mind thinking. Apparently, he later called up the relevant authorities to look into conserving the property because it appeared to have a place in the consciousness of people who visit Singapore, even though Singaporeans at the time did not see the hotel as anything special.

Eventually, on 4 March 1987, Raffles Hotel was recognised as a national monument. Together with the adjacent land which faces North Bridge Road, it was tendered out for restoration and development by the Urban Redevelopment Authority. A consortium of DBS Land and OCBC bought it and the rest is history.[3]

When the hotel celebrated its 120th anniversary in 2007, Mrs Lee had recovered sufficiently from her stroke and was up and about. We invited Mr and Mrs Lee to join us for the celebrations, and to our surprise both of them came. There was a cake with 120 candles which they blew out.

But what surprised us even more was when Mr Lee, who was 84 years old then, asked to say a few words. He said to the guests that they might have been wondering why he and Mrs Lee had agreed to attend the anniversary celebrations of a hotel — a commercial building. (At that time, Raffles Hotel wasn't even under Singapore ownership.) He then told everyone it was because the Raffles was where he and Mrs Lee held their wedding reception.

Full stop. That was all he said. He had given a rationale, as well as a personal, explanation.

After blowing out the candles and cutting the cake, he and a small group of about ten people went to the Raffles Grill for a simple dinner. They did not join in the rest of the festivities.

I have never talked about this incident until now. I always thought it was not correct for me to commercialise Mr Lee's connection to the hotel. But I share this story now to show how much he valued his wife and the affection and love that existed between them.

However, while he and Mrs Lee had their wedding reception at the Raffles Hotel, I don't think that was the prime reason it was preserved. After all, their old school, Raffles Institution, made way in 1985 for what is now Raffles City. I think the sentimental reason for preserving the hotel was largely augmented by the "iconic" value of the property, whereas the physical buildings of Raffles Institution had little practical value.

Raffles Hotel restored and birthday dinners

The hotel was closed for restoration between 1988 and 1991. Six months before it was ready to open, Richard Helfer[4] and I decided we would not have a VIP open it because it was not a new property. It was already 105 years old. We wanted to make the hotel important to the local community, rather than merely a tourist attraction, and so we decided to invite Singaporeans and Singapore residents from the different communities.

We wanted the opening ceremony to be held in the month of September 1991 and consulted a *feng shui* practitioner to choose a good date. The man suggested the evening of Monday, 16 September. We did not think anything of it at the time but it later dawned on us that this was the date of Mr Lee's birthday. People thought we had deliberately chosen the date because of that. But the truth is, we didn't.

We decided to invite Mr Lee to look at the restoration works, which he did. Richard and I took him around in early September and showed him the different suites. He asked Richard the cost of the suites. Richard replied that it would cost $600 a night for the small suites and $6,000 for the largest. Mr Lee was sceptical and said we surely wouldn't be able to attract people with such rates. Standing in the smallest suite, he also remarked that it was too tiny. But Richard reminded him that it was actually 65 to 75 sq metres in size and only looked small because there were many people in the room with us, including security officers and our staff members. Subsequently, when the hotel opened and the suites were booked, Mr Lee acknowledged to Richard with a smile that he had been right about the rates after all.

During the show-around, we took the opportunity to ask Mr Lee if he wanted to celebrate his birthday at the hotel. We told him it would have to be on the 15th as the opening party was planned for the 16th. He said yes. So, the day before the hotel officially opened, he celebrated his birthday over dinner at the East India Rooms with his family and close friends, numbering not more than 20 people. I won't even say if we had our licence yet.

From 1991 until 2014, I have followed the hotel through its days when Raffles Holdings owned it to when it went under private equity ownership, and then to Qatari owners.[5] I have seen it through five general managers.

Every year, I worked with Mr Lee's private secretary, Ms Wong Lin Hoe, to arrange for Mr Lee to hold a dinner event at the hotel. We called it his "birthday party" but it wasn't really because it was not held in September. He would hold it in October or November; the latest was in January one year. The venue was always the East India Rooms, except for two years when the space was not available and the dinner was held at the Casuarina Suite and the Drawing Room. The dinners were always organised by Ms Wong. Around July every year, she and I would start having a conversation and preparations for the dinner would begin.

The menu didn't change much over the years. It was always a simple four-course meal comprising a starter, soup, main course and dessert. Mr Lee's main course was usually beef, while a choice of fish and one other selection would be offered to guests. There was wine sometimes, as well as beer and soft drinks. The dinners started punctually at 7.30 p.m. and end by 10 p.m.

That dinner tradition continued even after Mrs Lee had a stroke and recovered and, eventually, after she passed on. I believe Mr Lee liked the dinners and found it comforting to have family around him, as well as old friends like Lim Kim San and Yong Pung How.

He had a guest list of 20 people in the first ten years or so, but the numbers eventually increased to 40 people as his family grew bigger and he started including personal staff, doctors and some younger ministers. The last of these Raffles Hotel dinners was held in December 2014 where he had 40 people across four tables. That night, he went around from table to table to show his appreciation for the care they had given him.

Mr Lee and air conditioning

Once, Mr Lee was at the Casuarina Suite hosting a Taiwanese VIP. It was a weekend event. Now, I would usually make it a point to be around for his events but I happened to be away that time. On Monday, I went to the office. At 8.30 a.m., the phone rang. MFA's Chief of Protocol was on the phone.

He told me there had been a power outage in the area on one day over the weekend, at about 4 or 5 p.m, and that the power had come back on by 6 p.m. However, because the event was at 7 p.m. and the air conditioning was not running at full capacity, the room wasn't cooled enough. As a result, the room temperature was not at 22° Celsius (72° Fahrenheit), which was what Mr Lee liked. Mr Lee felt it and asked the captain to adjust the room temperature. However, instead of explaining the power outage, the captain merely fiddled with the thermostat which, of course, had no effect. Mr Lee then asked the Chief of Protocol and the hotel's catering manager whether he could change rooms. Again, the catering staff failed to explain that this wouldn't have made a difference as the whole hotel was affected. Mr Lee was annoyed. By 8 p.m., the rooms had cooled sufficiently for Mr Lee to feel comfortable and the party went on smoothly. It was reported to me that the Taiwanese VIP helped to defuse the situation by saying something like, "hen hao, wo men Tai Bei tai leng le" "很好，我们台北太冷了" ("That's very good. Taipei is too cold.").

I explained the circumstances to the Chief of Protocol. I believe Mr Lee's principal private secretary also called me about the matter. They asked why all this was not explained to Mr Lee at the time. Later in the morning, I received a note from Mr Lee's office. I quickly replied, saying in two paragraphs that it was the hotel's fault for not explaining the situation to him adequately and my fault for not training the staff well. I also explained that because of the earlier power outage in the hotel's vicinity, there was nothing we could have done to adjust the temperature.

A couple of days later, I saw Mr and Mrs Lee at the hotel and he told me he had accepted my explanation. But he asked why the hotel staff didn't just tell him. After all, he said, he was a reasonable man.

How was I supposed to answer that question? Luckily, Mrs Lee quickly stepped in and said, "Harry, it's obvious this was the first time it had happened here so they will learn from this and improve." Basically, she was telling him to let it go. He did not talk about the matter anymore. We sometimes did not give him enough credit that he would listen and be reasonable. Probably, sometimes, we were too unnecessarily afraid of him.

Mr Lee and his constant concern for Singapore

Whenever he had his annual dinners at the Raffles, I would make it a point to be there to welcome him and his guests. I continued to do this even when I was no longer connected to the property. As I walked Mr Lee to the East India Rooms, he would always ask me how the hotel was doing, who its current owners were and what their plans were. I tried to answer as best as I could. Because I wasn't privy to all the information, there were times I could not give him a firm answer and I would give him an educated guess. Maybe he was just striking up polite conversation with me, but I don't think so because he was not a man for small talk.

The last time I saw Mr Lee was at a dinner at the China Club. This was on 5 January 2015, a month before he was admitted to hospital. The occasion was organised by his niece Kwa Kim Li and hosted by Changi Airport Group chairman, Liew Mun Leong. Other guests present included Cheng Wai Keung, Chairman of Wing Tai Holdings; Stephen Lee, Chairman of Singapore Airlines and former President of Singapore National Employers Federation; former PPS Lee Seow Hiang; the hotelier Ong Beng Seng; Dr Gordon Tan; and myself.

China Club serves Cantonese cuisine. Mun Leong, however, made special arrangements for Mr Lee to have Japanese food. Mr Lee ate well and appeared to have enjoyed his meal. We chose China Club because of its location on the 52nd floor of Capital Tower. It offers panoramic views of Singapore, including Tanjong Pagar, the constituency Mr Lee had looked after for 50 years. Mr Lee took a long look at Tanjong Pagar from the restaurant. Stephen Lee stood by his side pointing out "beautiful Singapore" and our landmarks to him.

Conversation during the dinner was not too heavy and included discussions on SG50 celebration highlights. We all encouraged Mr Lee

JENNIE CHUA | 111

to attend the jubilee events that were being planned as we believed his presence would add very special meaning to the occasions and for the participants. We spoke openly about the respect and affection which Singaporeans have for Mr Lee and reminded him of the spontaneous applause and cheers for him whenever he made his entrance at the National Day parades. Conversations on SG50 led naturally to questions about the future of Singapore, essentially "whether there will be a Singapore 50 years from now".

We could see that Mr Lee was listening intently and heard us. But he did not really respond to our chatter.

Mr Lee passed away on 23 March 2015. I related the dinner conversations to Ho Ching at the wake at the Istana and to Prime Minister Lee Hsien Loong at a community dinner a few weeks later. This was followed by a letter, which I sent via email, to PM Lee who included extracts from it in his 2015 National Day Rally.

"As it was the start of 2015, we talked at length about the celebrations for SG50. We took turns to encourage Mr Lee to attend as many SG50 events as possible. Actually, we hoped he would be there for the SG50 National Day Parade. Mr Lee listened to our exhortations, but stopped short of saying yes to our suggestions.

At each of our gatherings, it had become a tradition to ask Mr Lee, 'Will there be a Singapore many years from now?'

Once, Mr Lee said, 'Maybe.' On another, Mr Lee said, 'Yes, if there is no corruption.' This was classic Mr Lee — ever-believing in Singapore, yet ever-cognisant that there was always work to be done, that we should never take things for granted.

Continuing with our tradition and in the spirit of SG50, that evening, we asked him, 'Will there be a Singapore 50 years from now?' Mr Lee's answer took us all by surprise. That evening, for the first time, Mr Lee said, 'Of course there will be ... even better!'"

While it is indeed a resounding vote of confidence that Singapore is in good hands, it was also Mr Lee's way of telling us that we have to work hard to ensure that there is a better Singapore after his work is done.

Notes

[1] Domestic helpers from China, so-called because they wore white tops with black trousers.

[2] This is how Lee Kuan Yew is pronounced in Cantonese.

[3] In 1987, the government declared Raffles Hotel a national monument. In 1988, DBS Land and OCBC forged a partnership under the cooperation of Raffles Hotel (1886) Pte Ltd to undertake the redevelopment of the hotel. The successful tender design called for the tearing down of the old Jubilee Theatre and Medical Hall along North Bridge Road. Raffles Hotel (1886) Pte Ltd was 56.67 per cent-owned by Raffles Centre Pte Ltd, a wholly-owned subsidiary of DBS Land. The remaining 43.33 per cent interest was held by Raffles Hotel Ltd whose major shareholder was the Oversea-Chinese Banking Corporation.

[4] Richard Helfer was the founding chairman of Raffles International and chief executive officer of Raffles Holdings from 1989 to April 2003. Jennie Chua was Raffles Hotel's general manager during the hotel's restoration and subsequently chairman of Raffles International and CEO of Raffles Holdings.

[5] In 2005, Raffles Hotel was sold to US investment fund Colony Capital. A subsequent merger with Fairmont Hotels and Resorts led to the creation of Fairmont Raffles Hotels International. In April 2010, Raffles Hotel was acquired by Qatar Diar, the sovereign wealth fund of Qatar.

LIEW MUN LEONG

Chairman, Changi Airport Group

❝What are you going to do after you retire?**❞**
– Lee Kuan Yew

The first time I met Mr Lee was in May 1975 when he came to Changi to tour the site of the future airport on the eastern tip of Singapore. I was a mid-level engineer at the time so I didn't get to speak to him. He had an awesome and intimidating personality (his aura continued till his advanced age). We were fearful and yet excited that the "Thundercloud", which was what we used to call him, was coming to visit us. We could feel his aura from afar!

It was Mr Lee who had decided that the new international airport should be built in Changi instead of expanding Paya Lebar Airport. He singlehandedly pushed for it. In 1974, we had already started the planning, design and construction works to expand the existing airport at Paya Lebar. I was then a young construction engineer busily building new aircraft parking aprons and looking into the 11,000 families that had to be resettled to make way for a second runway.

By some good fortune, when Mr Lee was in the US and flew over Boston's Logan Airport, he noticed that it was cleverly built as an "offshore airport". It dawned on him that building a new airport with reclaimed land at the coast of Changi would give us the flexibility to expand the aerodrome into the sea to meet future expansion needs. There were other advantages too. People would not be affected by high level aviation noise as noise would travel out into the sea. And there would be no need to impose height restrictions on buildings, thereby freeing up many hectares of much needed land for future development of our city. I remember thinking to myself, *Wow! Why didn't our senior airport planners, engineers and external consultants bring up such ideas? Instead they had to come from the Prime Minister himself!*

But there was uncertainty over this strategic shift to Changi. Some quarters within the government questioned whether the Public Works Department (PWD) could effectively manage such a large-scale project and complete it within an ambitious six-year time frame. The aviation forecast then was that we urgently needed the new airport by 1981. Rightly or wrongly, the common perception then was that PWD was an old, conservative and bureaucratic department inherited from the colonial British system. Some politicians were sceptical, saying, "They have only built drains, roads, bus stops, government offices and schools. Do they have the expertise and human resources to build such a mammoth international airport and complete it in time by mid-1981 when more than half the site at Changi is to be reclaimed from the sea?"

Mr Lee subtly directed "Three Wise Men" — our description, not his — to study the feasibility of building an airport at Changi within the time constraints. The three men were Howe Yoon Chong, chairman of the Port of Singapore Authority (PSA); Teh Cheang Wan, CEO of the Housing and Development Board; and Woon Wah Siang, chairman of Jurong Town Corporation. They had led many successful major developmental programmes in Singapore and therefore had the credentials to assess if the project was feasible and whether it could be achieved by PWD.

Howe Yoon Chong took leadership on the matter and confidently recommended that the Changi Aiport project could be executed —

and in time — by PWD, with PSA undertaking the reclamation work from the sea. He persuaded all permanent secretaries and heads of government agencies to sign a document, called the Singapore Changi Airport Development, to cut bureaucracy and unnecessary red tape and to pledge their support to make the project a success. Mr Lee later appointed Sim Kee Boon, another legendary permanent secretary, to take charge of the project. Mr Lee had the knack of choosing the right talented and courageous civil servants to champion his cause! He knew that Howe Yoon Chong could mobilise the civil service to undertake the national project. In selecting Sim Kee Boon to oversee the execution of the airport project, he spotted Mr Sim's discipline and eye for details and his strong people-mover spirit.

Changi Airport's Terminal 1 with its first runway system was successfully completed on time by 30 June 1981. Exactly on 1 July 1981, the entire airport operation moved overnight from Paya Lebar to Changi. Changi Airport was officially opened on schedule by Howe Yoon Chong, by then Defence Minister, in December 1981.

Today, 34 years later, we now have started our work on the third runway and Terminal 5, which will be built on reclaimed land. We can truly appreciate the ingenuity and foresightedness of Mr Lee to build the airport at Changi. Without Mr Lee, there will be no Changi Airport today.

Mr Lee's continuous involvement with Changi Airport

Right from the beginning, Mr Lee was very involved in the building of the airport. He wanted the airport to be built within a garden city. He wanted a lot of trees to be planted, instructing that he wished "to see a jungle when driving to the airport". The trees had to be counted every day and I remember sending daily telexes to Sim Kee Boon, detailing how many casuarinas and rain trees we had planted.

We built the first runway at Changi as an extension of the existing British-built military taxiway. It was then 2,000 metres long and we had to extend it to 4,000 metres by expunging Tanah Merah Road. Mr Lee wanted to see where the extension would be. He wanted to have an aerial view but he did not want to fly in a chopper. So we arranged to have him flown up in a Skyvan, a military passenger transport plane which could fly at a higher altitude. We were not sure if he would be able to make out what was on the ground from that height, so we decided to mark the site activities with big yellow aviation balloons which I tied to bulldozers and construction equipment. It worked! Several decades later, Mr Lee was the Guest of Honour at Changi Airport's 25th anniversary celebration. During the welcoming speech I gave as Chairman of Changi Airport, I nostalgically reminded him of the yellow balloons on the first runway site in 1975. He said he remembered them.

Back in November 2012, a group of us invited Mr Lee for dinner. It was just six weeks before I stepped down as President and CEO of CapitaLand. As soon as he sat down, he looked at me and asked, "What are you going to do after you retire?"

I was surprised he was aware that I would be retiring. I said, "MM, I am not retired yet but I will be helping Seow Hiang[1] to look after Changi Airport when I retire from CapitaLand next year."

He kept quiet. Subsequently, at almost every dinner after that, he would ask, "How is Changi?"

The airport was always at the top of his mind and he never stopped thinking and caring for it. Up till a few months before he passed away in March 2015, Mr Lee continued to take an interest in Changi Airport. One evening, I invited him to visit the airport to update him of developments, particularly the "Jewel" site.[2] He was not very mobile and so we took him around in a buggy and via the Skytrain connecting Terminals 2 and 3. I asked him if he had enjoyed the train ride. He said, "Yes, but too short!"

Mr Lee's interest in people and talent

I began to interact more closely with Mr Lee when I was CEO of Singapore Institute of Standards and Industrial Research (SISIR). It was 1990 and he had just stepped down as Prime Minister and taken on the role of Senior Minister (SM). He wanted to visit SISIR, a statutory board, to find out more about what it was doing. I asked his office why he had chosen to visit SISIR as his first stop after stepping down as PM. I was told that, as SM, he was interested to learn about the quality of our talent pool in Singapore, particularly our scientists, engineers, creators and innovators. He figured SISIR, being an R&D institute, would be a good place to start.

Briefing him was an enormous challenge for me. He asked numerous questions about our mission, our goal, our talent pool, the types of research projects we were undertaking, the needs of industries and the research institutions that we were benchmarked against. His questions came fast and furious, and the huge amount of efforts we put in to prepare for them paid off.

I wanted to impress him with the science and technology research talent we had in SISIR. With the assistance of the Economic Development Board (EDB), I had just recruited 52 very bright Chinese scientists and engineers who had studied for their doctorates in Europe and the US but were reluctant to go back to China following the Tiananmen Incident of 4 June 1989. I had visited them in their universities and persuaded them to join SISIR as research fellows. The long-term intent was to persuade the successful ones to remain in

Singapore as citizens. I was very proud of my recruitment "catch" and I suggested that Mr Lee could meet three of these scholars over coffee, since he had always shown an interest in foreign talent. When we were all settled down for coffee, Mr Lee opened his bag and took out a file containing the scholars' CVs. One of the scholars was Dr Wang Ming from London's Imperial College.

Mr Lee asked him, "How are you adjusting to Singapore?"

Dr Wang replied, "My wife, daughter and I are adjusting and settling well in Singapore, sir."

Mr Lee immediately remarked, "But your CV says you have two children."

"I have one daughter only, sir," said Dr Wang.

Later, we realised there had been a mistake in the CV. We were stunned that Mr Lee not only read the CV, he remembered how many children Dr Wang had.

Mr Lee further asked Dr Wang where they were living and where his wife did their household shopping. Dr Wang replied, "We now live in Tanjong Pagar and my wife shops at the wet market near our HDB flat."

"How do you travel to work?" Mr Lee asked again.

"I bought a car, a Toyota, and drive to work," was Dr Wang's reply.

The next day, Mr Lee's principal private secretary, Ho Meng Kit, rang up and said he wanted to know how Wang Ming, who had only just arrived in Singapore to work, had enough money to buy a car and a flat. The answer was that Dr Wang and his wife (another Chinese scholar recruited by NEC in Singapore) had worked as tutors in their university in the UK and had built up enough savings.

Half a year later, I got a call from Philip Yeo, who was then chairman of the EDB. By that time, Singapore had recruited quite a number of

Chinese scholars to teach at the National University of Singapore and Nanyang Technological University, and Mr Lee wanted to know how they were adapting to Singapore. Mr Lee was very curious because the findings had revealed that the Chinese scholars at both our universities did not seem to have settled down well in Singapore, unlike those at SISIR and the Institute of Molecular and Cell Biology, another research institute. They were settling down well and highly motivated at these two research institutes. Their morale was detected to be comparatively higher. Mr Lee wanted to know the reasons for this difference.

My answer to Philip was that there were hundreds of very bright doctorate professors, local and foreign, at our universities. It could be that many of the Chinese scholars were merely lecturing to students and not necessarily tasked with challenging research projects. The attention they were getting from the universities may not therefore be so personal. I was simply making conjectures. At SISIR, we gave personal attention to our scholars as many were our star researchers who could boost SISIR's technological capabilities. They were given interesting industrial research projects to work on. We made sure they were accommodated and settled down well. We even threw mooncake festival parties for them. I also made it a point to speak to them whenever I visited the laboratories. I believe all these, as well as personal touches such as knowing their names and being familiar with their research projects, made them feel more useful and inclusive.

Mr Lee was anxious that the foreign talents we attracted to Singapore were happy working in their jobs. He wanted them to stay.

The pragmatism of Mr Lee

When I was CEO of CapitaLand, we were contemplating selling the Raffles Hotel Group which consists of Raffles Hotel and a number of other hotels under the Swissotel brand. I remember people warning me against it. Raffles Hotel itself is iconic and beloved by many Singaporeans, they said, especially Mr and Mrs Lee who celebrate their family functions there regularly. If you sell it, you will lose your head, they warned me. But Raffles Hotel Group was not delivering acceptable financial returns and would need more than S$2 billion to further grow it to globally competitive size, so we decided to go ahead with the sale. The question was how to inform Mr Lee, not to get his approval but to let him know about our proposed divestment.

The board of directors of Raffles Group was to meet on a Saturday to make the final decision on the divestment. Up until the Friday night, I was emailing Mr Lee through Temasek about the proposed sale. He asked many questions. I answered them as best I could. That went on all night. By 2.30 a.m., I gave my answer to the last question and went to bed after that. I got up at 6 a.m. and checked my email to find his final comments on the sale. His email thanked me for keeping him in the loop. He said that if it had to be done in the business interest of the company, so be it. But he added that we should make sure we look after all the hotel staff and Jennie Chua, then the president and CEO of the Raffles Group. That was an important message. To me, it shows his pragmatism in business, balancing financial reality with emotional sentiments.

Raffles Hotel is an important icon of Singapore. However, it did not deliver the due investment returns to the public listed company which owned it and, indeed, needed to call for huge investment which we could not afford. We finally had to put our emotions aside and let the financial decision be made rationally. After all, the hotel would still be physically around at Beach Road in Singapore, although the owner may not be the same. Mr Lee understood the importance for us as a public company to follow financial discipline. He was pragmatic about us divesting Raffles Hotel Group. But he also showed his personal concern for the hotel staff when he reminded us to look after them after the divestment, which took place in July 2005.

A few years ago, during a Q&A session at a global conference, a foreign participant asked Mr Lee what had made Singapore successful. Mr Lee cited four factors: governance, meritocracy, anti-corruption and pragmatism. It took me some time to understand why he mentioned pragmatism as a success factor for Singapore.

Pragmatism is about finding practical solutions to problems without foregoing one's values. Mr Lee was my true teacher on that. You can identify many of his pragmatic solutions in the way he set policy decisions in the early days of nation building in Singapore. He was unapologetic about his pragmatic policies, no matter how unpopular they were. National Service, population control (first "Two is Enough", then "Have three, or more if you can afford it"), adopting English as the first language and using the mother tongue as the second language, HDB public housing, NEWater, agreeing to the Integrated Resorts, and his willingness to change his policy thinking for more workable solutions for the greater good — all these are testaments to his pragmatic leadership. I liken him to Deng Xiaoping who famously said, "It didn't matter if a cat was black or white, as long as it could catch mice!"

Mr Lee's concern for Singapore's commercial successes

Mr Lee never stopped caring for Singapore, even after he stepped down as Prime Minister. One hot Sunday afternoon, he took a walk at Clarke Quay with Mrs Lee to see what was happening there. They ran into former Ambassador Tony Siddique, who told them that he had invested in a restaurant/club there.

Clarke Quay was very quiet and business appeared slow and sleepy (this was before the area was transformed into today's bustling F&B entertainment precinct). Mr Lee told Tony Siddique, "This place, as it is, will die. Can you suggest to Mun Leong to seek help to transform it to something like the famous Lan Kwai Fong in Hong Kong?"

I reached out to Allan Zeman, the owner of Lan Kwai Fong, to see if we could interest him to do that, but he did not think it would work well here.

Eventually CapitaLand radically renovated the whole place with new and bold designs, putting special efforts to reduce the exposure to heat by installing colourful polymer shelters, and brought in new F&B concepts and entertainment attractions. We even managed to attract the world famous Parisian Crazy Horse to start a show there. Clarke Quay eventually turned out to be a commercial success, a "must-visit" place for most tourists. Few people, however, know that it was Mr Lee who triggered the whole transformation. Several years later, Mr and Mrs Lee visited Clarke Quay again one evening to find out its latest developments.

Mr Lee's interest in retirement and the older workforce

A few years ago, I sent a Harvard Business Review Paper to Mr Lee. Entitled "It's time to retire retirement", it argues against compulsory retirement based on age and discusses the virtue and economics of not retiring too early. I am against compulsory retirement too and, indeed, we had successfully employed several silver haired executives in their late fifties and early sixties to work in CapitaLand.

Mr Lee emailed me to say that he had read the paper and had suggested to Patrick Daniel, then Managing Editor of Singapore Press Holdings, to send a reporter to interview me and the "silver haired" employees. He copied his email to the Cabinet and Patrick Daniel, who arranged for a young reporter, Rachel Chang, to conduct the interview. A full-page article of the interviews was subsequently published. Mr Lee saw the value of keeping the older workforce in active employment and knew that they still had the ability to contribute to our economy. He truly valued talent, both young and old.

Mr Lee's inexhaustible curiosity

It is well known that when you are in Mr Lee's company — whether on official business or an informal gathering — you had to be very prepared to answer his questions, which were oftentimes unexpected. What's more, his queries were never limited to the business at hand.

As CEO of CapitaLand, I once hosted a dinner at Raffles City where Mr Lee was Guest of Honour. I had to "study" and commit to memory all the little details related to my business so that I would be able to answer any question he may ask. He could ask about the property market, business cycles, projection of business trends of Singapore and global markets — anything! It was as though I was preparing for a tough professional examination!

At the dinner, as expected, he asked about the price of property in Singapore, Shanghai and Beijing. Among other questions, he also asked about our performance and profitability. I was doing fine until his last question. He said, "Steve Green[3] told me that Americans are much better at making money from property than Singaporeans. Is that true and why?" He caught me off guard with that question. I briefly explained to him that it was probably true, because in America the real estate market was more closely connected to the financial markets and the real estate companies could tap into the capital market very aggressively for funding and to create financial products.

On another evening, we went on a buggy tour of Clarke Quay with Mrs Lee, then Chief Justice Yong Pung How and his wife, and Lee Seow Hiang, his principal private secretary (PPS) then. Mr Lee wanted to see Clarke Quay's transformation after its extensive renovation. We stopped at the famous discotheque, Ministry of Sound. Whilst Mrs Lee stayed at the first floor, Mr Lee climbed up to the second floor to watch the youngsters enjoying themselves dancing to bizarrely loud music.

He surprised me with the question, "Have you done that before?"

I told him, "Yes, a long time ago, sir, when I was much younger."

He commented, "That is tribal!"

He then requested to visit Crazy Horse as he wanted to find out how it was faring. We went there and met the owners, a husband-and-wife team, who told him business was not as good as they had expected. He asked many questions and instructed Lee Seow Hiang to help resolve the operational problems they faced, especially the restrictions on promoting and advertising the show. I think his concern then was that since Crazy Horse was world famous, its failure to take off might presage the likelihood of success of the Integrated Resorts when they were opened in the coming years.

The loving couple, Mr and Mrs Lee

In 1998, Mr Lee was our Guest of Honour at the opening of Sheraton Hotel in Suzhou, China. After the official dinner, I asked him if he and Mrs Lee wanted to take a walk around the rock garden we had created. The rocks were brought in from the famous West Lake. He agreed. It was very dark and we had to use a torchlight to guide them. Mr Lee's security officer was with us and we walked very slowly. It was quite tricky as some of the stones were jagged and slippery. As we walked in the dark, I silently regretted my stupid suggestion as Mr Lee was already in his late seventies. But they enjoyed the walk and luckily there were no mishaps. After that, we all retired for the night.

The next morning, I asked the security officer if Mr and Mrs Lee slept well. He said yes but they had woken up early, at about 3.30 or 4 a.m., and gone for a walk in the garden! Apparently they had enjoyed the earlier walk so much that they wanted to experience it by themselves again. Luckily, nothing untoward happened during that walk either. It was heartwarming to see how loving they were as a couple, and how they still enjoyed and treasured their quiet moments together. They were still very much a romantic couple!

In 2008, Mr Lee was invited by the Chinese government to attend the Beijing Olympic Games as a special state guest. He wanted very much to take Mrs Lee along but she had just suffered a third stroke and was bedridden. We studied various ways to safely move her around, such as modifying an MPV to suit her needs, and looked carefully into the logistic arrangements. We had it all planned but Mr Lee decided in the end not to risk it. He went alone.

In Beijing, his then PPS Chee Hong Tat told me Mr Lee had a free slot in his schedule and asked me to arrange for ten eminent non-government people in China to have lunch with him. He wanted to have a conversation with them to gather their views, I guessed. I managed to assemble several top Chinese bankers, business leaders, entrepreneurs and even one of China's top nuclear scientists to lunch with him at the China World Hotel. Most of them were not conversant in English so we arranged for a translator to be present. Mr Lee spoke with them for two hours without the aid of the translator. He sparred freely with these very brilliant minds in Mandarin over a wide range of subjects. The Chinese guests were all very impressed with him and thanked me for inviting them. It was a rare opportunity for them to meet Mr Lee, whom they respected very much.

I learnt later, that after dinner that night, he went back to his room and read a book, over Skype, to Mrs Lee. He remembered to do that after a hard working day with the Chinese.

Mr Lee in his later years

Age had inevitably taken a toll on Mr Lee over the years. In the last few years before his passing, he had become less mobile and was not speaking as much as before. But despite his feebleness, he continued to take an interest in Singapore and world affairs, and in the conversations whenever we met at social gatherings.

In recent years, some of us met up with him regularly for meals on a social basis. His niece, Kwa Kim Li, made the arrangements and accompanied him. As he was quite immobile, it was good for him to get out of his home occasionally and we were more than happy to keep him company. He wasn't speaking much by then, but we knew he listened attentively to our conversations and once in a while he would chip in a word or two. His memory was still very good.

Sometimes we would try to tap into his wisdom by asking him his views or his prediction of an outcome for a current event. His responses were usually short and often monosyllabic, but they were always thoughtful, sharp and precise. During the 2008 US Presidential election, for instance, we asked him who he thought would win the election: McCain or Obama? He answered, "Obama."

When asked why he thought Obama would be the winner, he simply said, "Likeability."

I deeply treasure those precious times that we had with him. I learnt much from Mr Lee even from his short and succinct comments and answers to our questions. There were still many lessons that could be distilled from his replies. His one word, "pragmatism", triggered me to think about his management and leadership style.

He made his last public appearance at the Pyramid Club's annual dinner in November 2014. To me, as the best demonstration of his inner strength, he was prepared to be seen in public being fed by an assistant during dinner — and he appeared nonchalant about it.

Our last, and probably the most memorable, dinner with him was on 5 January 2015, at the China Club. This was about ten weeks before his passing. As 2015 was our Jubilee Year, we wanted to share a jubilee cake with him at the dinner. He was in very good spirits, ate well and smiled a lot that evening. His face was pinkish and he appeared in good health. We arranged the next dinner with him to be on 11th February. Of course, nobody knew then that that would be his last dinner with us. Perhaps the most heartening exchange that evening was his response to the question we asked: "Mr Lee, do you think there will be a Singapore in 50 years?"

His response was, "Of course there will be … even better!"

This was his final endorsement of the future of Singapore which he dedicated his life to.

Notes

[1] Lee Seow Hiang is Chief Executive Officer of Changi Airport Group.

[2] Project Jewel is a new retail and lifestyle complex at Changi Airport. It will be a central hub connecting Terminals 1, 2 and 3 and will be completed in late 2018.

[3] Steve Green was US Ambassador to Singapore from 1997 to 2001.

LIM SIONG GUAN

Principal Private Secretary, 1978–1981

"Never look down. You are dealing …
as a representative of Singapore.**"**

– Lee Kuan Yew

I served as the first ever principal private secretary (PPS) to Singapore's founding Prime Minister from May 1978 to June 1981. People often ask me what it was like to serve Mr Lee, as he was known to be very tough and demanding of high standards of work. They always react with surprise when I tell them that the three years as his PPS were the freest three years of my working life!

In all my other career appointments, I could determine the agenda for thought and action. My diary was continually full as there was always more that could be done to improve and innovate than there was time and people to drive the change. However, when I was serving Mr Lee, I could only operate within his agenda. I could not create new work on my own. The most important service I could offer to those I interacted with was to convey and explain what the Prime Minister had in mind. Thus, I had time on my hands to read books and think deeply about issues of life and the government of nations.

From Mr Lee I learnt the principles of governance that undergirded the transformation of Singapore from the early days of self-government in 1959, to subsequent independence in 1965, and her development and evolution into a modern metropolis. He taught me that building a nation was not the same as building a city; a city is made of plans and concrete structures, but a nation is made of people united to work together for a bright future for all. Mr Lee also taught me that a leader not only needed to have clarity of views and single-mindedness of purpose, but also the capacity to communicate clearly and convey complex problems simply so that issues are understood by the man in the street.

I well remember my first meeting with Mr Lee as his PPS. He told me that in the course of my work, I would be dealing with foreigners, and he advised, "Always look the foreigner in his eyes. Never look down. You are dealing with him as a representative of Singapore. Conduct yourself as his equal." As I look back, I plainly see that in this wise instruction lay the reason for what has made Singapore so much of what it is — well regarded by the world, respected, self-aware, pushing always against the boundaries of possibilities.

Mr Lee, the master teacher

I sat in for all of Mr Lee's official meetings. It was his way of training me to develop understanding and judgement on the broad range of issues of government.

When he was dealing with the merger of the then Nanyang University with the then University of Singapore to form the National University of Singapore,[1] he took great pains to explain to me the issues involved, especially since he was sending me to discuss the matter with Wee Cho Yaw, the chairman of the Nanyang University Council.

His meetings with ministers and senior officials overseas were especially eye opening. I was always impressed with his clear grasp of wide-ranging topics, his ability to draw together disparate points to form a cogent case for discussion and present issues in a way which conveyed win-win possibilities.

He infused in me deep lessons on leadership and governance. I learnt always to be on the lookout for talent and to do whatever I could to allow people to achieve their potential. Singaporeans have to be relentless in striving for excellence and to desire to be the best in everything we do. For Singapore, unlike many other countries, survival and success are two sides of the same coin. There are countries that are independent but not sovereign, and countries that are sovereign but not independent. Singapore must seek to be friends with all who would be friends with Singapore, and never forget that no one owes us a living and that no one else is responsible for our security. The drive to be exceptional in the way we think is not an option: it is destiny for Singapore.

Mr Lee, the perfectionist

From the start, Mr Lee was very clear in his mind that Singapore would not be a concrete jungle. His passion to create a garden city where there were plenty of trees and flowering plants was infectious. I remember his questioning again and again on how to get greenery to grow even under the flyovers that were being built all over the island.

He was not satisfied to just outline the big picture on issues and always insisted on getting into the details of what he considered critical. Thus when he launched the National Productivity Movement in 1981,[2] he looked at it from all angles — schools, workers and businesses.

Once, he called together all the senior civil servants for a forum at the Regional English Language Centre. He wanted to discuss the low standard of English language in the civil service, particularly in the drafting of Cabinet papers where he felt that ideas were not clearly expressed, grammatical errors were too many, sentences were too long, and words were badly chosen. We were told not to camouflage ambiguity and uncertainty with words. We all ended up having to attend classes on writing simply and directly. *The Complete Plain Words* by Sir Ernest Gowers, first published in 1954, became a serious benchmark and reference for us all.

The three years I spent as Mr Lee's PPS were essential in preparing me for my next appointment as Permanent Secretary in the Ministry of Defence, and my later appointments as Permanent Secretary in the Prime Minister's Office, the Ministry of Education and the Ministry of Finance. If I had to describe the man in just three words, I would say he is strategic, patriotic and relentless.

Notes

[1] Nanyang University was merged with the University of Singapore in 1980 to form the National University of Singapore. An important reason was the government's desire to pool the two institutes' resources into a single entity with the English language as the medium of instruction, as it was a prevalent language for commerce and economic development in the world.

[2] The National Productivity Movement was spearheaded by the National Productivity Board which was set up in 1972, before which it had been the National Productivity Centre under the Economic Development Board.

JAGJEET SINGH
Grassroots leader, Tanjong Pagar

❝Mr Lee picked up his chopsticks and, one by one, he put the food on each of our plates.❞
– Jagjeet Singh

I never, in my wildest dreams, thought that I would one day work closely with this great man.

I grew up in Changi Village. My father worked as a civilian for the British at the nearby airbase. Our quarters were at the edge of the nine-hole golf course in Changi. The golf course is still there. We used to peer over the fence at Mr Lee playing golf with world leaders. I saw him there with Malaysian Prime Minister Tunku Abdul Rahman.

When Mr Lee came to play golf, he and Mrs Lee would stay at the Changi Cottage. When they were "in town", everybody in the village knew. In those days, there was not much security around them. They were free and easy and walked around the village. Their particular interest was this Hainanese bakery called A1. When A1 baked bread, the aroma would pervade the whole village. All the RAF[1] service wives would come out with their perambulators and babies, and queue up for the French loaves. Mr Lee once made a speech about that bakery and its impact on the whole village.

Every year in Changi Village, we had a sea carnival where traditional Malay miniature boats with big white sails were released to catch the wind. You just let them go, and see which one reached Changi Point first. Changi Point was a Malay village near the present Mindef[2] ferry terminal. This carnival was one of our traditions, and we always looked forward to it.

I was close to the village headman and helped with the carnival. So there is this picture of Mr Lee firing a shotgun to start the race. And there I was next to him in my Rover Scout's uniform doing crowd control; I was 16 or 17, just out of school at that time. In those days, the Ministry of Culture used to print huge information posters of the latest happenings and put them on the notice boards of bus shelters all over the country, especially in the rural areas. That was our Internet. That picture of me next to Mr Lee holding the shotgun found its place on bus shelters everywhere around the island. Mr Lee looked very strong and vigorous. He had a warm aura around him; you could tell that this man is a special human being. I thought that was the closest I would get to him. That was in 1961, I think.

Sometime in 1976 or 1977, I moved to Spottiswoode Park near the Tanjong Pagar train station. My wife worked for the Port of Singapore Authority (PSA), and since PSA had two blocks of staff housing at Spottiswoode, we decided to live there. Later, another seven blocks were added to the estate. Not long after moving in, I got a call from Mr Ch'ng Jit Koon. He was the MP looking after the constituency then. He asked me to form the Residents' Committee[3] (RC) for Spottiswoode. We were only the third RC in Singapore. The first one was in Marine Parade, the second in Tanjong Pagar Plaza. Our first chairman was Dr Low Cze Hong, a prominent eye surgeon who was staying at Spottiswoode then.

Mr Lee was the MP for Tanjong Pagar and he was there at the first RC meeting. He had everybody's files with him, including our photos. We all sat like schoolchildren in rows in front of him. He opened the files, called our names, we stood up, and he asked us questions. Some people, he grilled. For me, he said, "Jagjeet Singh. School teacher. Moved into Spottiswoode Park. You don't mind serving in the RC?" I just said, "Yes, sir. Thank you, sir." Then he moved on to someone else. Dare you say no when the PM asks you to serve? I was going to be the secretary of the RC.

I was also the First Assistant Secretary (we had several assistant secretaries then) of Tanjong Pagar's Citizens' Consultative Committee (CCC).[4] There were many Chinese clans in the constituency, which made the estate more like a Chinese town. But just like back in Changi, I had no problems in Tanjong Pagar and mixed around quite well with the residents. Every year, in the Hungry Ghost month, I would be invited to represent the CCC at the Ghost Month functions, two or three in a row. I understood the things that have meaning for Chinese people, one of them being the Chinese zodiac in which each year is represented by an animal sign. And so every year we made Risis gold-plated animal figurines that corresponded to the zodiac animal for that year, and auctioned them off at these events. From this we were able to raise money for bursaries. Education was one thing we knew we could always get support for.

No one treated me differently. I remember one Chinese New Year when I was the Organising Secretary for the Chinese New Year celebrations. In those days, we used to hold media briefings before the Chinese New Year dinner. A Chinese reporter asked Mr Ch'ng, "How can a non-Chinese help organise the Chinese New Year dinner?" To which Mr Ch'ng replied sharply, "Why not? Next Deepavali, you can be the organising secretary."

You may not believe this. My job on the CCC was to do the minutes. But back then, the meetings were all held in dialects and Chinese. There were times when I did not catch anything even though I had studied Chinese in primary school. The next day, I would go to the District Office, and together with the District Secretary we would sort out the minutes. It must have worked because no one said anything. One day, during a meeting, the CCC chairman realised I must have been having some difficulty. He asked, "How did you do the minutes all this time?" I said that I managed them somehow! After that, they got a gentleman who could speak English to sit next to me in the meetings, and he would translate for me. Gradually as more people in the committee could speak English, the meetings were held in English. Soon I became a Vice Chairman, and then a patron.

My wife once told our children, "This is the meaning of patience and tolerance. Your father sits through these meetings, he doesn't know dialects. Yet at the end of the day, he is able to produce the minutes." My children used to laugh about this. I used to laugh about it too. But I got it done. I told my children, I was asked to serve, so I come to serve, I don't come to ask for things for myself or the family. Even today, my children are grown up and they follow this principle. My daughter also volunteers at the Meet-the-People sessions in Sembawang. Sometimes she tells me, "I am there to serve, like you, not to ask for things." We believe in this. Well, anyway, this is what it takes to be a grassroots leader.

Mr Lee, and Mrs Lee, cared about what was happening with us grassroots leaders. Seven out of ten times that Mr Lee came to Tanjong Pagar, Mrs Lee would be with him. She would ask me about my children, even after they had finished university. Mrs Lee was like that. She was also very strong like Mr Lee, but she also had this caring way.

How did I know Mr Lee cared?

There was a courtesy campaign event one day. I can't forget it. I had sold my flat and just bought a house in Seletar Hills. At the reception, right in front of everybody, the chairman of the CC Management

Committee told Mr Lee that I was moving out of Spottiswoode. And right there, in front of the whole crowd, Mr Lee turned to me and said in a stern way, "Have you done your mathematics? Buying a private property, do you know what you're getting into? You have two small children, have you thought about their future? You'll tie yourself up in instalments!"

What could I say? I could only say, "Yes, sir, I've done my mathematics." It was frightening. It was also my most poignant moment with Mr Lee. That was his way. He knew that I had two children, and he was concerned that I should manage things properly for my family. I think he didn't know that I had been prudent and saved up. I spent all my time doing grassroots work, I didn't have any time to spend any money elsewhere! Today, I have retired from teaching and now serve as a full-time school counsellor. I have studied different ways of parenting and teaching, and I can recognise Mr Lee's behaviour as his way of showing his care. He was nurturing in his own way.

One weekend soon after, Mr Lee went on a walkabout. I wasn't there on that day. People were trying desperately to reach me. We didn't have handphones then. The headline that came out in the newspapers the next day was: "Even if you move from Spottiswoode to Seletar Hills, you must come and continue to serve." Mr Lee had said this at the walkabout, and the press were all trying to find out who he was talking about.

Later, in the 1990s, I moved again, this time back to my childhood village in Changi. I asked Mr Ch'ng, "Should I resign from the Tanjong Pagar grassroots?" Mr Ch'ng replied, "You? I don't know. You better write Mr Lee a letter and ask him yourself." Of course, I did nothing! I still remembered what he said about serving. I was willing and honoured to serve.

One of the ways I served was to help with crowd control when Mr Lee came on his constituency visits. There were two kinds of people: those who wanted to go up to him, and those who did not want to be near him — the nervous ones. Over the years, I found that more and more people wanted to go up to him. People wanted to shake his hand or have him hold their babies. Sometimes I wondered if the baby got a bath again for the next few days.

Every event at Tanjong Pagar was a sell-out. Now I've been to other ministers' events, and there is often a lot of chatter. When Mr Lee spoke, the occasional cough and the whirring of the fans overhead were the only things you would hear. People came out in droves just to hear him speak and they clung on to his every word.

I went from that young boy who happened to stand next to Singapore's Prime Minister in the photo, to the old grassroots leader who tried to stay out of the picture, working behind the scenes to make sure everything would go smoothly for him, even when he became Senior Minister, and then Minister Mentor, and finally Mr Lee. I took my job seriously. What do you expect? Mr Lee is our national treasure.

I remember the first time I sat down at the same dinner table as Mr Lee. It was after the National Day Rally held at the National Theatre, near where the Van Kleef Aquarium used to be. It was also my first National Day celebration. The dinner was held outdoors under huge tents. There were large round tables and you were required to sit together with your MPs. We sat down; nobody dared to touch anything. Mr Lee then picked up his chopsticks and, one by one, he put the food on each of our plates. It was the first course, a cold dish with an assortment of appetisers on a big platter. One by one, around the table, with his own chopsticks, with his own hand, until every one of our plates had food on it. We just sat without moving. We didn't know what to do. Then our PM told us, "Come, eat." So we ate. After that, for the other courses, we dared to take the food ourselves, but all of us did so very gingerly. I will always remember this dinner, when the PM personally put the food on our plates and asked us to eat.

Since then, I have attended many dinners with Mr Lee. I saw this change in Mr Lee over the years. He grew more accepting than he was in the beginning. In the beginning, he was very stern. He started to banter with us more. We also got to know him better. Like how the man liked a good beer. I'm not joking — he really liked a good beer. We always made sure we had two chilled beers and two beers at room temperature on standby. Sometimes he asked for a warm beer. I don't know where that habit came from.

Towards the end, he didn't drink any more beers. But right to the end, he never wanted to show weakness. I remember a dinner function, some four or five years back, as he was going on stage to deliver his speech, and his security officer went forward to help him — I saw his hand on the side, waving the security officer away. Mr Lee was frail, yet that hand motion was very clear. He just wanted to do it himself. He managed to, but we were all so afraid for him. At our last National Day dinner, the security officer had to prop him up for the National Anthem. His voice was soft. But you could tell he was resolved to sing.

Every time Mr Lee came to Tanjong Pagar, I was like the parade commander. I arranged the people lined up to greet him according to the protocol list given to me. First would be one of the lion dance performers. Next would be the person to pass him the *ang pow* for the lion dance. Then all the ministers and VIPs in protocol order, then down the line to all the grassroots leaders and volunteers, and so on. And Mr Lee would make sure to shake every hand.

One year, I remember I was at the end of the line. When Mr Lee got to me, he took my hand in both his hands and said warmly, like he was seeing an old friend, "Ah, Jagjeet!"

Ah, Jagjeet. I remember this.

I remember I was quite surprised. I thought, eh, this is the first time this is happening! Usually, he would just shake our hands and move on. I thought back to that first time he said my name all those years ago: "Jagjeet Singh. School teacher. Moved into Spottiswoode Park." And I realised that, all this while, I wasn't just a name in his files, or just a face at his table. All this time, I had a place in his heart too.

Mr Lee's death feels to me like the loss of a senior relative. We all come here to walk a journey. He walked a good journey. And in his journey, he carried a whole nation with him. We were fortunate he was in our midst. He changed our lives in a way we never imagined. I was privileged to be able to join him on some small parts of his journey. I hope we always remember what he stood for.

Notes

[1] British Royal Air Force.

[2] Ministry of Defence.

[3] Residents' Committees (RCs) were first established in the Housing Board estates of Bedok, Marine Parade and Tanjong Pagar in April 1978. By June that same year, RCs were also set up in Ang Mo Kio, Boon Lay, Bukit Merah, Kolam Ayer and Toa Payoh.

[4] The Citizens' Consultative Committees (CCCs) are the umbrella bodies of all grassroots organisations in Singapore and come under the purview of the People's Association. The CCCs originated in the early 1960s when community leaders formed welcoming committees to assist then Prime Minister Lee Kuan Yew on his constituency tours to rally support among the people for merger with the Federation of Malaya. The first four CCCs were set up in March 1965 in the constituencies of Nee Soon, Punggol, Sembawang and Serangoon Gardens. By the following year, CCCs had been established in all 51 constituencies.

NG KOK SONG
Group Chief Investment Officer, GIC, 2007–2013

“Your assumptions are based on theory,
mine on experience.**”**
– Lee Kuan Yew

The very first time I saw Mr Lee Kuan Yew, I was a young boy growing up in Kangkar village in Johor. He had come to my village to campaign for Singapore's entry into Malaysia and I remember pushing my way through the crowds to catch a glimpse of him.

My first close encounter with Mr Lee, however, was in 1981 when I was working at the Monetary Authority of Singapore. The chairman of the US Federal Reserve Board, Mr Paul Volcker, had requested an audience with Prime Minister Lee. I was asked to escort Mr Volcker to see Mr Lee at the Istana and to take notes of that meeting.

In 1980, when the US economy was suffering from high inflation and investors worldwide had lost confidence in the US dollar, President Jimmy Carter appointed Mr Volcker as chairman of the Federal Reserve Board to set things right. He undertook a very strong tightening of monetary policy, raising interest rates to drive out inflation. He set the stage for a progressive decline in global inflation where interest rates went down to almost zero.

Mr Volcker was a man of great stature. I was very excited to escort him to meet another man of great stature. On the way to the Istana, I got a message from Mr Lee's personal assistant who asked me to request Mr Volcker to refrain from smoking because Mr Lee had by then become allergic to cigarette smoke. Now Mr Volcker was a heavy smoker of cigars; I didn't quite know what to say to him.

When I met Mr Volcker, I asked him for a favour: I said I would appreciate it if he did not smoke at the meeting because Mr Lee had an allergy to cigarette smoke. He kept quiet for a minute. Then he agreed to my request, on the condition that the meeting lasted no more than half an hour. Otherwise, he said, he would get very agitated.

So off we went to the Istana. I remember bringing Mr Volcker in and the two men sat down. I took out my notepad and pen, ready to record the dialogue, but Mr Lee looked me sternly in the eye and waved his finger. He didn't want me to take notes. He wanted the conversation to flow freely and he didn't want Mr Volcker to be inhibited by somebody taking notes conscientiously.

The meeting went on for one and a half hours! I kept looking at my watch. Mr Volcker was very involved and absorbed in the exchange about American politics and the economy. He asked Mr Lee about his views on the world, particularly on China and India. And he did not smoke the whole time! When I escorted him out, he said to a US embassy official waiting outside that he had just been in the presence of a great leader. I bade him goodbye.

When he had left, Mr Lee's principal private secretary (PPS) at the time, Lim Siong Guan, said to me, "The Prime Minister would like a set of notes from today's meeting."

I jumped into action. I asked for a place to sit down. He gave me a small room at the Istana and I quickly took out my notepad and began to unload everything from my mind. I jotted down the key points so that I could write more elaborate notes later in the evening. Mr Lee wanted to circulate the notes to the Cabinet. He wanted crisp notes, summarising the main issues with the key points expressed succinctly.

Mr Lee was very fussy about the way people in the public sector wrote. He did not like flowery language.

So that was my first impression of Mr Lee — a man of great stature. Even Mr Volcker viewed him as such.

After that, I would escort many other people to see Mr Lee. All those occasions were great opportunities for me to experience firsthand Mr Lee's thinking, his farsightedness and the way he saw connections in things that others don't see. This is why he was so greatly respected. That was the advantage all his PPSs had. One got to benefit from his wisdom and insights on a whole range of topics. It was an enriching experience for me over the years as I escorted people to see him and took notes at meetings.

Mr Lee, the teacher

During the Asian currency crisis of 1997–98, Mr Lee was Singapore's Senior Minister. He had had considerable years of experience dealing and interacting with our neighbours, Malaysia and Indonesia. Therefore, when the currency crisis came upon this part of the world, Singapore was asked to assist its neighbours in that difficult time.

By then, I was at the GIC (formerly Government of Singapore Investment Corporation). Mr Lee was the founding chairman of GIC since its inception in 1981 until 2011. Mr Lee knew me then as a senior GIC officer at regular board meetings. So, when the crisis broke and he wanted some ideas on how we could help, he roped me in as one of his advisors. It was quite a trying time and, if you remember, then Malaysian Prime Minister Mahathir Mohamad was under considerable pressure, as was President Suharto in Indonesia. My role was to come up with ideas and structure some proposals for discussions with the governments of Indonesia and Malaysia.

One day, I emailed a proposal to Mr Lee as my chairman at GIC and also to then Prime Minister Goh Chok Tong. Mr Lee came back very quickly with his views. I responded and was on tenterhooks that whole day because he had disagreed with some of my points. I was trying my very best to explain my view as a market person, and how we had to convince the financial markets, and the viability of some of the things that we wanted to do. We were constantly on our email.

The remarkable thing is that Mr Lee had learnt to use the computer and was typing his emails personally to me. The back and forth over email went on until the evening when Mr Lee asked his secretary to call me to see him at the Istana. He said he wanted to see me personally as he was getting frustrated with corresponding over email. I went over at about 7 p.m. — he worked until quite late. I was ushered into his office and his PPS at the time, Heng Swee Keat, was asked to take notes.

For the first half hour, there was no discussion. Instead, he gave me a lecture. He said, "Kok Song, you have expressed your views to me and I have expressed my views to you. So now, I just want you to listen to what I have to say. I want to explain to you the history of our relationship with our neighbouring countries and share my experiences and how we should structure our relationship on the basis of my past experiences."

So I listened. I didn't say much because he was digging deep into the past, offering many anecdotes to support his points. When he stopped, I asked to explain my point of view.

He listened to me very patiently and asked many questions, trying to understand my point of view. This went on for about 15 minutes until the phone rang. His personal assistant said, "Mrs Lee is here. She is waiting for you to go for dinner." He replied, "Please tell her to wait. I haven't finished with Kok Song yet." I quickly continued.

Then he said, "Okay, Kok Song, now I understand some of your points. I am prepared to modify my proposals to take into account some of them."

He made some suggestions. I said, "Yes, alright. But perhaps we could also amend those suggestions slightly." This negotiating went on for about another half hour. Finally, we arrived at an approach we were both comfortable with.

The meeting ended at about 8.15 p.m. On my way out, I saw Mrs Lee and apologised to her for making her wait. But she graciously said it was okay.

As I drove home, I was suddenly filled with this great sense of admiration for Mr Lee, not because of his views or the way he made decisions, but that he took the time to explain to me where he was coming from. He could have made a unilateral decision, but instead he felt it was important to explain things to me and to hear my point of view. He took me seriously enough to let me encroach on his dinner time. That encounter uplifted me. I felt that this man was really worth working for because of the respect he had shown me in his desire to explain things to me.

Of course there were times he would become impatient because he felt that I was missing something. And he would say, "Your assumptions are based on theory, mine on experience."

Mr Lee taught me many things about leadership. Sometimes, the leader must teach and share, and be prepared to admit he might be wrong and be humble enough to take in other views. The example he set solidified my own desire to really serve my country because this was a leader worth working for and working with. You can't say that of many other leaders. He was not dismissive of viewpoints and was willing to negotiate and compromise.

Mr Lee's softer side

My next personal encounter with Mr Lee was when my wife, Patricia, was diagnosed with fourth stage stomach cancer in July 2003. It was in the terminal stages and the doctor said the chances of her living beyond six months were slim. Eventually, however, she lived on for another 19 months.

Patricia had had only brief encounters with Mr Lee — at GIC events and when Mr and Mrs Lee invited us to dinner together with other guests. But Patricia was largely a shy person and her conversations with him had been limited.

One day, I was sitting beside her bed as she was undergoing chemotherapy at Gleneagles Hospital. She said, "I tell you something. I feel like I want to write a letter to Mr Lee."

I said, "What about?"

She said, "Nothing to do with you. Your job is just to deliver the letter."

I did as she said and four days later, there was a reply.

After that, there were several letters exchanged. When she first wrote to him, she addressed him as "Dear SM Lee" and signed off "Yours Respectfully". His first reply addressed her as "Dear Mrs Patricia Ng" and was signed off as "Lee Kuan Yew". Subsequently, she addressed him as "My dear SM Lee" and he would write "Dear Patricia", signing off as "Kuan Yew".

The reason I am sharing this is because the way Patricia felt about Mr Lee was probably how people of my generation and the older generation feel about him. They are proud to be Singaporean because of what Mr Lee did for the country. He gave us hope when the future was bleak. When we separated from Malaysia, he inspired us to believe in ourselves and defy the odds to prosper economically.

When Patricia fell ill, she felt that her time was short and she just wanted to write to him. We are so used to seeing him as a stern person. But the way he responded to her letters showed he had a tender heart. During her illness, he would always ask me about her. He would say to me, "Tell her not to give up. Soldier on."

I would tell Patricia this and she would be so delighted to know that he was thinking of her. It touched her and made her even prouder to be a Singaporean.

In 2003, Mrs Lee also became ill; she had a stroke in London. I remember one day, after a dinner and when the guests had left, Mr Lee once again asked about Patricia. I told him she had decided to give up on treatment. She felt it was pointless and was prepared to go.

He said, "You go back and tell her I asked about her."

And then he added, "Now both of us are in the same boat. You are looking after your wife and I am looking after my wife."

Patricia had made a meditation video called "From Panic to Peace" with Father Laurence Freeman, a Benedictine monk. I gave that to Mr Lee, and he was very struck by her peacefulness and serenity.

He would tell me about Mrs Lee's condition and how he would spend time with her in the evenings especially after her second stroke in 2008 and she became bedridden. It was trying on him and quite depressing. So, I shared with him my experience taking care of Patricia for the 19 months before she died.

Taking care of Patricia was a very significant time for both of us. When she passed away, I didn't grieve. I was sad, naturally, but I had had the opportunity to care for her during the time she was ill. I worked half a day only. The rest of my time was spent with her, and towards the end that made a big difference to her. She said it helped her overcome her fear of death because she felt she was loved.

I said to Mr Lee, "I think you also now have this opportunity to show your love for the woman you love. Despite your own fragility and busy schedule, you take time every evening to sit and read by her bedside."

He said she did not recognise other people, but she responded to his voice. I said, "There you are. She knows. She is feeling and experiencing your love for her." His wife's illness was something he had no control over, and he was depressed about it.

Mr Lee, the master of discipline

One day in 2010, Mr Lee asked to see me in his office at the Istana. I walked in and before I could sit down he said, "Who have you prepared to take over from you at GIC?"

This startled me. I thought I was being fired! I replied that we had a management leadership succession plan in place and if anything were to happen to me that night, there would be a Singaporean on hand ready to take over my position the very next day. I added that we also had candidates with the potential to shoulder the responsibility five to ten years ahead.

He said, "Very good. That's how we should do things in Singapore. Having an orderly leadership succession is a large part of how we inspire confidence in Singapore, and GIC should do the same thing."

He added, "You discuss with the board when you propose to retire and hand over to your successor. But you must stay around to help your successor succeed. Your job is not done even after you have handed over your responsibilities to your successor."

Then, he switched the discussion. He asked me how old I was. He said he was also in his sixties when he handed over the reins to Goh Chok Tong. He asked me about my health. I was quite startled. I said that, on the whole, I was alright, but that I had high blood pressure and occasional gout. He said, "That's okay. You can take medication for those."

Then I told him I had also recently been diagnosed with Type 2 diabetes. To this, his reply was more emphatic. He said, "What? You have Type 2 diabetes? Kok Song, don't fool around, take that seriously! I have had many friends, including Goh Keng Swee, who had diabetes. It's very serious. If you don't take care, you will need insulin injections. Your quality of life will go down."

He told me to watch my food and to exercise. And then he asked, "What is your weight?" I said I was about 80 kg.

He said, "What? You are shorter than me and I am lighter than you! You have to do something about your diet and you must exercise."

Yes, he was interrogating me like he was my doctor. He then rang his PA and asked for his food to be brought in. It came on a tray. This was where he became my dietitian. He said he ate several light meals a day. In the evenings and for supper, he usually ate yogurt, pear and pomelo. He also avoided rice or took only brown rice.

He got up from his seat and led me to a small room in his office. In it was a stationary bicycle. Showing me the settings, he said, "I exercise regularly. I go for walks and I swim in the evenings. During the day, I come into this room and I ride the bike. I put on BBC Radio and I ride. I was in Vietnam last week and I ate so much I put on two pounds or more. Now, I am determined to get rid of them, so I have been sitting on this bicycle for the last few days."

I said he was very disciplined.

He replied, "Of course you have to be disciplined! If not, you are going to get more problems later." He was giving me fatherly advice but he was also being very practical.

Mr Lee doesn't waste time on small talk. He was always very focused on improving things, whether it was his health, work or Singapore. I, however, am not so disciplined. So, every time I saw him, I would just squeeze my stomach in a bit.

Mr Lee's spiritual side

I meditate in the morning and evening. One day in February 2010, I was meditating at home when my mobile phone rang. I had forgotten to switch it off so I quickly put it on "vibrate" mode. But then, my house phone rang. Normally, my helper would pick up the phone but she had taken the dog out for a walk. Then I felt my mobile phone vibrating. Someone was really trying to get hold of me; I thought it must be something terribly urgent. I answered the call. It was Mr Lee's secretary: Minister Mentor, as he was at that time, would like to speak to me.

Mr Lee came on the line and said, "Kok Song, I heard from Health Minister Khaw Boon Wan[1] that you practise meditation."

I replied that I did and, as a matter of fact, I was just meditating when he called. He asked if he should call back later but I told him it was okay, so we continued speaking. He wanted me to show him how to meditate. He said he had started meditating some years ago when his son Lee Hsien Loong was recovering from cancer.[2] He said, "Meditation was part of his recovery process so I would join him. But I only did it on and off, and I am not making much progress now because I keep dozing off."

I offered to go to him to show him how to meditate. That way, I would be in a better position to explain what I do to keep awake during meditation. "We will do it together," I said, before asking him when he would be free.

"How about tomorrow night?"

So that was how it started. The next evening, I went to his office and showed him how I practised meditation as part of a Christian prayer. To me, it is not just a relaxation exercise. It's more than that. However, meditation is universal and the method is similar. If you are not religious, it is a method of coming to peace. I also gave Mr Lee a CD recording of my teacher, a Benedictine monk from Ireland called John Main who died in 1992. After that session, Mr Lee asked if we could meditate together again.

In the first three weeks, we had five to six meditation sessions. He was determined to learn to meditate. We set aside 20 to 25 minutes for each session. I would sit on the floor while he sat on a chair. I set a timer. I told him to go easy in the beginning, meditate maybe for ten minutes. He then asked how long I spent meditating each time. I told him about 25 minutes, to which he replied that he too would do 25 minutes. I would normally pack up my things and leave when the session was over, but he would sometimes ask me to stay on and we would chit-chat for a while. Every now and then, he would tell me to feel free to stop by whenever I had time to meditate with him. This I did on several occasions. But more often, I let him take the initiative because I did not want to impose.

After several months, I asked him if he had been practising regularly. He said, yes, he practised most evenings before going to bed as it helped him to sleep. I was quite amazed. I have taught meditation to quite a number of people but he was my best student because he was so open to what I had to share. Also, he was practising diligently, not just listening. He meditated almost every evening.

I told him I marvelled at his discipline. He said, "Kok Song, if I am not this disciplined, Singapore would not be where it is today."

He then recounted the time he had to learn Hokkien when he was campaigning in the early days in order to connect with the people at the rallies. He said people laughed at him the first time he tried to speak Hokkien in public but they respected him for trying to communicate with them. "That's the kind of discipline you need. Anything that is worthwhile doing, you must be disciplined about," he said.

In August 2013, I introduced Mr Lee to my living teacher of meditation, Father Laurence Freeman, a disciple of John Main. They hit it off wonderfully, so when Father Freeman came to Singapore I asked Mr Lee if he would do an interview on record with him as we thought it would inspire many people to take up meditation. He said sure and he was also okay with us filming the session. This revealed to me again the incredible discipline that he had when he wanted to learn something. He would approach any task with seriousness and determination.

Mr Lee, ever the pragmatist

Mr Lee always approached things from a very practical standpoint, even meditation. He said that meditation helped him solve problems. He said he was not religious, but I think he was a spiritual person — if you define spiritual as being other-centred and wanting to do good. He would tell you he made mistakes in his life but that he never regretted them because he always did what he had to with the best intentions. Those are indeed the words of a very spiritual person.

I remember vividly the day I arrived at the Istana for a meditation session but was told he would be delayed by about one and a half hours. I was asked if I wanted to come back later. I said it was okay, I would stay and read a book while waiting. His secretary said he had gone to the Singapore General Hospital for treatment. During the day, rumours had been circulating that he had suffered a heart attack and was seriously ill in hospital. So I was relieved to hear he was coming back to meet me.

When he got back, we meditated as usual. After it was over, I said, "You must have heard the rumours circulating about you being seriously ill. And here you are, in front of me, looking quite well! Don't you think the government should put out a statement to stop these rumours?"

He said, "No, there is no point because one day it will be true."

Mr Lee on letting go

He once told me, "People think I am still in charge. But I have already passed on the responsibility. I am now just a radar for Singapore. I am trying to think and look at the world and see what risks, changes and opportunities we may face in the future. My job is to be a long-range radar, to look ahead and then share with the government and give them my advice."

I told him most Singaporeans feel that things will not be the same without him.

His reply was that life must go on. He added that he wished to live long enough to see the Marina Barrage and Gardens By The Bay completed, as well as the Kallang Basin transformed into a freshwater reservoir. He said, "The landscape of Singapore would be transformed. It would be a beautiful city. I wish to live long enough to see that happen." I was quite moved by that. Mr Lee lived for Singapore.

Some people accused him of not moving on. If this was so, it was because of his abiding concern for Singapore. He just wanted to do his best to make sure future leaders understood what it takes to keep the country going. I sense that consumed his attention constantly.

That's the reason he did not need to hold on to power. However, while he was still alive, he wanted to give every ounce of his energy to Singapore and to continue to contribute to a better country.

He was inspiring — awe-inspiring even. And he was irreplaceable, a true icon of Singapore who enabled Singaporeans to be proud of their country. Wherever you go in the world, people regard Singapore very highly because of him. Interestingly, his achievements are perhaps more powerfully recognised outside of Singapore than in the city-state he built.

Notes

[1] Khaw Boon Wan was Minister for Health from 2004 to 2011 and Minister for National Development from 2011 to 2015. He is currently Coordinating Minister for Infrastructure and Minister for Transport.

[2] Prime Minister Lee Hsien Loong was diagnosed with lymphoma in 1992. He was then the Deputy Prime Minister and Minister for Trade and Industry.

LAM CHUAN LEONG
Principal Private Secretary, 1981–1984

❝Just presenting a set of facts before Mr Lee was not sufficient to gain his acceptance.❞
– Lam Chuan Leong

Amongst the most memorable occasions of my time spent with Mr Lee when he was Prime Minister were the informal working sessions held over dinner, usually in the presence of overseas guests, some of whom were his long-time close personal friends. I was Mr Lee's principal private secretary from 1981 to 1984.

It was in these off-the-record meetings that he expressed some of his convictions and deeply-held principles. One of these abiding principles was strict adherence to the promotion of Singapore's collective interests instead of the interests of any specific sub-group, be they a company or an individual or groups of individuals. Another was the categorical freedom and protection he gave to civil servants to act professionally and free from any outside interference.

These were illuminating as they informed the basis for the various policies and decisions regarding Singapore's public policy. Staffers benefited from these deeper insights and were thus able to avoid the pitfalls of micromanagement or ad hoc decisions.

Mr Lee, the critical thinker

I remember once, during a discussion on the Suzhou Industrial Park[1] project, Mr Lee asked a question about the size of the budget we had allocated to this top-priority cooperative project with China. When I told him off-hand the sum of the budget, he was not convinced that the number was correct and explicitly asked if I had plucked the number out of the air to impress him. I explained that, by sheer coincidence, I had signed off the budget proposal to the Ministry of Finance the day before and offered to send him the details immediately after the meeting. Having satisfied himself that my answer was reasonable, he replied that it wasn't necessary to do so.

It was abundantly clear that just presenting a set of facts before Mr Lee was not sufficient to gain his acceptance. In his position, with the heavy responsibility of matters of state on his shoulders, he had to satisfy himself that whatever came before him must have impeccably sound foundations. He was constantly querying the basis, the sources, and the reliability of any information that came his way.

Mr Lee and the questioning of assumptions

Mr Lee was a meticulous and critical reader. In the early 1980s, he was reading a book — I believe it was by Hans Eysenck[2] — on the role of nature and nurture on human intelligence.

He noticed that in one part of the book the role of nature in determining IQ was given as 80 per cent, while in another part, it was stated that two-thirds of the IQ score was attributed to nature. He asked why that was so. I explained that the first statement is a general correlation statistic and given as the square of the deviations of the raw IQ scores. Thus 80 per cent is a contribution of nature to nurture in the ratio 4:1. If one takes the square root on both sides, the result is 2:1 and hence the two-thirds impact on the raw IQ score.

I was very impressed that Mr Lee took pains to actually create numerical examples of his own to verify if this was indeed the case.

It illustrated the enormous care with which he examined new ideas and propositions, and how he had to satisfy his own thorough understanding of them before using them as the bases for his decisions or thinking.

Mr Lee and his legacy

Mr Lee's dedication to Singapore's collective interests and future was abundantly clear. All his time and efforts were dedicated to thinking about what could be done to improve the lives of Singaporeans. In the process, he changed Singapore dramatically — our needs today are very different from those he encountered.

Particularly in the retrospective wisdom of three decades, his foresight into matters of public policy has proven to be prescient. His vision of a clean, green and pollution-free Singapore was in place long before the environmentalist movement or the climate change issue surfaced into prominence. His strong adherence to the free market system began controversially in the 1960s but has since become the bedrock of many countries that have tried to emulate our efforts in that direction.

However, foresight is only effectively transformed into concrete results when it is combined with the pragmatism and tenacity that Mr Lee possessed in abundance. Singapore's achievements owe an immense debt to a leader with these three qualities — foresight, pragmatism and tenacity — infused with an extraordinary sense of integrity to do what was best for the collective good.

Notes

1 The China-Singapore Suzhou Industrial Park (SIP) began in February 1994 as a bilateral project for Singapore to share its industrialisation experiences with China. It was backed by then Prime Minister Lee Kuan Yew and then Chinese Premier Deng Xiaoping. Singapore initially held a 65 per cent stake in the China-Singapore Suzhou Industrial Park Development Group (CSSD), with the rest by China. However, local officials in Suzhou set up a rival park close by (Suzhou New District Industrial Park), causing this venture to be in debt. Subsequently, Singapore cut its stake to 35 per cent to incentivise the local government to support the SIP. In 2001, one year after Singapore lowered its stake, the park made its first profit of S$3.8 million. Its stake in CSSD is now 28 per cent. Currently, the SIP is ranked the second-best industrial park in China and regularly tops developmental indices.

2 Hans Jurgen Eysenck (1916–97) was a German psychologist best remembered for his work on intelligence and personality. He received his PhD from University College, London.

BILAHARI KAUSIKAN

Ambassador-at-Large and Policy Advisor, Ministry of Foreign Affairs

**"Young man, do as I say. I was playing
these games before you were born!"**
– Lee Kuan Yew

I was privileged to belong to that generation of Foreign Service Officers who learnt our trade from the masters: Mr Lee Kuan Yew and his comrades. There were no formal lessons. When I joined the Foreign Ministry there was no formal training of any kind. We were thrown in at the deep end to sink or swim. We learnt by observation, almost by osmosis, while taking notes at meetings or accompanying Mr Lee and others on their trips abroad.

I have written in detail elsewhere about the specific lessons Mr Lee and his comrades imparted to us. I will not repeat myself. Instead I will try to recreate something of the atmosphere and spirit of the way we learnt by recounting a few anecdotes.

Of all I have written about Mr Lee since his passing, what has provoked the most scepticism was my contention that he was a very open person, thirsty for information irrespective of hierarchy, and tolerant of alternative views. Yet this was the first thing I learnt about him, even before I met him in person.

A week or so after I joined the Ministry of Foreign Affairs (MFA), I was tasked to write a brief for Mr Lee. I did so and after clearing the text with my bosses, sent it off. Within a few hours, back came a question from Mr Lee. I responded. Back came another question on my answer and so it went on for a few rounds. I thought nothing of it. I knew — or at least thought I knew — the answers to the questions posed and so replied without hesitation. It was only later when I casually mentioned the episode in passing to one of my superiors that the enormity of my offence was brought home to me.

I did not know that all responses to Mr Lee's questions required almost the entire Ministry huddling to craft some answer that would not arouse the Wrath of Lee. (MFA was then very small, the entire political section was about the size of one of our larger Directorates today). How dare I, the greenest of green Desk Officers, reply off my own bat? Mr Lee's questions were cunning snares into which, in my foolish and presumptuous innocence, I had fallen, and for which sin, at the very least, if Mr Lee was feeling particularly merciful, I could expect to be drawn and quartered. My career was certainly at an end.

I thought this was ridiculous. The questions he asked were of a factual nature. One either knew the answer or did not, and I did not understand how facts could be improved if arrived at by a committee of my elders. Nevertheless, they knew Mr Lee, and I did not, so I kept silent and resigned myself to death which I only hoped would be as painless as possible.

Nothing happened. Mr Lee was setting no traps. He just wanted to know.

Mr Lee suffered no fools. He often tried to intimidate you into agreement. But this is not the same thing as being intolerant. As I subsequently experienced, even when he did not agree, he listened. He never thought that he had all the answers. He never hesitated to change his mind if the facts warranted it. His views were always considered; his words chosen with deliberation. What Mr Lee said thus carried weight far beyond a small country's due.

This was brought home to me a year later when in the summer of 1982 Mr Lee travelled to Washington, D.C. I was then Desk Officer for North America and was on his delegation to take notes. The issue of the day was the Vietnamese invasion and occupation of Kampuchea, as Cambodia was then known.

The autumn before, an International Conference on Kampuchea was held at the United Nations in New York. Disagreement had arisen between ASEAN and China over what to do when the Vietnamese were finally compelled to withdraw. China wanted a return of the odious Khmer Rouge regime that the Vietnamese had displaced. This was unacceptable to ASEAN who maintained that the Cambodian people should choose their own rulers through UN-supervised elections. Singapore took the lead in holding to this position.

To our surprise, the United States took China's side. Perhaps in 1981 the prospect of a Vietnamese withdrawal seemed remote and the imperatives of US-China relations more compelling. At any rate, the US Assistant Secretary of State in charge of China, John Holdridge, attempted to bully and browbeat our Foreign Minister, Mr S. Dhanabalan, into changing our position. Holdridge threatened to call Mr Lee to complain — thereby exposing his ignorance of how Mr Lee and Singapore operated — and threatened "blood on the floor" if we did not relent. Mr Dhanabalan held firm and calmly invited him to do so. We maintained our position. The call was never made.

During Mr Lee's meeting with the Senate Foreign Relations Committee the next year, Mr Lee described America's China policy as "amateurish". Washington, D.C. is a gossipy place and word spread rapidly. Within hours, Holdridge called our Ambassador to find out what was said and to complain bitterly. As a young Desk Officer I was amused at the sight of such an august personality as an Assistant Secretary of State so thoroughly discombobulated. When he heard of Holdridge's complaints, Mr Lee, poker-faced, asked me as the note-taker whether he had really called him "amateurish". I showed him my handwritten notes. Mr Lee, still poker-faced, shrugged and said nothing.

The following year Holdridge was appointed Ambassador to Indonesia — an important position, but one in which he no longer held sway over America's China policy. And before his new appointment was announced, Holdridge anxiously enquired through an intermediary if Mr Lee had told then President Suharto anything about him. He was reassured that Mr Lee had not, and he went on to serve honourably in Indonesia.

Mr Lee was a lifelong anti-communist and risked his life in the struggle against the Communist United Front in which the Malayan Communist Party, supported by China, was the subterranean guiding force and most powerful component. But he recognised early on that China was a fact that could not be ignored. The point about this anecdote is not that he was anti-China but that his guiding principle, his laser-like focus, was always on the national interest of Singapore.

This, you may think, is the goal of any leader for his own country. But in reality, all too often too many leaders in too many countries confound personal interests or ego with the national interest. The devotion of Mr Lee and his comrades to the national interest is the exception not the rule and, I think, was recognised and respected as such even by those whose interests he opposed.

The story of Mr Lee's relationship with, and influence on, Deng Xiaoping has been told many times. But his pragmatic pursuit of Singapore's interest went beyond China. He supported the US war in Vietnam as buying valuable time for the non-communist states of Southeast Asia to put their houses in order and was instrumental in getting ASEAN to firmly resist the Vietnamese invasion and occupation of Cambodia. But Mr Lee always maintained that our problems with Hanoi were not bilateral. He recognised the determination and talent of the Vietnamese people and, notwithstanding his reservations about their political system, made clear he was willing to help them develop once they withdrew from Cambodia.

In April 1992, the ink barely dry on the international treaty that ended the decade-long Vietnamese occupation of Cambodia, Mr Lee, then Senior Minister, paid his first visit to unified Vietnam to offer help and advice. I had become Director for Southeast Asia and as we had not yet established an Embassy in Hanoi, it fell upon me to organise his visit which encompassed not just Hanoi but also Hue and Ho Chi Minh City. I made several trips to do so. What stands out was the great respect the Vietnamese had for Mr Lee notwithstanding his support for America's war against them, and their willingness to accommodate our every requirement for his visit.

This manifested in ways big and small, some even humorous. Practically the entire Politburo turned out for the first meeting to listen to Mr Lee. These were men who had defeated a superpower. They remembered our support for the US and had every reason to be bitter; some had even said that Singapore owed Vietnam a "debt" for our support of America. Yet they treated Mr Lee with great respect and hung intently on to his every word as he politely but clearly told them where they had gone wrong in their economic policies. But that was not the most vivid manifestation of the Vietnamese eagerness to learn from Mr Lee.

Vietnam had then just begun its reform efforts. Conditions were still primitive, the scars of war still evident, and organising a multi-city visit under these conditions very challenging. But perhaps only

Foreign Service Officers of a certain vintage will understand when I say that the most challenging aspect of organising that visit was to ensure an adequate supply of beer.

At that time, Mr Lee only drank a special type of Swan lager with only 0.01 per cent alcohol. Needless to say this was unavailable in Vietnam and in fact not easy to obtain anywhere. To ensure adequate supplies were at hand at every stop — and satisfactorily chilled — was a complex exercise in logistics. Somehow we managed, although our stocks were running low at a faster than anticipated rate as the weather was hot and the air-conditioning generally deficient. Still, by the time we reached our last stop at Ho Chi Minh City, I was congratulating myself. I have since learnt not to tempt fate.

I had not reckoned with the last official banquet, to be hosted by the city's Party Secretary and held in the old South Vietnamese Presidential Palace, a magnificent building but one in which the air-conditioning was not merely deficient but non-existent. It was a particularly sweltering evening. To keep cool, all of us, Singaporean and Vietnamese alike, were quaffing beer in more copious than usual quantities. But of course all of us except Mr and Mrs Lee were drinking Vietnamese beer — Ba Ba Ba — a tasty brew and to my mind far preferable to low-alcohol Swan lager. But our precious supplies of Swan lager were still disappearing at an unanticipated rate. With an anxious eye on the clock I did some hasty mental recalculations. Mr and Mrs Lee were due to depart for Singapore early the next morning. I concluded that we may just squeak through the evening. Then potential disaster loomed.

Seated across the table from me and next to Mrs Lee was some Vietnamese Party official whose name if I ever knew it, I have since forgotten. But he had been in every meeting in Ho Chi Minh City and must have been some Party bigwig. The intensity with which he observed Mr Lee's every action had caught my attention. That evening was no exception. He was watching Mr Lee so intently that he scarcely ate, although his enormous capacity for beer was undiminished. He suddenly noticed that the Lees were drinking a different beer from everyone else. His eyes lit up. I could practically see his thoughts appear, as in a cartoon, in a bubble above his head: *Ah, Mr Lee is drinking a different beer. Perhaps that is the secret of his genius.*

He beckoned a waitress and whispered to her. I watched in helpless horror as she brought him a precious can of our fast dwindling stock. I could hardly leap across the table and snatch the can from him. He examined the label with slow deliberation. Just as deliberately, he poured the beer into a fresh glass and examined the results, then carefully sipped. He looked thoughtful and sipped again. I held my breath. If he took a liking for the stuff we were doomed. Then to my infinite relief he pushed the glass away dismissively and called for a Ba Ba Ba. Whatever the secret of Singapore's success and Mr Lee's genius, he had clearly concluded it was not the beer. I breathed again and took a restorative gulp of my own.

Mr Lee supported the US presence in Southeast Asia as a vital element of the regional balance long before it was fashionable to do so — and at some political cost. He enjoyed close personal relations with many American leaders, among them former Secretary of State George Shultz. But he supported the US for Singapore's sake and when necessary did not hesitate to put his friendships on the line.

In 1988, as the Cold War wound down, we found it necessary to expel a US diplomat based in Singapore, one Hank Hendrickson who with the support and encouragement of his immediate State Department superiors had actively encouraged opposition to the PAP government, promising shelter and succour if they ran into trouble.

The communist regimes in East Europe were beginning to crumble and the Berlin Wall would come down a year later. The year before, the President of South Korea had been pushed from office by massive popular demonstrations, marking the end of the dominant role of the military in South Korean politics.

I doubt that Shultz himself authorised or even had prior knowledge of Hendrickson's activities. But as Secretary of State he bore overall responsibility for the actions of his officers, and he would have shared the general American belief that History was at last moving in the right direction. Events in the Middle East since 2003 have exposed the fallacy of such beliefs and have vindicated our conviction that it is foolish to attempt to nudge History in any particular direction in defiance of conditions in specific countries. But this was not so clear at that time and in authorising Hendrickson's expulsion, Mr Lee was certainly putting himself at odds with his old friend.

But he did not hesitate to take strong action, because he felt strongly about Singapore. On one occasion during the Hendrickson affair, to trap the Americans into an admission of their machinations, Mr Lee ordered me to do something that even I considered somewhat over the top. I did not think it would work and could even backfire. I said nothing — I am not *that* foolhardy and in any case the then Director of the Internal Security Department was kicking me under the table — but Mr Lee must have smelt my scepticism or seen it in my eyes. "Young man," he roared, "do as I say. I was playing these games before you were born!" It was a heart-stopping glimpse of the tiger's fangs up close.

I obediently set out to prepare what Mr Lee had ordered, but with extreme deliberation and certainly without an excess of zeal or haste. He cooled down. The order to set the plan in motion never came. And I am still here to tell the tale.

My friend and predecessor as Permanent Secretary of MFA, Peter Ho, has written of how Mr Lee had once told him: Reasonable men adapt, unreasonable men change the world. Singapore survived many perils and exists not just because of the towering intellect of Mr Lee and his team, but because of their passion. Passion is not always reasonable or agreeable. Passion can be terrifying. But Mr Lee could not have attracted such a formidable team or the support and admiration of so many international leaders, if he was the dictator some claim he was. People like Dr Goh Keng Swee or Mr S. Rajaratnam, among others, were not timid followers with no minds of their own. They followed him and the people of Singapore followed them because Mr Lee's passion for Singapore inspired them to dare to defy all odds.

Mr Lee and his team were passionately unreasonable about Singapore and were ruthless when they had to be. You cannot create something out of practically nothing by dint of gentle reason and bloodless intellect alone. And we will continue to survive and prosper only if enough Singaporeans continue to be passionately unreasonable about Singapore. Reason must be deployed to discipline but not conscribe passion. This is particularly so in the realm of foreign affairs which is not just another policy domain whose requirements can be satisfied (or avoided) by forming yet another committee. Successful foreign policy requires the passion to take calculated risks of analysis and action and not just bloodless and mechanical routine. Mr Lee and his comrades have bequeathed us the fundamentals of our foreign policy. These principles must now be adapted and applied to an external environment that is no less challenging than that they faced. This cannot be done just by bureaucratic rote.

STEPHEN LEE

President, Singapore National Employers Federation, 1988–2014

❝I do what I advise others to do! But everyone
is entitled to a treat every now and then.**❞**
– Lee Kuan Yew

I first met Mr Lee in 1981. He was then Prime Minister, chairing a meeting of senior executives to discuss productivity concerns. Later that year, he devoted a large segment of the National Day Rally speech to productivity, taking into account the feedback we had given him. Apart from that, I did not have much interaction with Mr Lee early in my working career. My distant impression of him was that he was stern but focused.

The first time I had a one-on-one discussion with him was in the mid-1990s when I was a Nominated Member of Parliament. He was then Senior Minister. I had chanced upon him sitting by himself in the members' room in Parliament House and took the opportunity to speak with him. We talked about the retirement age, which at that time was 55 and how that could be extended. We also discussed the concerns of employers. Mr Lee was interested to see Singaporeans working longer to supplement their income for retirement.

He was firm on moving ahead. One of his considerations was the unfavourable demographics. Twenty years ago, we had a younger population, but already he could see that the birth rate was declining and that it would be a matter of time before we had to extend the retirement age. He was far ahead and was already thinking of a retirement age beyond 60. Today, it is 62, with re-employment to 65, soon to be 67,[1] and perhaps beyond 67 in the future.

Thoroughness in thinking

My interactions with Mr Lee revolved mostly around business issues. I forged a closer working relationship with him when I was with the Port of Singapore Authority,[2] and later, Singapore Airlines (SIA).

Mr Lee had good listening skills. He often sought the views of others who were knowledgeable about a certain subject and he would listen attentively. Once he had made up his mind, he would fully support the initiative and those who would have to implement it.

While Mr Lee respected the businessman's viewpoint, he wanted to probe the reasons behind the decisions that were made. There were occasions when I discussed a business issue with him and suggested a certain course of action. He would question why I had chosen that course and whether I had considered alternatives. He was very thorough and quick to point out any gaps in my thinking. You had to know your subject well and be prepared to defend your choice of action when pressed. He had strong views but it was alright if you did not see eye to eye with him. You could give alternative views but you had better do your homework!

Forward thinking

Some of Mr Lee's colleagues have said that I was lucky to have worked with him in his later years when he had mellowed. I have every reason to believe that.

One remarkable thing about him was that he did not dwell on the past. He was always thinking ahead, even at his advanced age. I found this refreshing. He still had many ideas for Singapore's future.

Once, we were at Marina Bay. I asked him if he had ever envisioned the Bay to be like what it was today. He told me the initial idea, mooted some 30 plus years ago, was to build a dam at the river mouth to collect fresh water and to convert the area into a reservoir. In order to do that, the first thing that had to be done was to clean up the Singapore River. He said the rest came later. He was a very practical person as the idea for the Bay came about originally from the need for fresh water.

The Marina Bay is now a landmark and he took much joy in how well the idea had turned out.

Keen insight into labour management relations

I had the opportunity to chair two panel discussions where Mr Lee spoke. The first was at the Singapore National Employers Federation (SNEF) CEO Conference in July 1996 and the second at SNEF's 30th Anniversary CEO Summit in July 2010.[3]

The events were 14 years apart, yet one of the key points he made on both occasions was the importance of good labour management relations. He recalled the separation of roles of management and labour in some countries, and spoke of how management and labour in Japanese companies dressed alike in their company uniforms and worked as a team. Mr Lee strongly supported tripartism with the labour movement, government and employers working together to grow the economy to better the lives of workers.

The frequent traveller

Mr Lee was a frequent traveller on SIA during his many years in office. He was familiar with the airline's processes and procedures and would sometimes give suggestions on how to improve its services. He was observant and could be demanding when he felt things were not right.

Mr Lee did not watch in-flight movies. Still he made it a point to check if the entertainment system was in good order, if the chair was functioning well, or if other hardware was working properly. He noticed details like carpets that were slightly ripped at the edges. People wondered if he was naturally so fastidious. My conclusion is that he was not but that he understood what needed to be done to improve things. He pushed us hard to achieve a higher standard.

Mr Lee could be understanding as well. Once he asked for hot chocolate. The chief steward only had the 3-in-1 packet formula. When it was served to Mr Lee, he asked why there was so much sugar in it and requested that the sugar be removed. The steward panicked. He did not know what to do. How do you take the sugar out? Eventually, someone went up to explain the situation to Mr Lee. He accepted the explanation and changed his drink.

Treating himself to ice cream

Mr Lee could be quite relaxed when he wanted to be. In 2010, I was at a dinner with Mr Lee and several others. Seated between Mr Lee, who was then Minister Mentor, and myself was Ng Kok Song, who was then with GIC (formerly Government of Singapore Investment Corporation).

Part of the dinner conversation revolved around health and exercise, and Mr Lee gave some advice on how to eat healthily. When dessert came, we all chose a healthy Chinese item but he had two scoops of ice cream. I decided to pull his leg and said in an audible voice, "Kok Song, you should do what MM tells you to do but you should not do what he does." Upon hearing that, Mr Lee put down his spoon and protested, "I do what I advise others to do! But everyone is entitled to a treat every now and then." We had a good chuckle.

Appreciation of staff

There was one side of Mr Lee that many did not get to see. While he appeared fierce and stern, deep down he had a kind heart. For example, after every performance that was held at the Istana, Mr Lee would always walk up to the performers and musicians to thank them. Likewise for the cabin crew at SIA. He expected the crew to be well trained and to deliver their service professionally, and he always expressed his appreciation for their efforts to meet his expectations. Many of our cabin crew enjoyed serving him on board. In fact, many have asked to take photographs with him and he always obliged.

The people who have worked long with him — staff from the Prime Minister's Office, his Press Secretary YY Yeong, Private Secretary Ms Wong Lin Hoe, and many others — can attest to his kindness. I have attended a few dinners where he had invited his doctors, nurses, medical support staff, Chinese tutors, as well as security and personal staff. He was appreciative of their wholehearted support for him.

Notes
-----

[1] Singapore's employment age will be raised from 65 to 67 by 2017, as announced by Prime Minister Lee Hsien Loong in his National Day Rally Speech on 23 August 2015.

[2] Stephen Lee was chairman of PSA Corporation from 2002 to 2005.

[3] Stephen Lee was President of the Singapore National Employers Federation from 1988 to 2014.

Lee Kuan Yew (back row, extreme left) and Robert Kuok (back row, sixth from left) were classmates at Raffles College. Here they are, in this photograph taken in 1941, all dressed up for the Raffles College Ball.

LEFT: Mr Wee Cho Yaw, then president of the Singapore Chinese Chamber of Commerce & Industry, pinning the courtesy mascot on Mr Lee in 1982 at a National Courtesy Campaign event.

RIGHT AND BELOW: Mr Lee preparing to hunt wild boar in Kazakhstan and in discussion with President Nursultan Nazarbayev, 1991; to Mr Lee's right is his PPS Ho Meng Kit. Mr Lee first visited the Republic of Kazakhstan in 1991 to boost bilateral relations, and made subsequent trips in 1996 and 2003.

Mr Lee (seated) and Mrs Lee in Turkey, 1991. On the left are then Second
Deputy Prime Minister Ong Teng Cheong and his wife.

Singapore delegation to Islamabad, Pakistan, 1992.
FROM LEFT TO RIGHT: Tharman Shanmugaratnam, Ho Meng Kit,
Lim Hng Kiang and George Yeo.

Some of the letters exchanged between Mrs Patricia Ng (wife of Mr Ng Kok Song) and Mr Lee, and Mr Lee's letter to Ng Kok Song on the demise of Mrs Ng.

Mrs Patricia Ng

7 Aug 2003

Dear Senior Minister Lee

When National Day approaches each year, I feel very fortunate and blessed to live in Singapore and I have always wanted to express my deep gratitude to you but lacked the courage to do so.

Now, I feel a sense of urgency as this may be my last National Day as I have been recently diagnosed with advanced stomach cancer.

On this auspicious occasion of the 38th birthday of Singapore, I thank God that we have been blessed with a leader who has a gifted vision and the courage, will and ability to make his dream a reality. I have the deepest respect and admiration for you and regard you as truly the Father of our nation.

My husband, Kok Song, and I have raised three children in our thirty-one years of married life and we are all proud to be Singaporeans.

May you and your family be abundantly blessed for your commitment to our nation.

Happy National Day!

Yours respectfully

Senior Minister
Singapore

11 August 2003

Dear Mrs Patricia Ng Kok Song

Thank you for your letter of 8th August 2003 telling me that you feel a sense of urgency to write it because this may be your last National Day as you have recently been diagnosed with advanced stomach cancer. I am grateful and deeply moved that you write this letter at a time when you are burdened with the thought of leaving your loved ones behind.

I had heard from my son, Hsien Loong, that Kok Song's wife had been diagnosed with stomach cancer. I am sad at this cruel act of fate. I understand how and one still a minor. I am sad at this cruel act of fate. I understand how you and your family must feel. My family experienced it when we were told that Hsien Loong himself was diagnosed with cancer of the lymphatic glands. It was a traumatic blow.

It is so unfair. One small consolation is that modern medicine can make your suffering less unbearable.

My wife and I send you and your family our sympathy, understanding and support.

Kok Song will need them most of all. I have no words to describe our sadness or to comfort him, your family, your daughters and you.

Very sincerely

Senior Minister
Singapore

25 September 2003

Dear Patricia

Thank you for your letter 21 September and for the book "Universal Wisdom" by Bede Griffiths.

My wife and I are happy to hear that after your 6th chemotherapy session, your oncologist is very pleased with your medical progress and is hopeful for a remission. We hope you will enjoy many more years to celebrate your 80th birthday with your grandchildren and your family.

Many things in life can make or unmake a person. But the single most important factor is that someone who shares your life with you. In that respect my wife and I have been very fortunate. We are happy for you that you have a soul-mate in your husband Kok Song. It is a relationship that evolves with time and circumstance and grows with age.

Thank you for your kind words about Xiuqi. She is a nice girl. The best thing we hope for her is a happy marriage, not something one can assume these days for young women at university.

With all our best wishes for your remission.

Yours sincerely

P.S. Thank you also for the lovely gift of tulips.
h.y.

Mrs Patricia Ng

21 Sep 2003

My dear Senior Minister Lee

Congratulations on your 80th birthday which you so joyfully celebrated on 16th September 2003.

Although Kok Song and I were not able to be there with you, I can tell you that I strongly share the sentiments that you expressed that night. Mr Lee, you are very fortunate to have found a true soul-mate in Mrs Lee. We are truly blessed to have a partner through life to share our joys and woes and to truly be a part of our lives. I am also fortunate in having a true soul-mate in my husband and the thought that I would have him by my side at the end is a great comfort!

I hope to live to celebrate my 80th birthday too with my grandchildren and family! You are so blessed to have a granddaughter like Xiuqi who cares so deeply for you as to worry about your public image!

I hope you will enjoy the book "Universal Wisdom" by the late Benedictine Monk Bede Griffiths. He was a truly great spiritual teacher and at the end of his long life, he concluded that the most important relationship is love. He was a learned Oxford scholar and it took him a long time to embark on a spiritual journey. He truly inspired me by his great sense of presence. I felt you might enjoy his work.

Yours respectfully

---

16 February 2005

Dear Kok Song

My wife and I are saddened to learn of the passing of your wife, Patricia.

Her illness must have been stressful and painful for her and the family, but most so for you. Even though the prognosis was not good, when the blow strikes it is still a heavy knock.

There are some things that happen for which there are no explanations. My son, Loong, was devastated when he lost his wife two weeks after child birth when she was just 30. Life is like that.

It will take some time for your family and you to get over your grief and re-balance your own lives. It will come only after much pain and hurt.

With all our sympathies to you and your children.

Yours sincerely

Mr Lee in South Africa, 1992, where he met Nelson Mandela.
FROM LEFT TO RIGHT: James Fu, Lee Suan Hiang, Ho Meng Kit,
Lim Hng Kiang, Mr Lee and Nelson Mandela.

Mr Lee speaking at the official opening of UOB Plaza, August 1995.
It began to rain heavily just as Mr Lee started his address.

At Jurong Island, 2001. FROM LEFT TO RIGHT: Chong Lit Cheong, Lim Neo Chian, Mrs Lee, Mr Lee, Philip Yeo, Teo Ming Kian and Ko Kheng Hua.

Mr Lee with his principal private secretary Andrew Tan and his wife and son, in a photo taken in Mr Lee's office in 2004.

Mr and Mrs Lee in Hong Kong, 5 December 2005.

This was one of Mrs Lee's favourite photographs which she used to joke about being sandwiched between two Prime Ministers. The occasion was a PAP dinner held at Parliament House, 22 July 2006.

Mr and Mrs Lee having dinner at Nobu in New York, October 2006. Mr Lee was in the United States to receive the Woodrow Wilson Award for Public Service. STANDING FROM LEFT TO RIGHT: Mr Lee's doctor, Masagos Zulkifli, Liew Mun Leong and Ong Beng Seng. Seated are Christina Ong, Mrs Lee and Mr Lee.

Mr and Mrs Lee at their hotel pool in the United States, October 2006.

Mrs Lee and her aides by the shores of Lake Taupo in New Zealand, 2007. In her hand are some pumice stones she had collected.

Mrs Lee with a goose feather picked up by the lake. When asked by Mr Lee why she wanted the feather, she said, "千里送鹅毛" (a gift of a goose feather from across a thousand miles); in other words, it is the thought that counts despite the lightness of the gift.

Mr Lee and Mrs Lee at Sentosa. This photo was taken by his niece Kwa Kim Li on 14 February 2008.

Mr Lee officiated the opening of the Singapore Pavilion at the Shanghai World Expo in May 2010. Here he is meeting minority race children.

LEFT: Mr Lee checking in on Mrs Lee after a lunch meeting with Japanese politicians. He was in Tokyo to attend the Nikkei Conference, May 2010.

Mr Lee enjoying a day out shortly before he turned ninety, September 2013.

Mr Lee riding on a Skytrain, 5 September 2014. He was at Changi Airport to view the site for the Jewel project. FROM LEFT TO RIGHT: Liew Mun Leong, Kwa Kim Li, Stephen Lee, Lee Seow Hiang and Foo Sek Min.

Mr Lee celebrating SG50 with a small group of friends at China Club, 5 January 2015. STANDING FROM LEFT TO RIGHT: Ong Beng Seng, Cheng Wai Keung, Jennie Chua, Liew Mun Leong, Stephen Lee, Lee Seow Hiang, Gordon Tan. Seated next to Mr Lee is Kwa Kim Li.

LI KA-SHING
Chairman, Board of C.K. Hutchison Holdings

❝Of all the many people that I know,
Mr Lee was the one whom I respect the most.**❞**
– Li Ka-shing

My acquaintance with Mr Lee goes back several decades. We first met in the early 1980s and we continued to meet over the years, usually in Hong Kong and in Singapore.

Of all the many people that I know, Mr Lee was the one whom I respected the most. I admire him for his vision, his insights, and his thorough analyses of world politics and the economic environment.

My impression of him has not changed throughout all the years. His insightful views on politics and the economy of Singapore and the world have always impressed me. As has been evident over the years, his accurate views and judgements have solidified my staunch admiration for him. His keen insights made every one of our encounters memorable.

In 2006, at the opening ceremony of a library at the Singapore Management University,[1] I mentioned Mr Lee in my speech:

"You have put your heart and your will to elevate your country from strength to strength, through perplexing times and competitive challenges, unswervingly committed to the principle that progress gained through laying first constructive foundation is the best steadfast manifestation of all that we hope for and all that we hold dear, a true and ordered liberty, a humane and just society, fair and equal participation for all."

I was asked by Kishore Mahbubani, Dean of the Lee Kuan Yew School of Public Policy, to make a donation to the school. My first question was to ask if the request had come with Lee Kuan Yew's approval. When I found out it had, I immediately agreed to give a sum. That is the measure of the respect I have for the man.

I last met Mr Lee in May 2012 in Hong Kong. We had lunch in my office, and he was in good health and relaxed. We chatted about many issues.

Notes

[1] The Li Ka Shing Library was officially opened on 24 February 2006. The Li Ka Shing Foundation donated an endowment to the library for collections and to the Singapore Management University for scholarship.

TAN GUONG CHING

Principal Private Secretary, 1984–1987

❝Mr Lee never went around believing
he knew everything.**❞**

– Tan Guong Ching

The first time I met Mr Lee was when he interviewed me for the position of principal private secretary (PPS) to the Prime Minister. That was in early 1984.

He had interviewed a few other candidates, but as he had chosen me to be his PPS that meant the interview must have gone well. He was very courteous throughout. His questions probed my character and he wanted to know about my likes and dislikes, as well as the subjects I took at university. He was particularly struck by the fact that I had taken a course in anthropology; it was a subject that interested him because it is about communities and how they work and evolve. He was at that time grappling with the problem of large numbers of unmarried female graduates.

Mr Lee's private side

One episode I recall which captured a bit of the private side of Mr Lee took place during a state visit to China in September 1985. As part of the visit, we made a trip to the town of Qifu, the birthplace of Confucius, in Shandong Province. It was a long drive from Jinan, the capital of the province, where we were based, but the highway was broad and so the trip was very smooth.

The visit to Qifu was very revealing. I could not recall him ever being so happy. Mrs Lee was also with him. I then realised he was happy because he deeply revered the teachings of Confucius and was very thrilled to be staying in the same house that Confucius grew up in.

On top of that, it also happened that we were there on Mr Lee's birthday. This was so auspicious. We celebrated his birthday in Qifu with a simple cake as he did not want anything elaborate. He was already very health-conscious by then. He had given up smoking and was exercising regularly and watching his weight.

In another indication of how much Mr Lee revered Confucius, if you look at the photographs of his meetings with heads of state or heads of government taken in his office, you can see a statue of Confucius prominently on the corner table between him and the VIP.

Mr Lee was good at remembering faces while Mrs Lee had a very good memory for names. Very often, Mr Lee would ask her, "What is the name of that man we met at that place?" He could recall the person's face but not the name. Mrs Lee would invariably recall the name. They were a very good match.

Mr Lee's diet and exercise

Mr Lee exercised every day. He never missed a session, even when travelling. He would always ask if the hotel had exercise machines. If it didn't, he would bring along his exercise bike because it was easy to transport. He would also jog.

Mr Lee loved fruits and was partial to persimmons, pomelos and grapefruit. He also liked his fruits fresh, preferring to cut or peel them himself to ensure freshness. This applied even when he went abroad! We would give our hosts a list of things Mr Lee liked to eat and drink, and also politely inform them not to cut his fruits.

Once, we made a visit to Japan. The Japanese went out of their way to fulfil this requirement. But instead of just offering the whole fruit, they also brought in a chef who had a special skill. The chef peeled the fruits using only two knives; not once did he touch the fruits with his hands. That was indeed a sight to behold. You could tell that Mr Lee was really impressed by the demonstration.

When it came to drink, he would always ask for low-alcohol beer chilled to 14° Celsius.

He was very careful about his food. Mrs Lee watched over what he ate and would chide him whenever he overate.

Mr Lee as a boss

Mr Lee was a man who didn't need a conversation starter. But that was also because he was always prepared for the matter being discussed. Most of the time he would make mental notes of what he wanted to say before going into a meeting.

There would be a lot of work to be done when there were meetings where major issues were being discussed. But apart from that, note-taking, recording of minutes and preparing his schedule were things you took in your stride.

If you made a mistake, you had to let him know the moment you realised it. Most of the time, he would acknowledge your apology. It could be quite damaging if you didn't tell him and he made a decision based on your mistake. He would get very cross with you.

He looked after us quite well in the sense that he took an interest in our well-being, whether we were abroad with him or in Singapore. People see him as a tough boss but he was actually a very good boss because his instructions were always very clear. This meant you didn't have to do a lot of abortive work. If you had any doubts, you could clarify things with him and then carry on your work confidently knowing that it would not be called off. He was not a micromanager; neither did he breathe down your neck. But he expected you to perform the task to your best ability.

When my stint as PPS ended, I didn't get many opportunities to interact with him. But I continued to observe him at public events. You could see that his mind was still very sharp, in the way he analysed political issues and world events. That sharpness of mind stayed with him till the very end. His mind was sharp even though his legs were not as strong as before.

Mr Lee's integrity

Mr Lee never went around believing he knew everything. And that was why he sought the opinions of others. Before he made any major decision, he always sought second or maybe even third opinions. He didn't talk to just one person but to several persons to get their views. In that sense, he was a very careful man. He would discuss with a lot of people, especially people who had direct knowledge of the issue. He would also ask for data to back up any claims.

As a leader, he did not shirk from his responsibilities. He knew full well the buck stopped with him. He made the decisions and ensured that things were done no matter how tough or unpopular they were. He was really a Singaporean at heart and his whole life was really just dedicated to the improvement of the lives of Singaporeans and to the well-being of Singapore.

DR S. VASOO

Associate Professorial Fellow, National University of Singapore, and Former Member of Parliament, 1984–2001

❝Is there anything that you want to share?❞
– Lee Kuan Yew

Mr Lee and multiracialism

After I was elected as Member of Parliament (MP) for Bowen constituency in Ang Mo Kio New Town in 1984, I was advised by colleagues that when invited by PM Mr Lee Kuan Yew for either tea or luncheon meetings, one must not beat around the bush when asked for views; that he would expect a straightforward answer without mincing of words. One has to be open and give authentic views about social and political issues brought up for discussion. I was also told he could be a hard and straight talking person. Bearing these pieces of advice in mind, I looked forward to meeting him.

Not too long into my first term as a parliamentarian, I was invited to a luncheon meeting to be held in the modest dining room at his office. I was told by his Private Secretary that Mr Lee normally met MPs on a rotating basis. As a newbie attending the luncheon meeting for the first time, I had butterflies in my stomach but I reassured myself that it was indeed good of him to want to meet me and find out how I was doing as an MP in the ward. When he saw me, he called out my name assertively but with warmth and a reassuring tone. I felt comfortable as the hardy picture painted of him did not show on his face and instead he was supportive and encouraging in the way he greeted me. He was pleased to hear that I was making progress and we went on to discuss issues concerning the community and local politics.

One indelible matter he raised at this initial meeting was the discussion about the social landscape in the neighbourhood, specifically the integration of residents of different ethnic groups. I had brought up the issue of increasing concentrations of ethnic groups in the housing blocks, an observation that I knew caught his attention as I could see his eyes flash and his eyebrows lift. He added that he had been thinking about the matter for some time, and was concerned about the development of ethnic enclaves and how this would negatively counter his public housing plans for social and ethnic integration. He asserted that something had to be done quickly to tweak the housing policy to prevent ethnic ghettos from forming. That was indeed a bold proposal by Mr Lee — to maintain an ethnic or racial balance by amending the housing policies concerning the sale, allocation and resale of flats.[1]

His foresight was indeed marvellous. He took pre-emptive steps to deal with the long-term implications on racial harmony by setting directions to enhance better social bonding among the ethnic groups. He saw that if things were left to freer choice, the ecology of the housing estates could be affected and polarisation of ethnic enclaves would happen. This would not be a plus to social and community bonding. His quick intervention reflected his leadership. Mr Lee's relentless effort to promote racial harmony left a deep impression on me, a member of a minority race, that we cannot take racial harmony and issues at the surface but must implement innovative measures to promote congenial ethnic relationships among different races. His passion in wanting to make multiracialism work was indeed very visible, and I have been touched by his tenacity to do so and to remind people, particularly the young, not to slip up on inter-racial matters.

Mr Lee and the importance of community bonding

Mr Lee was very persuasive in getting Singaporeans of all social, economic and ethnic persuasions to live, school, play and work together respectfully and in dignity. He laid the foundations in the heartlands and in various institutions to ensure that we maintain good racial harmony. Cultivating good race relations was critical, and in many other countries this matter had not worked out well. Mr Lee had often pointed this out. He was deeply aware about the problem of race, having lived through the race riots in the 1960s. He knew full well how explosive race relations could be and constantly reminded people like me in the party, as well as community leaders, to manage issues concerning race carefully. He always reminded Singaporeans that it is very critical to see that our social policies and the various opportunities given to people are not biased towards any one racial or ethnic group.

We have become a global city but that does not mean we have fundamentally changed. In any case, we are still a multiracial society. From time to time, Mr Lee reminded Singaporeans of the need to maintain multiracialism. In all our pursuits to improve our livelihood, we make sure that we carry out what Lee Kuan Yew had always reminded Singaporeans: ensure that there is a fair playing field; be sensitive about the needs of various ethnic groups; see that policies are not lopsided in support of one group against the other; provide access to public services without discrimination. He constantly reminded Singaporeans and policy makers to observe these.

I hope that Mr Lee's message will be long lasting and etched in people's memory. When Singapore continues to do well, one may become complacent and overlook this whole need for racial harmony. We can become less sensitive about policies that overlook implications

196 | UP CLOSE WITH LEE KUAN YEW

on race relations. If we don't take proactive steps to nip ethnic tensions in the bud, a dormant volcano can suddenly be eruptive. And once that race relations volcano erupts, it will have severe ramifications on Singapore — nobody can gain from that. Singapore will go down, and everybody living in Singapore, regardless of their ethnicity, will be affected by this whole social eruption.

Mr Lee's contribution to Singapore was to make sure that all races had, and continue to have, equal opportunities. One may argue against this, but we have to be very mindful that the problem of ethnicity has fractured societies in many countries. Once fractured, it is not easy for a society to come up again. Mr Lee's efforts towards this will help Singapore to continue to be viable.

Mr Lee and Tanjong Pagar

In my course of working in Tanjong Pagar GRC[2] with Mr Lee, I found him to be a very caring person — although people often think he was fierce; perhaps that was because of his stern demeanour. But deep down in him, he had warmth. He always asked about me whenever I met with him. He would say, "How is it going? How is your family? Is there anything that you want to share?" So I think there was this tremendous warmth in him, if you got to know him as a person. And he would stick his neck out for you if he believed that you were right and you had good ideas to contribute.

Many of the projects in Tanjong Pagar GRC were carried out for the working class. One major project was to see how we could assist the *samsui* women living in Redhill and Bukit Merah. There were a number of programmes Mr Lee encouraged us to undertake for them, and these covered healthcare, home help, a meal voucher scheme, home repairs and organising leisure outings. Mr Lee had stressed that one should never give up on this special group of women who had contributed to Singapore during the hard times.

Bearing in mind Mr Lee's mantra to "never give up", a group of community service volunteers got together to befriend the women and follow up on their needs when they retired from construction work. As these women were less mobile, many outreach activities were carried out in the void decks of the blocks where they lived, an approach that increased their participation. A centre for the elderly was set up where they could meet to socialise and obtain social assistance when needed. Home help services and repairs to their homes were carried out by young committed volunteers who believed in promoting self-help among this group.

Mr Lee also saw the need to rejuvenate the older estates in these areas and pressed for housing renewal programmes to be initiated in Tanjong Pagar, Bukit Merah and Tiong Bahru. He could foresee that if nothing was done, the young would move out leaving only the elderly. This would make the areas less vibrant socially and economically. We needed to revive the estates to attract young families to live there.

I remember very clearly that it was in Tiong Bahru where the housing renewal programme began; this was followed by Redhill and Bukit Merah. It was one of the earliest steps taken after Mr Lee raised the alarm bell. We are all now talking about the ageing population, but Mr Lee had already thought about this issue some 20 years ago. He had the foresight to see this. It left a tremendous impression on me, that he had this capacity to grasp things and anticipate the consequences of a greying estate. If we didn't do anything about it, this could have a tremendous impact on the community. It would become less vibrant, less active and less resourceful.

Mr Lee's leadership qualities

If there is one quality of Mr Lee that I admire, it was his ability to identify and bring very good people, people of integrity, into his team, the community and various social institutions. To me, that is the most critical attribute that he had. That was a very strong factor for the survival of Singapore in those nation-building years. For Singapore to remain very vibrant, for the community to remain very strong, we need to have groups of people who are selfless, who have the integrity and the social responsibility to bring change and improve Singapore. Mr Lee's approach to build up institutions inspired me and many of my colleagues.

You see, people always think of him as a very hard person, very goal-driven, very specific, very rough, very directive. But I don't think so. Because in all the things that he did, we should ask: Did he do it for the public good? Was it for the interest of Singapore? The answer is yes. Although he was tough, he was also straightforward — it was all in the interest of Singapore, in the interest of the community. And look at the results that have come about, and what has happened to Singapore over the last 50 years, under his leadership. Singapore has transformed from a small entrepot trading post to a very significant country. From that very insignificant country in 1965, it has become a global city today. A lot of Mr Lee's imagination and thoughts — all in the interest of the public — have taken root in this progressive island-state. This is an important aspect of his effective leadership.

Mr Lee gave me this advice: Never give up. If you think it is right and if you see that it is going to be valuable for the community, and for the collective interest, just do it. In the long term, people will realise that it is for the public good and not your personal interest. I found this advice applicable even at the micro-community level when the main HDB upgrading plan for Henderson Crescent was to be undertaken.

A controversy had surfaced when I proposed sealing off a street that ran through the neighbourhood to vehicles, and relocating all the open carpark places to a multi-storey carpark facility. This would create more space to plant trees and green up the area, and to build a playground and community meeting points. The walkways would also be safer for pedestrians.

However the plan was met with vehement objections at a meeting dominated by car owners. Only a small group of non-car owners participated although they were a majority living there. I weighed the situation. If I pandered to the vocal minority who were vociferous, I would have done injustice to the majority. The striking catchphrase "never give up" did not elude my mind. I pursued the matter steadfastly with the conviction that the changes were for the interests of the majority. We did a survey and then a ballot of all flat-owner residents. The majority of the residents supported the proposed changes to the neighbourhood. Today, the residents find the place congenial and environmentally friendly.

Mr Lee implemented many reforms which were not for his self-interest; they were for the interests of Singapore. Sometimes people, particularly his opponents, misread him. But if you were to ask Singaporeans of my generation, my mother's and my grandmother's generations, and others who have lived through his period of leadership, they would say that he did so much for the good of Singapore. They would say he is the father of Singapore.

Mr Lee, the green environmentalist

Every year without fail Mr Lee would make it a point to engage in the tree planting campaign he had started decades ago, long before the world became concerned about climate change. Looking back now, he anticipated the grave impact of climate change on Singapore as an island. Never have I come across a leader who took a very serious view on greening Singapore. He was a true environmentalist unlike many who merely pay lip service. I recall a discussion I had with him, in which he said without reservation that bold actions had to be taken to clean and green our environment.

Mr Lee attended many tree planting programmes in the various Divisions of the Tanjong Pagar GRC and these occasions gave him many opportunities to assess the ground issues affecting people's lives. He interacted with many heartlanders to hear out their views. I clearly remember that during a tree planting project in Telok Blangah Rise, where he planted a cluster of small red palm trees, he suggested to residents and grassroots leaders the idea of planting more mango trees. Why mango trees? His answer was simple and insightful — such an effort would encourage more residents to take ownership in looking after the trees and together they could enjoy the harvest. The good outcome of planting mango trees helped community bonding and this became obvious over the years since this initiative was implemented in that precinct. Mr Lee's idea bore fruit indeed: The residents of that neighbourhood enjoyed not only the fruits of their labour but also fellowship with one another.

Mr Lee's riverine legacy

My colleagues and all those who have worked with Mr Lee will remember him for the transformation of Singapore. The most impressive thing he achieved was the landscape change to the face of Singapore, from the squalor of villages and pig farms to the iconic housing board flats that we now have, where more than 80 per cent of the people own their homes.

The transformation of the Singapore River that I knew of when I was living with my grandmother in Hock Lam Street in Chinatown was indeed spectacular. During the late 1950s, I saw very few people swimming there. The river was smelly and the stench of rotten eggs pervaded the air. The water was black, polluted and poisonous. Nobody could even wade through that revulsive water. I remember this filthy river well. When I was in secondary one, I used to walk to my school, Gan Eng Seng School, via South Bridge Road, and whilst looking at the river, I had to hold my nose. Today, the river is so different. It is clean and lined with trees, and leads out to the Marina Bay. River cruises ply its length; people are enjoying the new Singapore River as a place of leisure. That's a sea change indeed. It left in me a lasting impression of the "never die" spirit of Lee Kuan Yew.

Mr Lee did a lot for Singapore. His leadership, tenacity and relentless capacity to get things done have left a deep impression on me and many Singaporeans. Some people may not agree with that. But I think most Singaporeans of my generation and others would vouch that he contributed more than his life to the development of Singapore.

Notes

1 In March 1989, the Housing and Development Board (HDB) implemented the Ethnic Integration Policy to promote racial integration and harmony in the HDB estates. Under this policy, ethnic quotas were set for HDB neighbourhoods and blocks to ensure a better racial mix.
2 S. Vasoo was Member of Parliament for Bowen from 1984 to 1988, Tiong Bahru from 1988 to 1991 and Tanjong Pagar GRC from 1991 to 2001.

MOSES LEE

Principal Private Secretary, 1987–1990

❝My PPS is going to have his fourth child
so we must encourage people like him!**❞**
– Lee Kuan Yew

I was Mr Lee's last principal private secretary (PPS) while he was Prime Minister. Prior to this, I had been asked twice before to consider a posting to his office.

The first time was in late 1980, but I said I wanted to do my postgraduate studies at Harvard first. The second time, Tan Teck Chwee, who was then the chairman of the Public Service Commission, said he wanted to post me to the Prime Minister's Office. At that time, I had two daughters and the younger was just a year old. I told Mr Tan, who was a family man, that I really wanted to spend more time with my kids and he understood.

Then in 1986, Dr Andrew Chew, who was head of the Civil Service, told me that I would be posted to the PM's Office. I was already in my early thirties. I had finished my postgraduate studies and was quite senior in my career already. I remember I had moments of anxiety about whether I could serve Mr Lee adequately, given what I had heard about him. I told my wife, "Sorry, now the family is your concern." Once you knew you were going to be serving Mr Lee, you instinctively knew you would have little time for yourself.

On my first day of work on 2 January 1987, he called me into his room in the afternoon. He sat me down, across from him at his desk, and proceeded to tell me in one hour what he planned to do for the next three years! He had already anticipated that he was going to retire and knew all the major issues he needed to address before then. Now, I have worked in so many places — in finance, national development, education — and nobody has ever briefed me their plans for the next three months! True to his character, he always planned far ahead, managed the processes tightly and paid attention to the smallest details to shape the outcome that he wanted. Nothing was left to chance.

His last remark to me on my first day of work was, "I don't care if you work days or nights, as long as you get the work done." He never really imposed on me or made things difficult for me. But that did not diminish the pressure and anxiety I felt serving him.

Mr Lee and his strength of conviction

I joined the civil service in 1974 and my first face-to-face meeting with Mr Lee was in 1976. At that time I was at the Ministry of National Development (MND) and was secretary of a committee called the Garden City Action Committee (GCAC).[1] The committee was chaired by the then Permanent Secretary of National Development, Mr Cheng Tong Fatt.

There were some issues with the Ministry of Finance over how much money to allocate to the Garden City project. We, of course, wanted as much money as possible. "A Clean and Green Singapore" was our mantra and we were responsible for this.

Mr Lee heard about the problems we were having and he called a meeting of all the key people — permanent secretaries and key division people. The purpose of that meeting was to impress upon everyone his determination to green Singapore and that we had to push on and not hold back our efforts.

Despite his busy schedule and duties, he was always concerned with the small details. He highlighted to us that trees planted in urban areas would be fighting for space with cars and pedestrians, and so we needed to ensure the trees could breathe and aerate. He told us we would have to create aeration space for the trees to grow properly. I recall him saying, "How can you breathe if there is a plastic bag over your head?"

Today, we use gratings but we did not have them then. He said he was prepared to spend $2,000 per tree to make sure each tree could grow and breathe properly. (I distinctly remember that figure, $2,000, because at that time, my salary was just a little over $1,000!) That showed how determined he was. You could see flashes of fire in his eyes! He looked the permanent secretaries in the eye and said, "Is there a problem?" You could hear a pin drop.

There I was, a young scribe, bewildered at the intensity of the man. I look back now and realise that the man was so far-sighted. In the 1970s, he was already thinking about what the future city would look like. That was quite a remarkable first meeting, even though I was just sitting and listening passively to him.

Mr Lee and his open-mindedness

The second time I met Mr Lee made an even greater impression on me. One day, I got a call from his secretary to say the Prime Minister wanted to see me. I was still at the MND and this was probably in 1980 when the hot debate was whether Singapore should have a mass rapid transit (MRT) rail system or an all-bus system. I was told he would be seeing us in a group. He wanted our views on what we thought about the issue.

There were about five or six of us, young people from different agencies, in the room. He asked us, one by one, if we should have an

MRT. I told him my view, which was that every big city has an MRT. I had been to London and used the Tube and found it to be the most comfortable and convenient way of moving people. I added that I was quite clear about that because I was a bus commuter and our buses were fighting with taxis, bicycles and lorries on the roads. My view was we had to have an MRT if we were to build for the future.

The interesting thing was that it was not our views he was soliciting, but how we *felt* about the matter. He wanted to get a real feel of how things were being perceived on the ground. As young officers, we felt honoured and privileged that he had chosen to ask us, though ours was just one of many forums he had on this issue. To me, that showed how open-minded he really was; in the sense that, when he looked at a specific issue, he really studied it extensively, getting all kinds of feedback, both positive and negative, before ultimately making a decision. Unlike my first encounter with him, this time he came across as patient and receptive, mainly listening to get the most out of us.

Mr Lee, the lifelong learner

While most people who knew and interacted with Mr Lee could not help being impressed by his considerable breadth and depth of intellect and wisdom, I often wondered how many appreciated the fact that he was truly a lifelong learner. This was one of the first attributes of Mr Lee that struck me when I started work as his PPS.

He was constantly challenging, questioning and probing, absorbing new ideas, viewpoints and information which would be useful for charting the future of Singapore. Depending on his current area of interest, I fed him with data, facts and technical details as well as diverse expert opinions. He would also ask to meet a wide range of people whom he could engage and spar with, from subject experts to ordinary folks from the business and social community. He never ceased to amaze me by asking questions that none of us would have anticipated, and raising new angles and perspectives for which sometimes the experts did not have ready answers.

Equally amazing was his ability to recall. His brain was like a supercomputer, storing a huge amount of important and relevant facts and data to be recalled at will. Once, he asked me to check up on a particular statistic that was told to him at a meeting more than a year earlier. I was the note-taker and had forgotten all about it, but he was correct up to the decimal point!

His knowledge of plants was legendary. I remember he once observed that all our lampposts were so plain and wondered why we couldn't train creepers and flowering plants to grow up the lampposts. He also asked how we could make trees grow under flyovers, and suggested that we could install pipes to direct rainwater there or plant trees that do not need too much sunshine. This man, in the midst of thinking about our country's survival in the 1970s and '80s — in the midst of domestic and international politics, and issues regarding the army, our security and our economy — was also thinking about plants! It was quite amazing.

Mr Lee, the world statesman

Mr Lee travelled widely to broaden and deepen relationships with other countries. In doing so, he developed personal ties and friendships with world leaders and influenced outcomes to provide space for Singapore to survive and prosper.

I have travelled with him to meet leaders of the world and I have witnessed their interactions. He was always able to piece together diverse incidents, events and personalities to present a refreshing viewpoint of current issues and future trends frankly and objectively. All the leaders wanted to tap his mind for his views on their own issues and to find out how he saw the world. Before each official visit, he would have studied the leaders he was going to meet and had a clear view of the strengths and weaknesses of their systems. It was therefore no surprise that many leaders sought his advice on their domestic issues and problems. They knew that he was not just a politician and that his rich experience in developing Singapore had valuable lessons for them.

Mr Lee, the pragmatic visionary

Mr Lee was unique as a visionary who could foresee issues and trends decades and even a generation ahead, and yet was solidly grounded with a pragmatism that enabled him to transform ideas and ideals into reality. There are many great thinkers and visionaries in our time, but very few are also able to implement and build equally well. Perhaps it was his ability to pay attention to the smallest details that ensured that Singapore worked and at the highest standards possible. When he went on his walkabouts or visits, invariably he would offer new ideas or suggest areas for improvement which officials wished that they themselves had thought of first.

Greening Singapore was always top of his mind. The Parks and Recreation Department at that time had many suggestions and ideas from him. While walking or jogging around the Istana grounds, should he notice trees and plants not thriving well, he would follow up with short notes to the curator on his diagnosis and suggest treatment. He wanted trees to be planted along the East Coast Parkway so that when they matured the treetops would form a shaded canopy thus lowering roadside temperatures. To beautify the streets, he proposed erecting wire mesh casings on lampposts on which flowering creepers could grow, but that had maintenance issues. Bare concrete retaining walls were covered with green creepers to improve appearance.

Mr Lee and his dedication to Singapore

Much has already been said about Mr Lee's great love affair with Singapore and how he dedicated his entire life to ensure its success. However, I realised very early on that it was a passion taken to extremes. He never rested, and was continuously looking for ways and means to further Singapore's interests and ensure its survival and progress — above everything else.

Whether he was meeting local officials, business and community leaders, or receiving foreign visitors, he was always looking out for ideas and solutions for Singapore. He enjoyed hosting small poolside barbeque dinners for old friends and visitors. On those occasions when I was present, I chewed softly and kept my ears wide open, for the discussions would eventually turn to Singapore and the world, and there would be follow-ups after the dinner.

His mind was constantly thinking, even while exercising. Sometimes, I would get calls from him while he was in the middle of rowing or when he was on his bicycle. He would be panting on the other end of the line! His exercise regime was legendary. There was no rest for him. There was nothing trivial about him. That was why a lot of people said it was very hard for him to make small talk.

One incident stands out in my memory. We were on an official trip to Fiji. This was in November 1988. After Fiji, we went to Sydney where we attended a dinner given by Nick Greiner, the Premier of New South Wales. Mr Greiner was giving a speech and Mr Lee was expected to give one too. We received word that the Premier's speech would not be substantive, just a small welcome address. So we prepared a similarly light speech for Mr Lee.

The Premier spoke first. He talked about areas of cooperation and of working together with Singapore. It was a substantive speech, not a courtesy speech! The speech we had prepared for Mr Lee was obviously inadequate. I still do not know if we were misinformed or if the Premier changed his mind at the last minute. But what were we to do? The speech we prepared was of no use then.

Then, Mr Lee went on stage and gave the best speech I had heard in a long time. He prefaced it by saying he had thought he was to give a courtesy speech, so he would not be using his prepared response but would speak instead on whether Singapore would survive the next 100 years.

He gave his account of our challenges. We were completely enthralled. We had never known until then how deep his concerns were. This was after he had made his famous remark about how, even if he were buried, he would still rise from his grave if something was wrong with Singapore.[2]

To me, hearing him talk so comprehensively about Singapore's future proved to me he was always thinking of our survival. All of us knew that, but most of us didn't know the extent to which that drove him, in terms of whatever he did. That speech summed up everything he was about: His whole life had been about making sure Singapore survived, long after him, and long after you and I were gone.

I actually thought he was a better speaker when he spoke off the cuff. It was always a joy and pleasure to hear him expound on any topic because he made it so compelling for us to listen.

Mr Lee and his attention to details

People say it must have been difficult to work for him but actually I think he was the easiest person to work for. Some bosses tell you to do something but change their minds later. He, however, would make his instructions as clear as possible, whether it was about a political issue or something personal.

There was one trip, I think it was probably in Fiji, where he had a tooth problem. We didn't know how to treat it so he dictated and described the condition of his tooth to us so that it could be sent to a dentist for assessment. The notes came up to about three pages long!

The pressure of the job was indeed great, not because the tasks were complex but because the issues he dealt with were often life-changing ones, urgent and immediate, and the margin of error very small. So I had to make sure I got it right the first time, all the time.

Mr Lee's softer side

The day-to-day working relationship was businesslike and formal, and there was no small talk on personal matters, family or stuff like that. I could not imagine troubling him with personal problems or career matters, knowing that he carried such important and weighty issues every day.

However, while he was all work, it was Mrs Lee who provided the balance by adding the human touch with the staff. She would make small talk, asking about us and our families to put us at ease. More importantly, she was an important moderator and always looked out for us. One day after dinner, after seeing his guests off, Mr Lee turned to me and started giving instructions. Mrs Lee quickly intervened and said, "Harry, it is late. Let him go back and sleep." It had not occurred to him that it was late. So he said alright, and got into his car.

I remember talking to then Cabinet Secretary Wong Chooi Sen after a Cabinet meeting where the discussion was on procreation benefits for couples who chose to have a third child. When the Ministry came back with their paper, the decision included extending to the fourth child the same benefits given to the third child!

I asked Mr Wong what happened as the Cabinet paper had not mentioned anything about benefits for the fourth child. Apparently, Mr Lee had said, "My PPS is going to have his fourth child so we must encourage people like him!"

Mr Lee never asked about my personal life so he probably found out about my wife's pregnancy from Mrs Lee. Mrs Lee really put everyone at ease. At functions, even the wives would be tense but she would make small talk and ask them about their children. They complemented each other very well. She was more than his equal, intellectually. But there was a softer maternal side to her which was very evident in the way she dealt with the staff.

One day in August 1990, just after National Day, I left my office to go to the toilet. When I came back, I was surprised to find him sitting in my room. I greeted him. He said he had to move because someone was in his room fixing something.

Then, he asked me how long I had been with him. I told him, three years and eight months, and he replied it was time for me to move on. He asked me where I would like to go. I said that all my predecessors had gone on to become permanent secretaries but I would personally like to be posted to a statutory board. I wanted to gain operational experience. I said I would just leave it to the system to decide where I could be best deployed.

The next thing I knew, about two weeks later, Andrew Chew came to me and said I was to go to the Singapore Broadcasting Corporation

(SBC). Mr Lee had obviously acted immediately on our conversation. I was very touched that he took the trouble to make it happen for me. So I left in September for SBC.[3]

Mr Lee, the role model

On my last day as his PPS, when I went to say goodbye, I told him I was going to SBC. Straightaway he spoke to me for ten minutes on why SBC was important. He was telling me what he, as Prime Minister, expected of SBC and what the government expected. It was to be a channel for communication as well as an avenue for culture and values to be transmitted. All this gave me a valuable perspective on the job and made it more meaningful for me. I felt hyped up and inspired.

I consider my stint with Mr Lee the highlight of my civil service career. He was in his sixties, at the prime of his political career, and Singapore had made spectacular progress in improving the lives of its people. He had fire in him with an intensity he brought to every detail and every task. During those years, he bridged the gap between Singapore and the rest of the world.

For those of us who had the privilege of working so closely with him, we could not help being inspired by his dedication and sacrifice and wanting to do our best to contribute to Singapore's success in our own small way.

I believe that it was Singapore's good luck that we had Mr Lee on our side. If he had been born somewhere else, we would have told a different Singapore story. But Singaporeans know that our success is not due to luck. It is the work of Mr Lee Kuan Yew, a giant of a man who dedicated his life to give us peace and prosperity over the last 50 years. His passing on 23 March 2015 was a great opportunity

214 I UP CLOSE WITH LEE KUAN YEW

to celebrate his life's work, and to give Singaporeans, especially the younger ones, a compelling history lesson of how we got here. In my humble opinion, the best way to honour his legacy is for all of us to stay united and continue his work to build the best home over the next 50 years.

Notes

1   GCAC was a coordinating body tasked with the greening of Singapore, especially the urban areas.
2   National Day Rally speech by Lee Kuan Yew, 1988: "Even from my sick bed, even if you are going to lower me into the grave and I feel something is going wrong, I will get up."
3   Moses Lee was General Manager of Singapore Broadcasting Corporation from 1990 to 1994 and Deputy Chairman, Singapore International Media Pte Ltd, from 1994 to 1995 after SBC's corporatisation in 1994.

HO MENG KIT

Principal Private Secretary, 1990–1994

**❝I see a rain tree that is not doing so well.
Can you check with National Parks?❞**

– Lee Kuan Yew

I became Mr Lee's principal private secretary (PPS) in August 1990. He stepped down as Prime Minister in September 1990 so I served him in his capacity as Prime Minister for a month and then transitioned to serving him as Senior Minister until I left in September 1994. I was with him for four years which made me his longest-serving PPS. Most PPS terms are for two to three years. Halfway through my stint, he asked me if I wanted to extend my service. How could I refuse? It was such an honour and the job was so interesting. Also, frankly, it was an immense privilege working for him because I saw the world through his eyes — it was a perspective which was so historic at that time.

Till today, my time as his PPS is the stint I am proudest of. Invariably, that is the first thing anyone who reads my CV notices. People always ask me what he was like and what it was like working for him. I always say I learnt a lot. He was like a teacher to me; it was the equivalent of getting two Masters degrees at the same time.

I was in Mindef, in the Armed Forces, when I got a call informing me that I had been shortlisted, along with two others, to be his PPS. The three of us were summoned to the Istana to be interviewed by Mr Lee. I was so nervous. After the interview, he said he would not decide yet and wanted all the candidates to take an examination. I was not sure if that was the first time the PPS entrance examination was introduced. In any case, his office told me to return to the Istana to take the examination.

A couple of days later, I went to the Cabinet office. I remember going in at about 9 a.m. with the other two candidates. We took the examination in the Cabinet Room, completing it in about two hours. At that time, Mr Lee's work day began at noon, usually with a lunch appointment. We had to clear the Cabinet Room before he arrived. The examination question was this: Mr Lee will be giving a speech on the Growth Triangle, the economic cooperation area between Singapore, Malaysia and Indonesia. How should he pitch his message in his speech? I answered the best I could and sent my paper back to his secretary.

About a week later, I was told that I had been selected. I don't know what the criteria were. He could very well have selected the worst answer!

The first two months were very busy. Moses Lee, my predecessor, was still around but only for about three weeks as he would be going to the Singapore Broadcasting Corporation (SBC). It was an important job ahead because SBC was going to be corporatised.

Mr Lee was also quite busy during that period as he was trying to complete his last duties as Prime Minister before handing over the reins to Mr Goh Chok Tong. The most important matters for him were to settle two issues with Malaysia, that of water negotiation[1] and the Malayan Railway land.[2] As his PPS, I was involved in the negotiations, despite not having the full background to these technical talks. I spent a lot of time reading the files but many details were not held with our office. Also, not everything important was recorded. The relevant Ministries were helpful in providing whatever information I needed as these were important matters between us and Malaysia. It was a steep learning curve for me. I was thrown into the deep end but it was good learning. It prepared me well for my PPS duties.

Mr Lee as Senior Minister

As Senior Minister (SM), Mr Lee was no longer accountable for the day-to-day functioning of government. However, in the first few months, when he was adjusting to his new role, he was involved in some operational issues. One of the issues he was concerned with (and very upset about) was chewing gum. He would get regular reports from the housing authority and town councils about chewing gum stuck on lifts, lift buttons, walkways and void decks. The reports included complaints from residents and the added cost to clean the mess. So one day he asked me to write a Cabinet paper to ban the importation of chewing gum. This was one of the few Cabinet Memos from SM's office for an operational issue. The approach to ban chewing gum was reflective of his style — top down, but it was effective.

Freed from day-to-day work, Mr Lee now had more bandwidth to look into more strategic matters. In fact, these were the longer-term issues, which as SM, he would help PM Goh deal with. I recall at least two strategic initiatives Mr Lee started during my stint with him as PPS. The first was regionalisation, to grow Singapore's Second Wing.[3] For Singapore to grow, he felt her economy should be spread across the region. The second initiative was a programme dealing with the long-term problem of ageing and rising healthcare costs. He felt if we did not change our habits and live a healthy lifestyle, our healthcare costs would balloon and our quality of life would be affected.

He also wanted to teach the younger ministers how to use campaigns to change the behaviour of Singaporeans as he had often done when he was PM. So another Cabinet paper on healthy living which included a Trim and Fit[4] programme for obese children was tabled. Now we have the Health Promotion Board in the Ministry of Health leading in this area.

Mr Lee's most memorable trips

Mr Lee once said to me that I was the most widely travelled of all his PPSs. Between 1990 and 1994 he had time, and was fit, to travel.

Many world leaders wanted him to visit them. The world had changed because of the fall of the Berlin Wall and many countries were looking into how to successfully transit to a market-based economy. Singapore was seen to have made an excellent transition from Third World to First. Mr Lee was its architect. He received many invitations to travel and provide advice. Travelling with Mr Lee was the most fascinating part of my job. I saw how respected he was internationally and how he made friends and influenced people. He cemented Singapore's importance to all the countries he visited.

CHINA

Mr Lee had a special place for China because it was reforming and he knew China would be a very important friend of Singapore. One memorable trip was to Western China to see the developments there.

I was with him in Dunhuang, a strategic point along the Silk Road in Gansu Province. The Chinese specially opened the Mogao Caves for the delegation. It was fascinating visiting these ancient sites in those early days when they were closed to the public. After Dunhuang, we went to Urumqi but could not get to Kashgar as it was snowing there and the plane could not land. I noticed that PM Lee Hsien Loong had a similar itinerary when he visited Western China in 2013. This time, PM made it to Kashgar.

Mr Lee started the Suzhou project in 1994. Before that, there were many trips to China to ascertain the best place to start this government-to-government industrial project — Shanghai, Tianjin and Shandong Province. The warm relationships between Chinese leaders and Mr Lee helped seed the good bilateral relations that we now have with China.

SOUTH AFRICA

In 1992, Mr Lee visited South Africa. It was a country most of us had never been to. It was a spectacular country. But I think the political context was important. This visit occurred after Nelson Mandela had been freed and he was to take over power from F.W. De Klerk.[5] Mr Lee met both men and advised them to continue to give a place to the white Africans simply because they could run the country, having done so for some time.

It was during this trip that he received news that then Deputy Prime Minister Lee Hsien Loong had been diagnosed with lymphoma.[6] His private staff on that trip did not know the full details as it was a personal matter. It was very much business as usual for the rest of the trip. That was the man. It must have been an upsetting development for him but he just carried on working, right in the middle of Africa. I am sure he must have been thinking about whether to cut short the trip, but he didn't.

KAZAKHSTAN

Kazakhstan, which was part of the former USSR, declared independence in 1991. Not all the people there were Kazakhs or Russians. There was a small group of Koreans who had settled there. A Korean contact had written to Mr Lee, inviting him to visit and be an adviser to the country's leader, Nursultan Nazarbayev.

Mr Lee was quite intrigued. He wanted to know where this Korean community had come from. Later, we learnt that Stalin had deported the Koreans to Kazakhstan in the 1930s and '40s.

So, maybe out of curiosity, he went to Kazakhstan just to have a look at the country. I remember our first visit; we could not figure a convenient way to get to the then capital Alma-Ata (later renamed Almaty). It was a new country in Central Asia and there were no direct flights to Southeast Asia. So I liaised with the Sultan of Brunei's office and asked if we could use one of his private jets. We flew there via Karachi and north over the Himalayas.

It was fascinating to be in Kazakhstan right after the breakup of the Soviet Union. In the past, all roads led to Moscow, but now the country wanted to forge a new path of its own — and its leaders wanted Mr Lee's advice. In the end, however, he decided not to be their formal adviser. But he did visit the country again. Today, we have good relations with Kazakhstan. The Singapore brand is strong in Kazakhstan.

I saw the more adventurous side of Mr Lee when he went hunting for wild boars with the Kazakh officials. They had set off after lunch. Mr Lee was supposed to return by 5 p.m. and we were worried when he did not show up. He came back at about 7 p.m. It was dark by then. He had enjoyed himself. In fact, he had shot a huge wild boar. I think the Kazakhs had it stuffed and sent here. It probably is in the State's safekeeping somewhere.

VIETNAM

Mr Lee had a strong interest in Vietnam. It was an important country in Southeast Asia with a large and young population. It was also trying to reform. But we had our past encounters with Vietnam, having opposed their invasion of Cambodia. Mr Lee made several visits to

Vietnam — to Hanoi, Ho Chi Minh City and Hue. These visits built up our relations with Vietnam and reset our relationship with them to a new level. The Vietnamese officials respected him. Our links with Vietnam are excellent because of the strong ties cultivated by Mr Lee.

TURKEY

The then Turkish Ambassador to Singapore was very keen for Mr Lee to visit his country. Mr Lee's visit in September 1991 coincided with the Turkish people campaigning for elections. Opposition parties were promising the people: "Elect me and I will give you two keys — one to your house and another to your bank!"

Mr Lee was appalled that they would say that. You cannot go around promising what you cannot deliver. So he advised Turkish leaders not to set such expectations for their people. Everywhere he went, he carried the same brand and the same message. Regardless of the country, he was always consistent.

PAKISTAN

In 1992, Prime Minister Nawaz Sharif wanted Mr Lee's advice on his country's fiscal problems. Mr Lee said he would be willing to give advice but they needed to tell him their problems first. Pakistan sent its top Finance Ministry official to Singapore to provide details and to learn what to do. It was very intense work.

On our side, we needed a person who not only could provide the financial advice but also do a good job. That person was Mr Tharman Shanmugaratnam.[7] Mr Lee selected him to work with the Pakistanis on their fiscal issue. He had already spotted the potential in Mr Tharman in those early days. Mr Tharman did a fantastic job. We tried to help in a very genuine way. Until today, the Pakistan High Commissioner still calls on me, asking our businesses to invest. We have been friendly over the years.

Mr Lee as the ultimate diplomat

We were very careful not to be seen as taking sides in all the countries we visited and always heeded the advice of the Ministry of Foreign Affairs (MFA). Our dealings were always with the current government but we would always find time to meet important opposition leaders. When we went to the United States, for example, we made it a point to call on both Republican and Democratic leaders. In Pakistan, when Prime Minister Nawaz Sharif was in power, we sought a special meeting with Benazir Bhutto.

The four years I spent with Mr Lee were characterised by much travelling and the building of Singapore's relationship with many friends around the world. Because of Mr Lee, I saw places I would not have been able to see on my own. I not only had access to these places, I also listened in to his conversations with great leaders like Henry Kissinger, George Shultz, Nelson Mandela, Jiang Zemin and Mahathir Mohamad. I was privileged to be present when history was made. For example, we were in Moscow and waiting in a *dacha* (villa) for a call on Mikhail Gorbachev but he was delayed defending his policies of glasnost and perestroika. Mr Lee was accompanied by Mr Wong Kan Seng[8] on that visit. Soon thereafter, the Soviet Union was dissolved.

Mr Lee travelled well. He planned meticulously and paced himself well. He had absolute control of his schedule. He had a very lean team of personal staff with him usually consisting of one secretary, two security officers and a doctor. If it was an official visit, the Press Secretary and I would go along. If it was a private one, we would not. And, of course, Mrs Lee would go most of the time.

He was also a very relaxed traveller, always very curious about his environment and the activities that were planned for him.

I did not have to prepare official briefs or notes for him; MFA would do that. But I would take notes at the meetings. However, Mr Lee would take his own notes at sensitive "four eyes" meetings. He never procrastinated or wasted time. After the meeting, he would dictate the meeting points onto tape and put the tape recorder into the red box for his secretary to transcribe. The information would then be sent to his Cabinet colleagues. It was the same arrangement even when he was travelling, except there would be no red box and his secretary would have a lot of transcribing to do when he returned.

Of course, for an issue that needed more time, early preparation would be done way ahead of time. I learnt from Mr Lee to be very detailed and meticulous in preparing in advance, to look at issues from all sides, to know who should be consulted, what questions should be asked, and so on.

Mr Lee's moods

You would have heard about his temper and it was very real. He was very sensitive to his environment. One day, something happened in his Istana office and the temperature in his room went haywire and it got warm. He was angry with the Istana staff, called them in, interrogated them and wanted to know what had happened. Luckily, they quickly fixed the problem.

On another occasion, we were in Ho Chi Minh City. This was a time when few had gone there to invest and there were no decent hotels. The only acceptable one was a floating hotel; it was actually a ship converted into a hotel and docked on the banks of the Saigon River. Mr and Mrs Lee had a suite but it faced the afternoon sun. One day, he returned early and found that the afternoon heat made his room too warm. He was insistent that the ship should be unberthed and moved so that his room would not face the sun. Mrs Lee kept saying to him that it could not be done as it was moored and fixed. Fortunately, she was there to tell him that!

Mrs Lee helped tremendously in managing many of his personal affairs when they travelled. She would get his things packed and looked through his speeches. She was good at softening the ground for us. When he queried why certain things could not be done a certain way, she would say, "Harry, they are thinking about it this way, offering a different perspective." She did this often, not just overseas, but in Singapore as well.

Mr Lee, the adventurous eater

He was adventurous with food as long as it did not affect his health. He ate lamb in Urumqi and had camel paw in Dunhuang. He loved fruits and was very curious about new kinds of fruits and vegetables. If he liked them, he would ask for some to be packed and taken home. He took home mangoes from Pakistan, flat peaches from Shandong and hami melons from Xinjiang.

Mr Lee's dedication to work

We worked six days a week. Saturday was a full working day, no half day. Mr Lee was very dedicated and singularly focused on Singapore, and very simple in his lifestyle. He walked the talk. Very few of us can do that.

He was constantly switched on, thinking and caring about the well-being of Singapore. I remember receiving an instruction one day: "I am passing Orchard Boulevard and I see a rain tree that is not doing so well. Can you check with National Parks? Maybe the pavement is not right and water is not getting to the roots."

Whenever possible, he would distil his daily happenings into words. When he was suffering from a toothache, he dictated to his secretary the nature of the pain, even attempting to describe the pain in words. All this would be transcribed and sent to his dentist. He was very detailed and efficient.

Mr Lee's concern and compassion

In December 1992, my fourth child and second son, Samuel, was born. He was born with a rare syndrome where his blood platelets are trapped in a giant hemangioma in his stomach wall. He was bleeding at birth. As it was a rare condition, his diagnosis and treatment were not typical, and he was in hospital for almost three months. I was looking after him while doing my job. It was a tough time then, juggling the uncertainty of Samuel's illness and not allowing this to affect my duties.

Mr Lee knew about my situation and would ask frequently about Samuel. He wrote to me hoping that the illness would be treatable and that Samuel would not be permanently affected. He was concerned.

Samuel is now 22 years old and in his second year of studies at an Institute of Technical Education. He is fully functional although he walks with crutches. He is a happy young adult. He passed his 'O' level examinations, plays the violin and swims.

After four years as Mr Lee's PPS, I got to know him well. At the end of my service, he just said thank you and I left the office. It was official and businesslike. I don't have a photograph taken with Mr Lee. None of the PPSs have asked to take a picture with him at the end of their tour; at that time we maintained a respectful and official distance. In his later years, he would probably have agreed.

The last time I saw Mr Lee, he was in a wheelchair. It was about two years ago at the launch of his book, *One Man's View of the World*, at the Istana. He was considerably weaker but still a proud man. He stood up, walked to the stage himself and made a speech. That was the last time I saw him in person alive.

Notes

[1] Singapore and Malaysia have signed four agreements to regulate the supply of water from Malaysia to Singapore. They were signed in 1927, 1961, 1962 and 1990. The 1990 water agreement was signed on 24 November 1990 between the Public Utilities Board (PUB) of Singapore and the Johor state government. It will expire in 2061. This agreement was a follow-up to the memorandum of understanding signed in 1988 between the two countries' prime ministers at the time, Lee Kuan Yew and Mahathir Mohamad.

[2] The railway Points of Agreement (POA) is an agreement between Malaysia and Singapore over the issue of the future of railway land owned by the Malaysian government through Malayan Railways in Singapore. It was signed by then Prime Minister of Singapore Lee Kuan Yew and then Finance Minister of Malaysia Tun Daim Zainuddin on 27 November 1990.

[3] In February 1991, then Prime Minister Goh Chok Tong had a blueprint for Singapore entitled "Singapore: The Next Lap". It was a broad agenda for Singapore's long-term development, which included ideas and proposals to make Singapore a nation of distinction. The first wing was to focus on Singapore's own growth. The second wing was to focus on the growth of the region around Singapore.

[4] The Trim and Fit programme was a weight loss programme that targeted child obesity in Singapore schools between 1992 and 2007. It was introduced as part of the National Healthy Lifestyle Campaign.

[5] Nelson Mandela was President of South Africa from May 1994 to June 1999. Frederik Willem de Klerk was State President of South Africa from August 1989 to May 1994.

[6] Lee Hsien Loong, then Deputy Prime Minister of Singapore, was diagnosed with lymphoma in 1992. He underwent a three-month period of chemotherapy and has been in remission since.

[7] Tharman Shanmugaratnam was then Director of Economics at the Monetary Authority of Singapore (MAS). He was Managing Director of MAS before he left to join politics. He was Minister for Finance from 2007 to 2015. He is currently Deputy Prime Minister and Coordinating Minister for Economic and Social Policies, as well as Chairman of MAS.

[8] Wong Kan Seng was then the Minister for Community Development and Minister for Foreign Affairs.

YATIMAN YUSOF

Parliamentary Secretary for Foreign Affairs, 1986–1996

❝This is nice fresh fish. Where did you learn how to fish?❞

– Lee Kuan Yew

Many things have been said about the late Mr Lee Kuan Yew's prowess as a powerful leader, an iconic political figure who made the hard decisions and the key driver behind Singapore's unprecedented success in the short 50 years of nation building. Only a handful have had the privilege of knowing him as a person. Even fewer have had the opportunity that I was most fortunate to have — to be housed together with Mr Lee in a small two-storey building at Moose Lodge, New Zealand, set against the mountainside and overlooking the beautiful Lake Rotoiti.

It was only a few months into our appointments as Parliamentary Secretaries when Tang Guan Seng and I were chosen to be part of Mr Lee's 12-member delegation for the first two legs of his visit to New Zealand, Fiji and Australia in April 1986.

When we arrived in Auckland on 5 April, we were flown on the Royal New Zealand Air Force twin-prop Andover to Rotorua, and received by the New Zealand Prime Minister, Mr David Lange, and his three Cabinet Ministers. From there, Mr and Mrs Lee, Guan Seng and I, together with a security officer and a doctor, were driven to the official guest house at Moose Lodge. The rest of the delegation stayed at the Hyatt Kingsgate Hotel.

Surrounded by a thick green pine and spruce forest and connected only by a lone country road, this quiet serene setting was where Mr and Mrs Lee, Guan Seng and I spent hours together over lunch, breakfast and dinner whenever we were free from official engagements. The intimate sitting and dining area on the ground floor magnified the closeness.

Prior to this trip, we had learnt from our senior colleagues of Mr Lee's inclination to engage us for discussion. But that was not a surprise to me as I had covered Mr Lee's visits to Sri Lanka, London and Washington as a journalist, and he would gather us for discussions when he managed some time between official meetings. His favourite topics: feedback on policies and politics. It was with this knowledge that, as a greenhorn in politics at that time, I did my homework and got up to speed on various current issues, so as to be ready for robust, meaningful exchanges of local policies and world politics. I must be well prepared for this, I thought.

As usual, Mr Lee had his daily morning jog before breakfast. When we tucked into our first meal of the day, it slowly dawned on me that I was clearly mistaken. Despite his mind being heavily occupied with bilateral trade issues with New Zealand, Mr Lee took an interest in our personal lives and our conversations were light-hearted banter of private matters close to our hearts. I had initially credited this to Mrs Lee's motherly presence. However, at some point I wondered whether it was Mr Lee's preference to have two young, newly-elected parliamentarians with him. There was no way to be sure, but such sentiments were not misplaced given that their son, Mr Lee Hsien Loong, had been elected slightly more than a year earlier.

It started innocently, with Mrs Lee commenting that she loved eating duku and mangosteen. She thanked me for the fruit basket that

I had delivered to their home, having hand-plucked the fruit from my *kampung* in Johore. I also learnt that Mr Lee liked duku too. She then suggested that the green strips lining East Coast Parkway be converted into a fruit orchard, so that city children would know what durian trees look like. We laughed when she shared about how our children draw chickens as they saw them in the supermarket; and they could not be blamed because they were not privy to seeing chickens free-roaming as we had, growing up in Singapore when it was nothing more than a *kampung*.

Mr Lee then asked about our children, how old they were, and the schools they attended. When I told him that I had four children aged 14, 10, 5 and 3, Mrs Lee remarked in Malay, *"Awak tak dengar loceng ke?"* ("Did you not hear the bell ring?")

I laughed, slightly embarrassed, and said that I just loved having children and they brought me much joy, but shared that on most occasions I do not take all four children out together for outings.

Mr Lee responded, saying that I was afraid of being teased by people who saw me with my many children, when it was the norm to "stop at two".

When they heard that I had sent my children to the neighbourhood Bedok Boys Primary School, Mr Lee said that whichever school we chose, what was important was that the children were comfortable with the social and learning environment. There was not a trace of elitism, cynicism or judgement in his tone.

On the second day at the lodge, as I was not involved in the morning meeting, I decided to go fishing for trout at the lake. The lodge owners, an elderly couple who co-managed the resort, offered me a small boat, fishing line and bait. Three hours later, I returned with two reasonably large rainbow trout. The lodge owners offered to grill one, and steam the other. So for dinner, the four of us were treated to a well-prepared rainbow trout dish, complete with greens and potatoes on the side.

"This is nice fresh fish," commented Mr Lee. "Where did you learn how to fish?" he asked.

"I was just lucky," I said, avoiding the answer.

"But you are not *orang laut*," said Mrs Lee, using the Malay term for "people of the sea". I said I used to go fishing from time to time when I was a teacher.

Our stay at Moose Lodge was not all peaceful, however, and was marred by a shooting incident of a traffic officer named Mr Robin Dudding who was shot dead. The gunman, who was seriously injured, was successfully apprehended by the police. Mr Lee was shaken by the incident. Not because it had happened so near to him, or that it could have possibly put him in harm's way. He was shaken by the tragedy of the situation, a tragedy to which his visit may have contributed in some way. When we met again, prior to our departure to Fiji, Mr Lee was still unable to put the incident behind him. He said that had he not stayed at Moose Lodge, Mr Robin Dudding would not have been on duty at the turn-off to the lodge, and he would not have died. I tried to convince him by saying that it was fate; but one could tell by his expression that he still felt bad about it.

I later found out that Mr Lee had penned a condolence note to the traffic officer's wife. In his note, Mr Lee said that he was shocked by the tragedy and expressed grief over the loss suffered by her, her children and their friends.

On 9 April, we continued our second leg of the journey to Fiji to meet with Mr Lee's good friend, Ratu Sir Kamisese Mara. Mr Lee's delegation, which was due to arrive at Nadi Airport on the western part of the main island at mid-afternoon, was delayed, arriving only in the evening. This meant that an elaborate series of traditional Fijian welcome ceremonies prepared for Mr Lee's arrival had to be unceremoniously cancelled.

The following day, Mr Lee arrived ten minutes earlier to meet Ratu Sir Kamisese and personally apologised to the Fijian leader. He later also expressed his profound apologies at a press conference. This was a personal glimpse into the seriousness with which Mr Lee took interpersonal relations — in this instance, the cultural slight that he might have caused — which had made him not only well respected but also well received amongst leaders in many parts of the world.

By and large, the meetings in Fiji went well. Mr Lee had working meetings with the Fijian leader and his Cabinet. Singapore offered airport ground service to Fiji on top of assistance in areas of port development and management. Over dinner, Mr Lee and Ratu Sir Kamisese talked about the golf they had played in Jamaica. Sitting across the table from them, I could sense the great chemistry the two leaders shared, over a mix of politics and friendship.

Towards the end of our stay in Fiji, we hoped to enjoy the view of the Pacific from The Fijian, a top resort hotel on Yanuca Island. There was ample time as we were scheduled to catch the Air Pacific flight at Nadi Airport to Brisbane only at 3.10 p.m. As we were strolling down the beautiful white sandy beach, we received an alert by the hotel staff to return to our rooms immediately. He said that a cyclone was about to hit the island and we had to make haste to the airport.

We raced to the car as the rain started to fall heavily. I was told that the host had offered Mr and Mrs Lee a helicopter to take them to Nadi but Mr Lee had courteously declined. So this meant that the delegation had to cross the island by car. The motorcade had Mr Lee's car in the middle accompanied by a security car; Guan Seng and I were in the second car; and behind Mr Lee's car was another security station-wagon followed by other cars carrying officials and journalists.

En route, we hit a flooded stretch, and Mr and Mrs Lee had to be transferred to a Land Rover that had pulled up about a metre away. Both were caught in the rain, and their clothes were drenched. Before the Land Rover drove off, I was able to pull out my camera and captured a few shots of the Prime Minister and Mrs Lee in the vehicle.

Upon catching sight of this, Mrs Lee quipped, "Yatiman, you could not forget your journalist past and still shooting pictures." Mr Lee managed to smile amidst the mayhem, on seeing my behaviour.

"My apologies PM and Mrs Lee. Nobody can get these kinds of shots!" I said and continued clicking away.

So Mr and Mrs Lee, both cold, wet and shivering, got into the Land Rover, only to have the vehicle engine stall midway. Policemen and soldiers jumped to action immediately, escorting and pushing the Land Rover to safety.

While on the way to the airport, a police security personnel accompanying Mr Lee's motorcade was involved in a head-on collision. Members of the Singapore delegation stopped to help him. He was bleeding profusely and succumbed to his injuries and died. Mr Lee was informed of the accident when he reached the hotel in Nadi for a rest stop. He was again shaken by this unfortunate turn of events, as it turned out that it was the very same security officer who had accompanied him on his daily morning jogs throughout his stay in Fiji.

We parted ways when we arrived in Brisbane safely, Mr Lee and Mrs Lee continuing their third leg of their official visit in Australia, while Guan Seng and I headed back home to Singapore. This short span of six days when we journeyed together gave me tremendous insight into Mr Lee's character, a person whose emotional quotient was almost as strong as his IQ, as he juggled a demanding schedule — tragic mishaps included — between serving the nation, spending time with his family and developing friendships that last a lifetime, yet still keeping great dignity and calm.

YEONG YOON YING
Press Secretary, 1993–2015

❝Without her, I would be a different man,
with a different life.**❞**
– Lee Kuan Yew

On 2 October 2010, my family was celebrating my grandson's full month at home when the phone rang. It was an urgent call from Mr Lee, asking me to help compile a video montage that chronicled some of Mrs Lee's best moments. She had just passed on.

With a heavy heart burdened by sadness over her demise, I spent the whole night scouring through MediaCorp's archives, as well as my personal collection, to look for the most appropriate clips which could be refined into a congruous storyboard. Mr Lee watched the video the next morning and I remember his eyes turning red.

Even though he had mentally prepared himself for her passing, his true feelings for Mrs Lee were revealed during the funeral service. What touched me the most was the title of his eulogy: "The last farewell to my wife." The very poignant eulogy said, "Without her, I would be a different man, with a different life."

To me, that sentence summed up their 63-year marriage. They indeed enjoyed a blissful marital life, one which was anchored by mutual trust and respect. Theirs was a bond that other couples should emulate.

Mrs Lee was a quiet and calm person. She hardly raised her voice. She knew Mr Lee's temperament best and had her ways of soothing and calming him down whenever he was unsettled or anxious. All his staffers were very grateful for this.

I recall one of my first trips to China as Press Secretary, in 1993 or 1994. The programme was very tight. On one occasion, Mr Lee asked his private secretary to pass me some information for follow-up. Realising that I was just about to have my lunch after a long and hectic morning, Mrs Lee immediately said, "Harry, YY is having her meal. The work should wait." Mr Lee then told me, "YY, no hurry, give it to me this evening."

On another visit to China, Mr Lee was to make an important speech at the Confucius Conference. The hall was full and a dozen journalists had broken up our entourage. From afar, Mr Lee instructed me to extend a copy of his speech to a "John Wong". Standing beside me was Mr Lee's physician, Dr John Wong. Mrs Lee, sensing my confusion, quickly told me, "YY, not this Dr John Wong. Mr Lee meant Dr Aline Wong's husband, Prof John Wong." In the course of my career, I have been grateful countless times to Mrs Lee for saving me from embarrassment.

She was the one who took good care of Mr Lee. She was always by his side at both private and public engagements. If a prepared speech was required, Mrs Lee would be his first reader and final vetter. Her language was simple and elegant, just like her. We knew that all the speeches she vetted would have no grammatical errors, and we would always feel assured whenever she came on a trip with us.

She was the perfect example of "贤妻" (good wife). Because she took care of all his personal needs, Mr Lee could dedicate all his time and his whole life to managing the country. He knew that she was his rock, supporting him along the way and making sure that his daily needs were well taken care of.

Mrs Lee would always sit in during Mr Lee's Chinese lessons which were held daily. At times, she would surprise us by using Chinese idioms brilliantly. I recall a trip to New Zealand in 2007. After all the official calls were over, Mrs Lee visited Lake Taupo, the largest lake by surface area in the country. She picked up some pumice stones to take home as souvenirs. She also picked up a goose feather, which prompted a puzzled Mr Lee to ask, "Choo, what for?"

Mrs Lee replied in Mandarin, "千里送鹅毛" (a gift of a goose feather from across a thousand miles). Everyone was silent. Those well versed in Chinese understood her. Mrs Lee was trying to explain that her act of giving someone a feather meant "物轻情意重" (it's the thought that counts despite the lightness of the gift).

I was amazed and asked her where she learnt this 典故 (allusion or saying).[1] She told me she had learnt it by sitting in on Mr Lee's lessons. She showed time and again that she, like her husband, was a "lifelong learner". In Chinese, this attitude can be expressed as "活到老，学到老" (one is never too old to learn). Understandably, she supported Mr Lee's belief that Singaporean Chinese should also know Chinese and that the learning of Chinese can open up a window to a rich culture.

As far as I can recall, Mrs Lee granted only a handful of media interviews throughout her life. The only TV interview was with Radio Television Hong Kong, whose crew filmed her and Mr Lee visiting their alma mater, Cambridge, for a documentary aired in 2002.

Mr Lee, with his distinguished international profile and standing, was one of the greatest politicians of his time. But deep down inside, he was a very private person and so was Mrs Lee. I recall his candid reply to the television interviewer's question on whether he and Mrs Lee held hands when they were young.

Mr Lee said, "We had a lot of work to do. We did not hold hands. We were too busy then."

The interviewer pursued this by asking, "But holding hands does not take up much time. Were people very conservative at that time?"

What I found priceless was Mrs Lee's sharp response to this: "Not everybody, just us. We don't do these things, not then."

While drafting his speech for his 80th birthday, Mr Lee thanked everyone who had fought for Singapore with him. However, I noticed that there was no mention of Mrs Lee. I pointed this out to him and when the final text came, he had added a sentence:

> "At the end of the day, what I cherish most are the human relationships. With the unfailing support of my wife and partner, I have lived my life to the fullest. It is the friendships I made and the close family ties I nurtured that have provided me with that sense of satisfaction at a life well lived, and have made me what I am."

In October 2003, after Mrs Lee suffered her first stroke in London, Mr Lee flew back in time for Tanjong Pagar's Tree Planting ceremony. From his voice and expression, the audience could sense his anxiety and sadness. To me, this was the turning point in Mr and Mrs Lee's roles. Mrs Lee once said, "Before my stroke, I took care of him. Now, I enjoy being pampered by him."

Mr Lee would stay by her side at the hospital, not only to give her moral support, but also to accompany her during her physiotherapy sessions. Doctors noted Mrs Lee's remarkable recovery which was partly attributed to his presence and support, especially in helping to ensure that she kept to her exercise regime.

Mr Lee was a champion of exercise and keeping fit. He always encouraged Mrs Lee to exercise because he wanted her to have a quality life in her old age.

I recall a trip to the United States in 2006 when Mrs Lee was tired and wanted to skip her afternoon swim. She gave the excuse that since that day was a public holiday in Singapore, she should be allowed to also take a break from swimming. Mr Lee advised her against it, saying that the swim would help her to have a good night's sleep. He then added that he would join her for a swim later that evening. The smile on Mrs Lee's face after hearing that is still etched in my mind. While I have never heard them say "I love you", their actions revealed everything.

After her second and third strokes in 2008, Mrs Lee could no longer accompany Mr Lee on his overseas trips. In a media interview, Mr Lee shared that when he was not travelling, he would read to her before he went to bed every night. If he was overseas, he would talk to her over the phone and let her know who he had met and what had been discussed. The helper at home would turn on the speakerphone so that Mrs Lee could hear his voice. I took a picture of Mr Lee speaking over a mobile phone to Mrs Lee in 2010, after a lunch meeting with Japanese politicians. It was such a touching sight.

I have seen many loving couples during my public service days, but I would say that there were few as compatible as Mr and Mrs Lee. Not only did they excel in their professional lives, they were also successful in their personal lives. To me, they were the epitome of the ideal husband-and-wife team.

Mrs Lee once said, "I did things the way I wanted and I didn't get involved in the things I didn't want to get involved in. I think I had the best of both worlds."

In my 21 years of working in the Prime Minister's Office, I have observed and felt much. Therefore, I have chosen not to write about Mr Lee, but about Mrs Lee. I must sing for the unsung heroine behind the great man. Without Mrs Lee, Mr Lee would have been a different person, as he himself has acknowledged.

Let us salute the late Mrs Lee, who has helped one Prime Minister of Singapore and nurtured another. We, as Singaporeans, have benefitted much from her contributions.

Notes

[1] This particular allusion is of a variety known as 歇后语, which is an idiomatic two-part double pun. Part one is akin to a riddle, while part two is usually a double pun based on part one. The second part is often omitted.

ALAN CHAN

Principal Private Secretary, 1994–1997

"Harry! Harry! Cool down!"
– Mrs Lee

The first time I came up close to Mr Lee was in 1969, at the Raffles Institution's Founder's Day celebrations. Because of the riots in Kuala Lumpur, he needed a forum to give a speech and so he picked that particular day. Another minister had been invited to give away the prizes but Mr Lee borrowed the occasion to give a sombre analysis of the political climate. I listened attentively as a 16-year-old boy. His words woke me up to the seriousness of the situation. It was an eye-opener.

Mr Lee and the Chinese language

The first time I formally met him was when he interviewed me for the position of principal private secretary (PPS). I was one of four candidates. The first thing he said to me after looking at my CV was, "Chan Heng Loon, you don't qualify. You have a C6 in Chinese. I am looking for a PPS who is good in Chinese."

I explained that the low grade was my biggest disappointment because I knew I was strong in Chinese but something happened to me during the 'O' levels and my results had suffered. He asked me some more questions to assess my proficiency in the language. I told him I had been reading Chinese newspapers, magazines and books since the age of six. He listened closely and carried on quizzing me on various Chinese publications.

He then added, "I believe what you said. Please go ahead and take the PPS exam."

A couple of weeks later, my predecessor, Ho Meng Kit, told me I was successful in getting the job. While Mr Lee's initial impression was that I was poor in Chinese, he had given me the benefit of the doubt after hearing my explanation. Indeed, I was to be tested very soon.

Within two weeks into the job, Mr Lee, who was Senior Minister at the time, asked me to go to Taiwan with him together with George Yeo. We met then President Lee Teng-hui and then Premier Lien Chan. There were long discussions and the conversations were all in Mandarin. I was in charge of taking minutes. Mr Lee said he wanted the notes verbatim the next day, and he wanted them written up in English with keywords in Chinese so that he could share them with the Cabinet. I had to work through the night. I handed him the notes at about 9 a.m. An hour later, he told me I had passed the test.

It was fortunate that I had been reading Chinese newspapers and magazines diligently, which helped me follow their conversation. I wasn't stumped by the terms "Qiandaohu 千島湖 incident" and "de chuan mo fu 德川幕府", which is the Mandarin term for the Tokugawa Shogunate, the last feudal Japanese military government.

During my PPS stint, we would visit China once or twice a year. I was often busy on the flight out, as I had to translate the briefs from the various ministries, for example, the Ministry of Foreign Affairs and the Ministry of Trade and Industry. I would get the briefs in English but had to translate all the key words into Chinese so that Mr Lee could use the Chinese words when he spoke to then President Jiang Zemin and then Premier Li Peng.

This was also the time of the China-Singapore Suzhou Industrial Park (SIP) project, which experienced many hiccups along the way. Mr Lee personally resolved many of its issues, even going to meet President Jiang. I believe that without Mr Lee's intervention there would have been many more obstacles and things would have been even worse.

After the SIP project was launched in 1994, every other city in China wanted the same. At one particular provincial capital, we were invited to attend a luncheon event. I checked out the venue and saw that the organisers had hoisted a huge banner with the words: "The establishment of Singapore Industrial Park in our city".

We never agreed to set up any venture with the province! I panicked and quickly reported back to Mr Lee, expecting him to rebuke me for this. But he just nodded and said, "Alan, it's not your fault. We're here as guests and they can do what they like. But brief the journalists that we are not backing it. Just play it down as far as Singapore is concerned." He understood the circumstances and accepted them. He even smiled and took photos with the provincial leaders with the banner as backdrop.

On my last day of working with Mr Lee, he thanked me for being an efficient PPS. I told him I would be going to the Ministry of Foreign Affairs (MFA). He said that was a good thing because MFA needed to build up its China desk, which was the main task that had been assigned to me. I had a very able director at MFA, Albert Chua, now Second Permanent Secretary for Foreign Affairs. He started a weekly study programme where we would have xue xi 学习 (learning period). In those sessions A, for example, would do a presentation on the education system of China, B would talk on the People's Liberation Army, C would share about the provincial government of Zhejiang, and so on.

This shortened the learning curve for all our new diplomats in China. I had been well trained in discipline serving Mr Lee. To ensure that our diplomats could speak impeccable Chinese, I imposed a ten-cent fine if any of my staff used an English word in a Chinese conversation!

Mr Lee, the constant learner

My predecessor, Ho Meng Kit, started the process of inviting bankers to regular discussion sessions with Mr Lee. When I took over as PPS, that task fell to me.

Twice a week, Mr Lee would meet with ten bankers each time — Singaporeans as well as foreigners — to get their take on key banking issues. If he liked any of their comments, he would ask the persons who made them to elaborate their thoughts on paper. After that, I would circulate the reports to the remaining people in the group. Each individual could also give their comments on the reports and these would also be recorded. In no time at all, we were looking at stacks and stacks of comments and reports.

The banking sector was foreign to me. Mr Lee was not trained as a banker but he had this incredible ability to grasp key points quickly. From his sessions with the bankers, I saw how he was able to absorb information from about 300 submissions and distill ideas from them. Subsequently, we would send these observations to the Ministry of Finance and the Monetary Authority of Singapore where they would develop them further. It was in this manner that we formulated the policies to liberalise the banking sector.

When Mr Lee was suffering from heart problems, he received numerous well wishes. Once, he received a book on health for heart patients. He told me to summarise it for him! It took me about a week — and he became quite an expert on his condition.

Mr Lee's discipline and determination

I witnessed Mr Lee's determination and discipline firsthand during the trying period of 1996 and 1997. First there was his 1996 lawsuit against *Yazhou Zhoukan* 亞洲週刊, a Chinese language newsweekly, which had published the comments by a lawyer, Tang Liang Hong, alleging impropriety in Mr Lee's purchase of two flats. While the publication quickly retracted the statement and paid a settlement fee, Tang, who would run as a Workers' Party candidate in the 1997 General Election, refused to apologise. In fact, six months later at an election rally, he repeated the allegations and stated that, if elected, he would raise the matter again.[1]

All this coincided with the period when Mr Lee was having heart problems and had to have a second stent put in. He was bogged down with health problems and was asked to slow down.

But he kept on going. Despite his ill health, he gave a talk at the Nanyang Technological University on 14 March 1996.[2] He was just recovering and his blood pressure readings were not good, but he felt it was very important that he addressed the students. He felt it was crucial that they heard the government's point of view. We had to make special arrangements for an ambulance; doctors were also on standby, although they sat discreetly in a corner. That day he spoke from 8.30 p.m. to midnight, engaging in long exchanges with the students. A normal person would have stayed at home and rested, but not Mr Lee. It was clear that, to him, duty trumped almost everything. When a mission was key, he always rose to the occasion.

Mr Lee and Mrs Lee

Mrs Lee was his constant companion and his sounding board. She also helped me often by reducing his sting and I was most grateful to her. When he was irritated by an issue or by his health, and I had to bring bad news to him, Mrs Lee would prepare him first. She would say to him, "Alan is coming in with some bad news but, remember, he is just the messenger." Many times, I would be at his desk in the office and she would be sitting in a corner, reading or knitting. When he was unhappy or upset about something, she would say, "Harry! Harry! Cool down!" She had a very strong human touch.

As he got older, of course, he became more mellow. My predecessors told me I was quite lucky!

Mr Lee, never one to take a rest day

Mr Lee worked seven days a week even though there were no personal staff members around on Sundays to attend to him. We did work a full day on Saturdays though.

There is this Whitehall red box that he had in his possession. The term "red box" informally refers to a ministerial box used by ministers in the British government to carry their documents; it is primarily used to hold and transport official papers from place to place. Mr Lee held a key to the box at home and his PA had a key in the office. There was always a lot of paperwork going through the box.

Mr Lee was a night bird. He usually slept at 2 or 3 a.m. and would wake up late. Before he went to sleep, he would put his work into the red box. First thing in the morning, the security officers would collect the box from his home and bring it to his office, and his PA would open it. I would attend to the documents and prepare what was needed. Then, I would fill up the red box and it would be sent back to him. This box would go back and forth throughout the day whenever he worked from home.

Mr Lee and getting down to the ground

Sometimes, on Saturdays at about 11 a.m., Mr Lee would send me an instruction to visit a certain precinct in the afternoon. He only wanted the town council manager and one ministry officer to be around — no MPs or anyone else. And certainly no media. By the time I called to inform the precinct, there was little time left for them to prepare for his visit. At the most, they could only ensure that the floors were swept. Certainly they could not repaint anything as he would be able to smell the fresh paint.

He also liked to make spontaneous private visits to the homes of families of different races. The town council manager would choose three families from different socio-economic backgrounds: those who lived in one-room flats to those in five-room flats. Mr Lee would talk to them and get their views. In Chinese, we call it "wei fu chu xun 微服出巡" (to go on an inspection in plain clothes).

I remember two households in particular. One was a Malay family living in a five-room flat. Their bathroom was like a hotel's, with twin wash-basins, hairdryer and all the amenities. It showed that they were able to live very well. The other family also lived in a well-decorated flat. The son, a surgeon working in Hualien, Taiwan, was not admitted into the National University of Singapore (NUS) but he was so keen to be a doctor that he went to Kaohsiung University where he qualified as a surgeon. I can only speculate that instances such as this would have set Mr Lee thinking. Subsequently, NUS increased the intake of students into its medical school and the Singapore government recognised the qualifications of more foreign medical schools.

Even on Sundays, when the staff wasn't working, Mr Lee would get his security officers to drive him around the housing estates. On Monday mornings, I would get a note detailing his observations.

He always felt the best way to get honest and direct feedback was to go down to the ground himself.

Whenever we travelled overseas, he would ask to go to the local market. He would look at the fruits and fish on sale and, immediately, he would get a feel of how prosperous or poor the place was.

I remember once we were in Dalian, China. At the market, he saw a pineapple and asked the vendor where the fruit came from. The vendor said it was from Taiwan. He said, "You mean there's trade between Taiwan and China?"

That was in 1994. It is a clear example of how the reality on the ground could be different from common perception. Unless you saw and experienced it for yourself, you would not get the real feel of things. On these market visits, Mr Lee would also ask the price of an egg and what people's monthly wages were. Everywhere he went, he made it a point to get firsthand information.

Mr Lee and his diet

Mr Lee ate a lot of fruits. Before leaving for a trip, he would first ask for a list of fruits available in the city he was visiting.

Once, before a trip to New Delhi, he asked why watermelon was not on the fruit list. I quickly sent a telex to our high commission who replied that they were afraid that the watermelon might be contaminated with the Hepatitis C virus. He said to me, "Silly fellow, you only get Hepatitis C from animal products." I relayed this back to New Delhi and a week later we received a formal letter from the Physician to the High Commissioner of the United Kingdom. The letter explained that in New Delhi, syringes are used to inject sugar water into the watermelons to sweeten them and these syringes may carry the Hepatitis C virus.

Mr Lee liked to drink beer, usually one glass or at most two. He used to drink Swan Lite Lager because of its low alcohol content. When this beer went out of production, Mr Lee switched to regular beer. He also enjoyed red and white wine. While he liked Japanese food particularly, he also enjoyed Western food. When he was having his health problems, two physicians supervised his meals, which would consist mainly of steamed fish, blanched vegetables and plain chicken soup.

In the evenings, he would either run or swim. When it came to exercise, he was quite a taskmaster. Mrs Lee had to report to him everyday what she did for exercise. Her routine was usually swimming or walking. Occasionally he would chide her for not doing enough.

Mr Lee and his dedication to Singapore

During my time with Mr Lee, there were constant requests from people to meet him or for him to attend functions. To these requests, he would always ask one question, "Will it help Singapore?" His instruction to me was: "If it doesn't, don't come to me. Drop it."

Just before I took up the PPS job, I paid courtesy calls to my seniors. I asked one of them how I should apply for leave. He asked me how I could think of such a thing when I would be working for a man who lived and breathed Singapore! This person told me that to be Mr Lee's assistant I should be prepared to serve him at all times because, at the end of the day, it was all for the good of Singapore. I never felt so small. Today, some 20 years later, that conversation still lingers in my mind.

Working for Mr Lee enabled me to strengthen my confidence. I left the job with a deeper understanding of the idea that once you have the DNA, and the conviction, in yourself to always do good for Singapore, you don't waver. You push on.

Notes

[1] Lee Kuan Yew, *From Third World to First: The Singapore Story 1965–2000 Memoirs of Lee Kuan Yew*, Singapore: Times Editions, 2000, p. 153.

[2] Speech by Senior Minister Lee Kuan Yew, "Will Singapore be another Slow-Growing Developed Nation?" Nanyang Technological University, Singapore.

PETER SEAH
Chairman, DBS Group Holdings & DBS Bank

❝It is a bay, you block the water from coming in and over time, you get fresh water.❞
– Lee Kuan Yew

Over a period of 20 years, I was privileged to get to know Mr Lee Kuan Yew through many meetings, private chats and over meals. Besides getting to know Lee Kuan Yew as the founding father, Prime Minister, Senior Minister and Minister Mentor, I also got to know Lee Kuan Yew the man, one who had compassion, who was open minded and always willing to challenge convention, accept different views and help if he believed in the cause. In private, he was relaxed and open and would talk about his family like any other father would.

Perhaps, by sharing a few anecdotes, I can better portray Lee Kuan Yew the man whom I have been fortunate to know.

Mr Lee's interest in the banking industry

I first met Mr Lee in 1994, in Davos, Switzerland, at the World Economic Forum. I was invited to tea with SM Lee and other Singaporean participants. When I got back to my hotel room, I received a call from Singapore that he would like to see me when I returned home.

My first meeting up close with SM Lee was at a lunch with him and two other Singaporean bankers. His interest then was banking and he wanted to know more about it. He asked probing questions. He had been told that local banks were wanting and lacked talent. It was a stressful lunch, especially when I expressed my disagreement with his perception. I explained the need for local banks to be more prudent because of their smaller capital base. He was a bit annoyed. I left the lunch feeling that he thought poorly of me although I noted that he did listen to my arguments. Anyway, I concluded that it was likely to be my first and last meeting with him.

I was wrong. He did accept my views even though he may not have agreed with them.

In 1997, he invited me to join the board of GIC (formerly Government of Singapore Investment Corporation) that he then chaired. This, to me, meant that he valued my views.

My years on the board gave me the opportunity to enjoy his intellect, decisiveness and his ever 'young mind' in guiding the company. He always listened to the views of other board members. He was compassionate and understanding to those who made mistakes. When staff were penalised for serious mistakes, and he was assured that there had been no integrity breach, he would instruct that they be taken good care of after the punishment. He made it clear that he would not tolerate issues of integrity.

In the late 1990s, Mr Lee was very vocal about the need for consolidation in the banking industry. As CEO of OUB, the smallest of the Big Four local banks, I knew that the writing was on the wall. I suggested to my board that we should take the initiative to merge with the smaller Keppel Bank. They disagreed.

I felt that I needed to take action. I was not prepared to just wait for a bank which I had invested 20 years of my life building up, to be taken over. In desperation, I wrote a paper to SM Lee with my views and proposals and asked for his help. I expected nothing. My wife, Mylene, similarly thought Mr Lee would not bother with it.

I was pleasantly surprised when I received a call to see him at his office. I didn't know what to expect. When I arrived, there was a young officer from the Monetary Authority of Singapore (MAS) to take notes. I could see that Mr Lee had used a red marker to underline and write notes on my paper. He questioned me in a rather harsh tone and said I was very bold to be complaining about my chairman whom he knew was well respected. I replied that I stood by everything I had said and believed that my proposals were the best option for OUB. He told me in a raised voice that I could lose my job for what I had done. I replied that having written to him, I was prepared for the consequences. He glared at me. I didn't know what was going to happen next. I expected the worst.

Then, he broke out into laughter!

I realised that he wanted to test my conviction and courage. He then said that he saw logic in my arguments and proposal, and asked what I wanted him to do. I requested his help to speak with my chairman to consider my proposals. He said that he would try his best.

As I left his office, the young MAS officer jokingly told me that I was lucky to walk out alive. I felt differently. I was truly impressed that Senior Minister had taken the time to read my paper, to engage me, to test my conviction. In spite of OUB being the smallest of the Big Four, he had been prepared to accept a different solution from the consolidation he envisaged. I was grateful for his time and I developed a deep respect for his open-mindedness and his willingness to help me because I stood by my convictions.

In the months that followed, he constantly reminded me to move fast, saying that time was running out. At most functions, he would ask to speak with me to find out whether I was making any progress. My wife was very impressed with his reaching out to me and his genuine

254 | UP CLOSE WITH LEE KUAN YEW

efforts to help me. She saw him in a different context at Istana poolside dinners, where he was warm and sociable. She became a great fan of his. I asked his views on options such as a strategic alliance with a major global bank, which he encouraged. But it was not to be. In 2001, OUB was taken over by UOB. SM Lee subsequently admonished me and said, "I told you to move fast."

The current strength and size of the remaining three local banks (UOB, DBS and OCBC) and their ability to take on the global banks here and in the region, plus their ability to support our financial centre, attest to his wisdom and foresight about the need for banking consolidation.

The unconventional Mr Lee

Another experience that attests to Mr Lee's willingness to go out of his way to assist when he saw that it would be for a good cause and for Singapore, was the acquisition of telecommunications company Global Crossing in December 2003.

Singapore Technologies Telemedia (ST Telemedia) had been trying to acquire a controlling stake in Global Crossing, which had filed for bankruptcy. Global Crossing had invested in the largest fibre optic network infrastructure globally. At US$250 million for a 61 per cent stake, ST Telemedia had considered it an attractive acquisition.

The process was, to say the least, challenging, especially in a new security paradigm following the 9/11 terrorist attacks. In tandem with obtaining clearance from the courts, we were subject to national security clearance from CFIUS (Committee on Foreign Investment in the United States). This process required getting approval from various government departments such as Justice, Treasury, Defence and the newly created Homeland Security.

The major stumbling block was the Defence Department that refused to approve for security reasons. As CEO of Singapore Technologies Group, I had to make the rounds in Washington, D.C. to lobby congressmen and senators for support. The most unforgettable meeting was with an Assistant Secretary at the Defence Department, who said in no uncertain terms that the transaction would never be approved. This was in spite of my reminding her that our Prime Minister (Mr Goh Chok Tong) had just signed a bilateral trade agreement with the United States in May 2003. We felt that, given the recent bilateral agreement, it was ridiculous for the US to reject our application.

I returned dejected and told my colleagues we needed help from the government. That, we knew, was going to be difficult. Indeed, our initial approaches were met with reluctance. The general government policy was not to get involved in private sector transactions. We came up with the bold idea of making an appeal to Senior Minister Lee. I had found him open-minded and thought he could perhaps understand the strategic implications to Singapore, beyond the commercial aspects.

SM responded in a fashion that really stunned us. He agreed that we should not accept such treatment and made calls to his various senior American contacts in the defence and security establishments. In doing so, he demonstrated that there were times when the government had to fight for the private sector, especially when it came to defending Singapore's national interests. His actions prompted other government leaders to join the effort to lobby for the approval of our application. The matter eventually reached the office of the US President and we had our investment approved. Today, we still hold the investment which has been merged into another telemedia company and the stake is worth in excess of US$3 billion.

The role model leader

SM Lee exemplified a leader who would do whatever it took to enhance and protect the interests of Singapore. He was never afraid to do things differently and to be unconventional. He displayed great courage. If I see him as a role model Singaporean leader, it is because of what he had done to earn my utmost admiration, respect and love.

I have unforgettable memories of conversations with him, and deeply appreciate his sharing of experiences and views on a broad range of subjects. He was generous in sharing his knowledge. I always enjoyed my dinners with him.

My last dinner with him was on 17 December 2014 which he hosted at Raffles Hotel. He was relaxed and ate well. In my last conversation with him, I asked him about his 40-year vision of Marina Barrage. How did he conceive it?

His reply was typically LKY, simple and modest: "It is a bay, you block the water from coming in and over time, you get fresh water."

That was MM Lee, as I called him when he became Minister Mentor in 2004, never wanting to take credit for the great visionary he was.

HENG SWEE KEAT

Principal Private Secretary, 1997–2000

❝Can you pass me the red box?❞
– Lee Kuan Yew

Mr Lee Kuan Yew had a red box. When I worked as Mr Lee's principal private secretary, or PPS, a good part of my daily life revolved around the red box. Before Mr Lee came in to work each day, the locked red box would arrive first, at about 9 a.m.

As far as the various officers who have worked with Mr Lee can remember, he has had the box for many, many years. It is a large, boxy briefcase, about 14 centimetres deep. The tradition of using red boxes came from the British government, whose ministers used them for transporting documents between government offices. Our early ministers had red boxes, but Mr Lee is the only one I know who used his consistently through the years. When I started working for Mr Lee in 1997, it was the first time I saw a red box in use. It is called the red box but is more a deep wine colour, like the seats in the chamber in Parliament House.

This red box held what Mr Lee was working on at any one time. Through the years, it held his papers, speech drafts, letters, readings, and a whole range of questions, reflections and observations. For example, in the years that Mr Lee was working on his memoirs, the red box carried the multiple early drafts back and forth between his home and the office, scribbled over with his and Mrs Lee's notes.

For a long time, other regular items in Mr Lee's red box were the cassette tapes that held his dictated instructions and thoughts for later transcription. Some years back, he changed to using a digital recorder. The red box carried a wide range of items. It could be communications with foreign leaders, observations about the financial crisis, instructions for the Istana grounds staff, or even questions about some trees he had seen on the expressway. Mr Lee was well known for keeping extremely alert to everything he saw and heard around him. When he noticed something wrong, like an ailing rain tree, a note in the red box would follow.

We could never anticipate what Mr Lee would raise. It could be anything that was happening in Singapore or the world. But we could be sure of this: It would always be about how events could affect Singapore and Singaporeans, and how we had to stay a step ahead. Inside the red box was always something about how we could create a better life for all.

We would get to work right away the moment the box arrived. Mr Lee's secretaries would transcribe his dictated notes, while I followed up on instructions that required coordination across multiple government agencies. Our aim was to do as much as we could by the time Mr Lee came into the office later.

While we did this, Mr Lee would be working from home. For example, during the time that I worked with him, the Asian Financial Crisis of 1997 erupted, ravaging many economies in our region and unleashing political changes. It was a tense period as no one could tell how events would unfold. Often, I would get a call from him to check certain facts or arrange meetings with financial experts.

In the years that I worked for him, Mr Lee's daily breakfast was a bowl of *dou hua* (soft bean curd), with no syrup. It was picked up and brought home in a tiffin carrier every morning, from a food centre near Mr Lee's home. He washed it down with room-temperature water. Mr Lee did not take coffee or tea at breakfast.

By the time Mr Lee arrived at the office, the work that had come earlier in the red box would be ready for his review, and he would have a further set of instructions for our action. From that point on, the work day would run its normal course. Mr Lee read the documents and papers, cleared his emails, and received official calls by visitors. I was privileged to sit in for every meeting he conducted. He would later ask me what I thought of the meetings. It made me very attentive to every word that was said, and I learnt much from Mr Lee.

Evenings were Mr Lee's exercise time. Mr Lee has described his extensive and disciplined exercise regime elsewhere. It included the treadmill, rowing, swimming and walking — with his ears peeled to the evening news or his Mandarin practice tapes. He would sometimes take phone calls while exercising. He was in his seventies then. In more recent years, being less stable on his feet, Mr Lee had a simpler exercise regime. But he continued to exercise. Since retiring from the Minister Mentor position in 2011, Mr Lee was more relaxed during his exercises. Instead of listening intently to the news or taking phone calls, he shared his personal stories and joked with his staff.

While Mr Lee exercised, those of us in the office would use that time to focus once again on the red box, to get ready all the day's work for Mr Lee to take home with him in the evening. Based on the day's events and instructions, I tried to get ready the materials that Mr Lee might need. It sometimes took longer than I expected, and occasionally, I had to ask the security officer to come back for the red box later.

While Mrs Lee was still alive, she used to drop by the Istana at the end of the day, in order to catch a few minutes together with Mr Lee, just to sit and look at the Istana trees that they both loved.

They chatted about things that many other old couples would talk about and discussed what they should have for dinner, or how their grandchildren were doing.

Then back home went Mr Lee, Mrs Lee and the red box. After dinner, Mr and Mrs Lee liked to take a long stroll. In his days as Prime Minister, while Mrs Lee strolled, Mr Lee liked to ride a bicycle. It was, in the words of those who saw it, "one of those old man bicycles". None of us who have worked at the Istana can remember him ever changing his bicycle. He did not use it in his later years, as he became frail, but I believe the "old man bicycle" is still around somewhere.

After his dinner and evening stroll, Mr Lee would get back to his work. That was when he opened the red box and worked his way through what we had put into it in the office.

Mr Lee's study is converted out of his son's old bedroom. His work table is a simple, old wooden table with a piece of clear glass placed over it. Slipped under the glass are family memorabilia, including a picture of our current Prime Minister from his National Service days. When Mrs Lee was around, she stayed up reading while Mr Lee worked. They liked to put on classical music while they stayed up.

In his days as PM, Mr Lee's average bedtime was 3.30 in the morning. As Senior Minister and Minister Mentor, he went to sleep after 2 a.m. If he had to travel for an official visit the next day, he might go to bed at 1 or 2 a.m. Deep into the night, while the rest of Singapore slept, it was common for Mr Lee to be in full work mode. Before he went to bed, Mr Lee would put everything he had completed back in the red box, with clear pointers on what he wished for us to do in the office. The last thing he did each day was to place the red box outside his study room. The next morning, the duty security team picked up the red box, brought it to us waiting in the office, and a new day would begin.

Let me share two other stories involving the red box.

In 1996, Mr Lee underwent balloon angioplasty to insert a stent. It was his second heart operation in two months, after an earlier operation to widen a coronary artery did not work. After the operation, he was put in the Intensive Care Unit for observation. When he regained consciousness and could sit up in bed, he asked for his security team. The security officer hurried into the room to find out what was needed. Mr Lee asked, "Can you pass me the red box?" Even at that point, Mr Lee's first thought was to continue working. The security officer rushed the red box in, and Mr Lee asked to be left to his work. The nurses told the security team that other patients of his age, in Mr Lee's condition, would just rest. Mr Lee was 72 at the time.

In 2010, Mr Lee was hospitalised again, this time for a chest infection. While he was in the hospital, Mrs Lee passed away. Mr Lee has spoken about his grief at Mrs Lee's passing. As soon as he could, he left the hospital to attend the wake at Sri Temasek. At the end of the night, he was under doctor's orders to return to the hospital. But he asked his security team if they could take him to the Singapore River instead. It was late in the night, and Mr Lee was in mourning. His security team hastened to give a bereaved husband a quiet moment to himself. As Mr Lee walked slowly along the bank of the Singapore River, the way he and Mrs Lee sometimes did when she was still alive, he paused. He beckoned a security officer over. Then he pointed out some trash floating on the river, and asked, "Can you take a photo of that? I'll tell my PPS what to do about it tomorrow." Photo taken, he returned to the hospital.

I was no longer Mr Lee's PPS at the time. I had moved on to the Monetary Authority of Singapore, to continue with the work to strengthen our financial regulatory system that Mr Lee had started in the late 1990s. But I can guess that Mr Lee probably had some feedback on keeping the Singapore River clean. I can also guess that the picture and the instructions were ferried in Mr Lee's red box the next morning to the office. Even as Mr Lee lay in the hospital. Even as Mrs Lee lay in state.

The security officers with Mr Lee were deeply touched. When I heard about these moments, I was also moved.

I have taken some time to describe Mr Lee's red box. The reason is that, for me, it symbolises Mr Lee's unwavering dedication to Singapore so well. The diverse contents it held tell us much about the breadth of Mr Lee's concerns, from the very big to the very small. The daily routine of the red box tells us how Mr Lee's life revolved around making Singapore better, in ways big and small.

By the time I served Mr Lee, he was Senior Minister. Yet he continued to devote all his time to thinking about the future of Singapore. I could only imagine what he was like as Prime Minister. In policy and strategy terms, he was always driving himself, me, and all our colleagues to think about what each trend and development meant for Singapore, and how we should respond to it in order to secure Singapore's well-being and success. As his PPS, I saw the punishing pace of work that Mr Lee set himself. I had a boss whose every thought and every action was for Singapore.

But it takes private moments like these to bring home just how entirely Mr Lee devoted his life to Singapore. In fact, I think the best description comes from the security officer who was with Mr Lee both of those times. He was on Mr Lee's team for almost 30 years. He said of Mr Lee: "Mr Lee is always country, country, country. And country." This year, Singapore turns 50. Mr Lee would have turned 92 this September. Mr Lee entered the hospital on 5 February 2015. He continued to use his red box every day until 4 February 2015.

(*This essay was originally published on 24 March 2015.*)

LEO YIP

Principal Private Secretary, 2000–2002

❝Mr Lee was not interested in form.
His focus was always on substance.❞

– Leo Yip

I met Mr Lee Kuan Yew for the first time in March 1999, when he
interviewed me to be his principal private secretary (PPS). When I
stepped into his office, I was struck by how simply furnished and
functional it was. As I was to understand later on, Mr Lee was not
interested in form. His focus was always on substance, whether
something really worked or not.

His first questions to me were about my family. What did my
parents do? What was my wife's occupation? What were my children
doing? His questions came steadily. He was less interested in what I did
in the course of my career. He was more interested in understanding
my thinking about what I did. He wanted to know what I had learnt
at different points of my career. Among others, he asked me the key
lessons I had learnt during my Masters programme at the JFK School
of Government at Harvard.

His questions were probing, and he would pause after each answer
that I gave and then pose a next question that forced me to think
deeper. Sometimes his pauses were long. Clearly he was thoughtfully
processing my answers. For me each pause was an uneasy silence, but
also a time for me to think deeper, in anticipation of the next question.
During that first meeting, I learnt about Mr Lee's expectation of me

to think deeply first about any issue that I needed to discuss with him *before* I went to see him.

Many people think of Mr Lee as a stern and no-nonsense person. That is true but I also found him to be a caring boss. It is a side of him not many know. Anyone who has had the chance to work for him would obviously have given his best to the job. Working long hours was part of the commitment. I tried to do the same. But Mr Lee, on more than one occasion, told me that I should get enough sleep, otherwise I wouldn't be able to function optimally. He did not have to say this and I truly appreciate that he cared enough to do so.

When Mr Lee decided that something was worth doing, he would ensure that it would be done well. He had this sharp focus and single-mindedness, and once he set his mind on an objective, he would see it through. The lesson for me observing Mr Lee was that if something is worth doing for Singapore, it is worth doing very well.

When Mr Lee was focused on an important issue, he would be seized with it. He would spend long hours reading up about the topic so that he could understand it better. He would ask for reports from different sources. He would meet and speak with people to get a strong grasp of the matter. One such issue was radical Islam and the discovery of the militant group Jemaah Islamiyah in Singapore. This was in 2001, after the September 11 attacks on the US. He spent many hours on understanding the ramifications of radical Islam on Singapore and countries in the region. He met with foreign officials, scholars as well as religious and community leaders to understand the range of perspectives and sentiments.

With Mr Lee, there was no room for superficiality when dealing with important matters. I saw firsthand how he worked hard to understand deeply the issues that were new to him, so that he could discern what they meant for Singapore and how Singapore could best deal with them. To understand any topic deeply, one simply had to be single-minded, and work hard to read, listen and learn.

The first time I came across a new meaning of the word "hoist" was when I worked for Mr Lee. He asked whether I had "hoisted in" a particular point or idea. For him, "hoisting in" a point was important. It meant fully understanding the idea, but also internalising it into my thought processes and recognising all its implications.

There is much to admire about Mr Lee. One of these was his strong sense of discipline. He kept to a strict daily exercise regime that would put many of us younger people to shame. He stuck largely to this routine even when travelling. His determination and discipline in learning Mandarin is well documented. When I was his PPS, he took Mandarin lessons every Saturday and sometimes on weekdays when he had the time. He kept up with this for decades. Many of us complain that we do not have the time to do many things, even if they are important. From Mr Lee's self-discipline, I learnt an important lesson — we will find a way if, and only if, we can muster the will to want to do something.

As his PPS, I had the valuable opportunity to understand Mr Lee's thinking and motivations. Whenever he reviewed any new issue, development, trend or opportunity, Mr Lee was solely and deeply focused on its impact on Singapore. This reflected how deeply he cared about, and cared for, Singapore. It also reflected his total dedication and commitment to the survival and success of Singapore. Whether it was the advance of Internet technology, the threat of terrorism or the rise of China, Mr Lee's pre-occupation was with understanding and assessing how this would affect Singapore, in terms of opportunities or challenges.

Over the two and a half years that I worked for Mr Lee, I sat in on numerous meetings that he had with world leaders, both overseas and in Singapore.

The leaders would seek out his views, not just on Asian and regional issues, but also on global developments. He did not have just a deep sense of history, or a broad and long-term perspective of issues, but also a perceptiveness about how today's developments would shape the future. He cut through the noise and zeroed in on the key issues that mattered. He saw through fads that did not last, and focused on the deep dynamics and trends that would shape the long-term development of societies and nations.

At many of these meetings, I marvelled at the goodwill for Singapore that Mr Lee generated with these world leaders, through his influence and perceptive analysis. Of course, not everyone agreed with all of Mr Lee's views, but even those who did not agree with him would acknowledge the weight of his arguments.

Even at his age — he was in his late seventies when I served him — he would try to keep up to date with new trends, including technology. He would read widely, listen carefully, and sometimes seek the help of specialists or experts to better understand the new developments. As a result, even in his old age, he maintained a young mind. Like everyone else, he had his mental models and lenses from which he viewed the world. But he made the effort to absorb fresh perspectives, new information and novel ideas to refresh and update his own understanding and thinking. To me, this was one key reason why his views continued to stay current, and not outmoded.

Mr Lee belonged to a select few of great nation-building leaders in Asia who emerged in the post-World War II years of national independence movements. Here was a man who built a nation with his team, and who galvanised a people to work together to take a country from Third World to First.

His life's work in building a successful nation is in itself a study of successful leadership. Even then, when preparing to give a speech on leadership, he wanted to understand all the leadership theories out there. He would ask me to research for him the various leadership models, what worked and what did not. He wanted to know about successful leadership models that worked in countries and large organisations. He studied the research carefully. With his track record as a nation-building leader, he did not have to. After all, what else did he need to learn about leadership? But in his humility, he did so.

We all know Mr Lee as a masterful orator who could swing a crowd and rally a people with his powerful speeches. He spoke off the cuff with ease. But in preparing for his speeches, he placed great attention on detail and made the effort to get every point right and well communicated. For important speeches, he would go through multiple versions and drafts; he would polish them again and again. He wanted to be sure that he would achieve the best outcome when communicating his message to his audience.

It was a great honour to have worked for Mr Lee and to have learnt directly from him. This was a man always seeking to make Singapore better for Singaporeans. This was his life's work. Of all the lessons I learnt working for him, I must say the biggest one is to work very hard to do more for Singapore. He was very inspiring and I was very much inspired. After all, this was a man who had given his entire life in the service of our country and fellow Singaporeans.

ANDREW TAN
Principal Private Secretary, 2002–2004

❝My memoirs could take two to three years
to complete. And you might not get a promotion.**❞**
– Lee Kuan Yew

The interview

"Sit down," the man behind the table instructed as I entered his office through the side entrance which had double doors. It was 1994. Over the course of the six years that I worked for him, this would become a familiar ritual.

Butterflies in the stomach. This was how it felt each time you walked through those doors. You quickly learnt to ignore the feeling, but you never let your guard down.

Here was a man who suffered no fools or took to light banter. Whatever you had to say had better be significant. Otherwise, save those words. Many have sought to impress him with their knowledge. But few actually succeeded. He was not looking for clever arguments. He was looking for conviction in one's beliefs.

Each encounter required preparation. Nothing was left to chance. This was a man who used every working hour of the day to think deeply about the issues affecting the country, and to plan ahead. He was always several steps ahead of everyone. But that day, he was just interviewing a young civil servant with little experience — and totally clueless what to expect.

The pragmatist at heart

Prior to this interview to be Mr Lee's researcher for the first volume of his memoirs, *The Singapore Story*, I had interviewed Dr Goh Keng Swee on his role as Singapore's first defence minister. Dr Goh, a close Cabinet colleague of Mr Lee, had retired from politics by then.

He was an "anglophile", Dr Goh would say, referring to Mr Lee's close ties with British leaders of the day. If Mr Lee had his way, perhaps the British, rather than the Israelis, would have played a greater part in the build-up of Singapore's defence. But Dr Goh got his way. The two did not always see eye to eye, but that was the strength of their relationship.

Dr Goh did not think the British could help Singapore build up the armed forces in double quick time following Singapore's bitter separation from Malaysia. When the pound sterling was devalued and the British hastened their timetable for their withdrawal east of Suez, which included Singapore, Dr Goh publicly declared that it was a "disgraceful breach of moral undertaking". But it was through Mr Lee's close association with the British, with Prime Minister Harold Wilson in particular, that he was able to persuade the British not to pull out of Singapore too quickly, which would leave behind a power vacuum — and a fledgling small nation without any defences.

Mr Lee's practical approach to foreign policy bought Singapore several years of much needed time and space to build up its own defence, while ensuring the major powers did not abandon the region at that time.

Indeed, all this would have been inconceivable some two decades earlier, in 1954, when the People's Action Party was formed and a young Mr Lee came under the scrutiny of the Special Branch on the suspicion that he was anti-British and pro-Communist or, if not, at least sympathetic to their cause. The British had kept a dossier on him as they thought he would be subversive to their interests.

But even as he fought against British rule in his early political career, Mr Lee was a realist and pragmatist. None of his other Cabinet colleagues quite matched his hard-headedness and hard-nosed appreciation of what was necessary for Singapore's survival. These instincts guided his approach to governing Singapore over the next few decades which have attracted both admirers and detractors.

The importance of choosing the right people

The interview did not take long. He had seen my CV, saw that I had studied history and had interviewed Dr Goh. However, there was one thing he wanted to ascertain. "My memoirs could take two to three years to complete," he said. "And you might not get a promotion."

He was gauging my reaction or, more precisely, my motivations in wanting to work for him.

"For someone who has devoted his entire life to building Singapore, what are two to three years on the project?" I quipped. Little did I know that this response would land me with, not two or three, but six years of duty, first working on his memoirs, and later, as his principal private secretary, with a posting in between.

This encounter exposed me to the importance that Mr Lee attached to assessing the character of a person and his intrinsic motivations. He would assess government and business leaders — whether during his overseas trips or when they paid courtesy calls on him. Were they serious players we could work with or best to give a polite hearing? He was a good judge of character and I soon came to realise that the success or failure of any endeavour often hinged upon the selection of good people.

For example, Singapore's first industrial township project in China, the Suzhou Industrial Park, which began in February 1994, was as much about bricks and mortar as it was about getting the right people on both sides to make it work, and ensuring personal, institutional and political interests were all properly aligned. As our experience has shown, this was more easily said than done, but fortunately, we succeeded in the end because we persevered. And Mr Lee played a crucial role in staying the course.

A unique generation, a product of their times

My three years working on his memoir was a big learning experience as I tracked his early life and political career and came to understand the forces that shaped his generation. The overthrow of British colonialism by the Japanese, the hardship and deprivation under the Japanese Occupation, the battle against the communists and communalists and, eventually, separation from Malaysia taught an entire generation of Singaporeans that no one owed us a living. We had to survive by our guts and wits.

But while the memoir was an important project, it always took second place to the more pressing affairs of the state. In particular, talks with Malaysia over the water agreements were still ongoing. He felt that he had a responsibility to resolve thorny issues that had ensnarled bilateral relations, making it difficult for future prime ministers to work together.

But he knew he had to finish the memoir and my stint would have to come to an end. What was remarkable was the effort he put in every evening to work on his drafts, with Mrs Lee helping him with the grammar and corrections. It was an endearing sight to watch them both at work — a husband-and-wife team.

My job was to make sure he got exactly the information he needed, no more, no less. He had a remarkable memory, which helped to narrow the search for relevant pieces of information. He could even recall his conversations with key leaders like Deng Xiaoping. He wanted to be sure of the facts and often, together with my team of two or three researchers, we would verify them from several sources. We also retrieved diplomatic records from overseas archives in Australia, the UK and US for their readings of the situation in Singapore. It was an exhaustive effort to ensure that the memoir could withstand scrutiny.

Looking back, I still marvel at the level of detail that went into researching for the memoir. More importantly, it became a history lesson for myself and my young team of researchers. We became even more convinced that the younger generation should get to know our history, parts of which had hitherto been glossed over in our textbooks. It was time we confronted our past and judged for ourselves the decisions that were taken in the light of prevailing circumstances.

Embracing the realities of our existence

I was posted to the Ministry of Defence after I finished working on the memoir. Shortly after the publication of *The Singapore Story* in 1998, the Malaysians were upset by some references in the book. The then Malaysian Defence Minister Syed Hamid, whose father, Syed Jaafar Albar, was mentioned in the book as part of the ultra-nationalists who had whipped up communal feelings leading to the 1964 riots, decided that RSAF jets could no longer train in or fly through Malaysian airspace with almost immediate effect. Fortunately, the RSAF had prepared for such an eventuality and activated their alternative flight paths. This episode showed how sensitive ties were back then. Notwithstanding, Mr Lee felt that Singapore's story had to be told the way it was.

My next stint was as principal private secretary (PPS) to Mr Lee, who was by then Senior Minister. This time, there was no interview. This was quite unusual as previous PPSs had been interviewed. They also had to be bilingual and take a written Chinese test. Mr Lee figured I would have failed the test anyway so he didn't even make me try. Nonetheless, I was inspired by his weekly Mandarin lessons and took up tuition for the duration of my posting. I believe he continued with these lessons for more than five decades. In multilingual Singapore, one can never neglect race, language and religion.

I was glad that Mr Lee was prepared to change the way Chinese as a second language was taught in schools. Those from English-speaking backgrounds like myself really struggled with the language, but as I grew older I came to appreciate the language and discovered more interesting ways to approach it without being turned off by all the rote learning.

During my time as his PPS, one of the biggest issues we had to deal with was the Singapore Airlines (SIA) pilots' union dispute with the management over pay and other benefits. This was in 2003. I watched how Mr Lee prevailed upon both the pilots and management, highlighting the stakes involved if the dispute was to boil over. Singapore could lose its relevance as an air hub if we undermined our own competitiveness particularly amidst stiffer competition from other air hubs and the onset of budget airlines. Mr Lee always saw the bigger picture. He was persuasive but also expressed in no uncertain terms that between saving SIA and protecting Singapore as an air hub, the government would choose the latter even if it meant sacrificing SIA. The two parties eventually returned to the negotiating table.

The other major issue was the threat of regional terrorism. This was the post 9/11 era and regional terrorist groups affiliated to

Al Qaeda had emerged in the region, most famously through the Bali bombings in 2002. Mr Lee would share his views with visiting leaders and stiffen their resolve to tackle the threat. Of great concern were the radical teachings expounded in madrasahs in the region. The security threat posed by the Jemaah Islamiyah was very real. Mr Lee held many meetings with then Indonesian President Megawati Sukarnoputri, shoring up support for her efforts to disrupt the militant terrorist group's regional network.

Indeed, whether on geopolitical developments in the region, such as the rise of China and India, or terrorism, many visiting leaders, including industry captains, were always keen to tap Mr Lee's views when they visited Singapore. It was as if all of them had been given the brief by their staffers that "no trip to Singapore is complete without a session with LKY". Mr Lee's wealth of experience and keen understanding of world affairs helped define a unique role for Singapore. Our leaders are knowledgeable and respected for their useful insights. This is a role our senior statesmen still play after they step down from power, and hopefully continue to do so.

Put in your best, expect nothing in return

The biggest lesson Mr Lee has taught me is the importance of setting high standards in whatever I do. Mr Lee took a keen interest in every aspect of Singapore's development. He rolled up his sleeves and went to the ground to understand the common man's concerns. He and his colleagues earned the trust of the older generation of Singaporeans by delivering on their promises of jobs, a roof over their heads and a better future for their children. Our first generation of leaders made tremendous sacrifices — in their personal life, career and family — to do what they believed was right for the nation. They got very little in return, except the satisfaction of seeing Singapore survive and thrive. For that, I have deep respect. But much more than this, all of us have a responsibility to carry on the good work of our pioneer generation in whatever way we can.

Towards the end of my stint as his PPS in 2003, I got married. It was only polite that I invited Mr Lee to my wedding, even though I knew he would likely decline the invitation, which he did. One evening, however, he summoned me to his room. The same side entrance and double doors took me to where he usually sat. But this time he was standing and Mrs Lee was seated across from him.

"I have something for you," he said. Before I could ask what it was, he shoved a small green box across the table to me. Fortunately, I caught the box before it reached the edge of the table. At that moment, Mrs Lee remarked, "Harry, this is not the way to give a gift!" I glanced at Mr Lee who seemed half-annoyed. We both had a good laugh. Running through his mind must have been the thought that I should be thankful I was getting a gift, never mind how it was delivered.

I will always remember this episode because, in a way, it sums up the thinking of first-generation leaders like Mr Lee: Do your best, give it your all. Expect nothing in return. And this was how he and the pioneer generation of leaders built this nation.

In case you're still wondering what was in the box, it was a small piece of jade with a little display stand. It looked like it had been kept for many years from the signs of ageing on the box and the wrapping. I always thought it a strange gift. But it reminds me of the frugality of our pioneer generation who felt that nothing should ever be wasted or taken for granted. Not in Singapore. It is now for the next generation to take us forward.

PETER TAN

Singapore Ambassador to South Korea, 2011–2015

**"Keep up with your Mandarin.
You will find it useful."**
– *Lee Kuan Yew*

Growing up, I had read about Lee Kuan Yew in the newspapers, and watched and heard him speak on TV and radio. He was often a topic of discussion in many homes, schools, offices and coffee shops. It was not difficult to feel his influence and see his fingerprints everywhere in Singapore.

As Prime Minister Lee Hsien Loong said in his eulogy at Mr Lee's State Funeral Service on 29 March 2015, "Mr Lee Kuan Yew built Singapore. To those who seek Mr Lee Kuan Yew's monument, Singaporeans can reply proudly: look around you."

Indeed, my educational path was influenced by Mr Lee. In 1988, I chose Japanese Studies as one of my majors in the Faculty of Arts and Social Sciences at the National University of Singapore. During orientation week, I found out that the existence of the course was due to Mr Lee who, in 1979, as Prime Minister, had brought up the idea of establishing a department of Japanese Studies with his Japanese counterpart, Prime Minister Ohira Masayoshi. The department was officially established in 1981. My association with Mr Lee then was distant but still I felt proud to be a product of his brainchild.

In May 1995, barely three months into my first posting in Tokyo, this sense of pride became more real. Mr Lee, who was Senior Minister at the time, was in Tokyo to attend the inaugural Nihon Keizai Shimbun's (Nikkei) "Future of Asia" Conference. Following his keynote address, as we walked him to the lobby, I saw a Japanese man carrying a camera walking hastily towards us. My instinct was to meet his path early, ahead of Mr and Mrs Lee, my boss Ambassador Lim Chin Beng and Mr Lee's security officer.

As the man approached, I planted myself in front of him, allowing sufficient space for the security officer to lead Mr Lee and the others away. From that distance, the man uttered loudly in Japanese, "Mr Lee, can I interview you?" Explaining that we were rushing to another meeting, I gave him my name card and told him, in Japanese, to call or send me a fax regarding the interview request.

Once in the waiting elevator, Mr Lee asked me, "Are you a *Monbusho*[1] scholar?" I was stunned momentarily. He must have overheard my interaction with the Japanese man. At that moment, I quickly recalled a senior colleague telling me, when I first joined the Ministry of Foreign Affairs, not to worry about Mr Lee asking us young officers questions because it would never happen. We were only "furniture in the background", he had said. I therefore did not expect a question from the man, especially not when I was still catching my breath after rushing to deflect the reporter only seconds before!

Ambassador Lim interjected in a timely fashion, as if to allow me some time to catch my breath. He said, "Peter has studied Japanese since his secondary school days." "Is that so?" was Mr Lee's immediate reply, to which I responded, "Yes, SM. I studied Japanese as my Third Language at the Foreign Language Centre and continued at the Japanese Studies Department in NUS." As if to jolt his memory, Mrs Lee then reminded him softly that he had discussed the setting up of a Japanese language centre with the Japanese Prime Minister in the 1970s. Mr Lee replied, "Oh, yes," and smiled. To me, that was as good as a stamp of approval. It was my badge of honour. At that very moment, I felt absolutely proud that I was a graduate of the Japanese Studies Department in NUS.

Mr Lee and his open attitude to viewpoints

Mr Lee was larger than life. And I was deeply privileged to have had the opportunity to work with him, both in Singapore and during my postings to Tokyo and Kuala Lumpur.

I sat in on numerous occasions when he met with foreign leaders and delegations. He did not say things for the sake of pleasing others. He was always focused and nothing he said veered from his fundamental thinking of what was good for Singapore, for bilateral relations and for the region. He was always direct, but polite. He was generous with his insights and gave honest assessments. His powerful intellect never failed to impress his guests.

In short, he was sharp, insightful and prescient. And because he had carefully thought through his core positions to arrive at a bottom-line conclusion, he would stick to that conclusion even though it might momentarily be unpleasant to one party or the other. All the foreign guests enjoyed their discussions with him.

In fact, over the years, many foreign contacts have told me that they had learnt much from their meetings with him. And I know they meant it. Former US Secretary of State George Shultz, who was one of Mr Lee's good friends, said, "I often travelled to Singapore and, with all due respect to the appeal of the city, the reason was to see Harry Lee."[2] I always came away from Mr Lee's meetings with his foreign guests feeling very proud to be a Singapore Foreign Service Officer and a Singaporean.

There is a misperception that Mr Lee did not listen to the views of others and that he was surrounded by yes-men. Those who have worked with him know this is far from the truth. The Mr Lee I knew was someone who did not care whether you were a senior or a junior officer. As long as you knew what you were talking about and could argue your case, he was prepared to listen. It was never about him and his views; it was always about Singapore. It was always about Singaporeans.

I was fortunate to have attended policy discussion sessions and watched him at close quarters dealing with several bilateral issues, such as the water package,[3] the bridge[4] and Points of Agreement (POA) negotiations[5] with Malaysia. It is true that he was a no-nonsense leader who suffered no fools. But he did not dominate any session. There was always healthy and robust debate during which he would challenge your ideas — not to intimidate you, but to ensure the issue was thoroughly debated and all perspectives explored. If your reasons were well thought through and you had a good case, he would listen and accept your viewpoints.

At the end of such sessions, I always came away feeling comforted that every decision was made with Singapore's best interests in mind.

Mr Lee's softer side

Many Singaporeans saw him as a stern and plain-speaking leader. But there was also a softer side to his tough personality.

Once, in 1997, I had the privilege of witnessing this softer side of the man. It was over dinner during one of his visits to Japan. At the end of the meal, a dessert of macha (green tea) ice cream was served. Now, he had a soft spot for ice cream but he also was very disciplined with his diet. And, as far as I can recall, Mrs Lee watched carefully over what he ate.

A few minutes before the ice cream was served, Mrs Lee had excused herself to go to the restroom. Mr Lee continued talking to Ambassador Lim, while enjoying his ice cream wholeheartedly. At that point, Mrs Lee returned and noticed that the dessert had been polished off his bowl. She gently remarked, "Harry, I see that you have finished your ice cream."

He smiled and then, without missing a beat, turned towards Ambassador Lim and said, "Chin Beng said it's a healthy ice cream."

Always the consummate diplomat, my boss quickly added, "Yes, it's low-fat and green tea is healthy."

At that moment, I realised that Mr Lee was also human. We need to enjoy life's simple pleasures every once in a while.

Mr Lee and his personal touch

In 2004, again in Tokyo, as Deputy Chief of Mission, I had gone to meet Mr and Mrs Lee at their hotel to accompany them to a dinner venue. When I stepped into their room, I noticed that Mr Lee was ready and looking quite intensely at a calligraphy scroll on the wall. On the scroll was a Chinese saying "乐在其中" (to find joy in what one does), rendered in the form of pictorial calligraphy.

Mr Lee turned around and asked Mrs Lee if she could make out the characters. She said she could not and then turned to ask me, as I was the only other person in the room. I read the saying to them in Mandarin and explained the calligraphy strokes and their meaning.

Just then, the security officer came into the room and told us it was time to leave for dinner. As I walked Mr and Mrs Lee to the car, he asked me, "Which school did you go to?"

I wasn't sure if he was asking about primary or secondary school or college so I just quickly replied, "St. Joseph's Institution." Furthermore, at that moment my only objective was to get them into the car as quickly as possible so they would not be late for the dinner.

"That cannot be!" was Mr Lee's quick retort.

I did not know quite how to respond except to repeat, "Yes, I was from St. Joseph's Institution, MM," before quickly ushering them into the car.

When they had left, I pondered his response and wondered if it had anything to do with my ability to read the calligraphy on the scroll. Did he think that SJI boys could not speak Mandarin?

After dinner, as I accompanied Mr and Mrs Lee back to the hotel, Mr Lee asked, "Do you speak Mandarin at home?" I replied that I spoke Mandarin and dialects with my parents. Immediately, he exclaimed, "That's why your Mandarin is good!"

My guess was right. He did not think boys from my school could speak Mandarin well. But that was not the point for me. I was pleasantly surprised that he had been thinking about the matter after a two-hour dinner meeting. I felt a little honoured that he had been trying to figure out how I, an alumnus of a Catholic mission school, could understand and speak Mandarin well enough to explain a Chinese pictorial calligraphy.

When the Ambassador and I sent Mr and Mrs Lee off at Narita Airport the next day, Mr Lee, as usual, thanked the Mission's staff for taking care of him and Mrs Lee. When he came to me, he said, "Keep up with your Mandarin. You will find it useful."

Those few words touched me deeply. His encouragement was another badge of honour for me. Now that he has left us, I want to let him know how I feel through this essay, "李资政,您在好几年前给于我的忠告,我至今还牢记在心里." (Mr Lee, I still remember dearly the advice you gave me several years ago.)

Mr Lee and his legacy

In the Foreign Affairs Ministry, foreign service officers rarely request to take photographs with our leaders. We do our work, stay out of sight and disappear into the background. So, today, I have no photos taken with Mr Lee. My two badges of honour, therefore, remain my most vivid memories.

I had hoped for Mr Lee to visit Seoul while I was there from 2011 to 2015. Many Koreans know of Singapore because of him. A taxi-driver in his sixties spoke of his respect for Mr Lee when he found out I was from Singapore. He compared Mr Lee to former South Korean President Park Chung-hee, calling them "builders of nations". Another time, two restaurant owners, one of a BBQ pork belly restaurant and the other of a *chimaek* (fried chicken and beer) restaurant, also went into endless praises of Mr Lee when they learnt I was a Singaporean. At the start of my presentations to Korean university students, I usually ask them what comes to their mind when they think of Singapore. They invariably answer "Lee Kuan Yew". Every time I listen to the Koreans talk about Mr Lee and Singapore, I feel proud to be a Singaporean.

I do not profess to have known Mr Lee on a personal level. I served him as a professional. But the sense of loss and grief I felt when he passed away is no less than if I were mourning a close relative or friend. Mr Lee has given us many reasons to be proud of Singapore. As Prime Minister Lee Hsien Loong rightly said at a tribute event in Ang Mo Kio on 25 March 2015:

"We are sad, we are sorrowful, our founding father has left us. But he has prepared us for this day, because he knew that to build well, Singapore must stand long after he is gone. And he has been preparing for that for many, many years."

284 | UP CLOSE WITH LEE KUAN YEW

Even in his death, Mr Lee brought Singaporeans together as a nation. To honour Mr Lee, let's strive together to make Singapore a better place to live in, as he did 50 years ago. Majulah Singapura!

Notes

1 Formerly known as the Monbusho scholarship, the Monbukagakusho scholarship is offered by Japan's Ministry of Education, Culture, Sports, Science and Technology.

2 Former US Secretary of State George Shultz's condolence letter dated 23 March 2015 to Prime Minister Lee Hsien Loong on the passing of Mr Lee Kuan Yew, as published online by *The Straits Times* on 24 March 2015.

3 Singapore and Malaysia have signed four agreements to regulate the supply of water from Malaysia to Singapore: in 1927, 1961, 1962 and 1990. The 1990 water agreement was a follow-up to the memorandum of understanding signed in 1988 between then Prime Minister of Malaysia Mahathir Mohamad and then Prime Minister Lee Kuan Yew.

4 In July 1996, Dr Mahathir announced plans to demolish the causeway and to replace it with a suspension bridge that would allow ships to navigate the Johor Straits. In August 2000, Mr Lee met with Dr Mahathir in Putrajaya to resolve bilateral issues. Through the negotiations, Singapore agreed in principle that the causeway would be replaced by a bridge and that Singapore will reclaim its side to the maximum to join up with the bridge as part of a package deal that included agreements on water, the "Points of Agreement" on the joint redevelopment of Malaysia's railway land in Singapore, and the relocation of Malaysia's KTM rail station to Kranji. Source: *Water Talks? If Only It Could*, published by the Ministry of Information, Communications and the Arts of Singapore, March 2003.

5 An agreement between Malaysia and Singapore over the issue of the future of railway land owned by the Malaysian government through Malayan Railways in Singapore. It was signed by then Prime Minister Lee Kuan Yew and then Finance Minister of Malaysia Tun Daim Zainuddin on 27 November 1990.

CHENG WAI KEUNG

Chairman, Wing Tai Holdings

"Why do the Chinese like chocolate cake so much?"
– Lee Kuan Yew

These are anecdotes of my encounters with Mr Lee Kuan Yew over the years. They are personal vignettes into his thoughts and feelings, revealing his keen intellect and strength of character — and the man he was away from the public eye.

Of trust and respect

I worked on a couple of projects with Mr Lee. He was a man who would make his views known and you would be wise to take heed. But if you still felt strongly about the matter and gave him good reason to support your case, he was not one to bully you into acquiescence.

I recall a specific policy matter in which Mr Lee and I had taken different positions. He must have thought about the issue carefully and come to his conclusion. But he heard me out and took in my considerations. After a series of extended discussions, he told me that while he still felt his approach was better, I could proceed with my recommendation on the matter.

Mr Lee deferred to my judgement. Since I was appointed to the task, he was willing to let me take responsibility and be accountable for my decisions. This is contrary to his detractors' criticisms of him. He showed respect to his colleagues in his own ways.

Naturally, you would have to earn his confidence and trust. When giving your views, you had to be sure they were untainted by self-interest as he could see through motives quite effortlessly. Mr Lee did not care for yes-men or staffers to butter him up. He sought out critical-thinking people who would dare challenge the norm.

An observant, questioning mind

Once, in the 1990s when we were travelling in China, Mr Lee was curious as to why the Chinese seemed to like American apples so much as he was served them everywhere. I told him that as a good host, the Chinese had most probably imported them especially for him.

On the same trip, at a dinner, he noticed that we were again served chocolate cake for dessert and asked, "Why do the Chinese like chocolate cake so much?" A senior Singaporean government official explained that because Mr Lee had mentioned the night before that he liked chocolate cake, he had specially ordered one for him that evening. Mr Lee was a bit vexed and said, "Just because I said I liked it last night does not mean I want chocolate cake every day!"

The comment might have sounded light-hearted, but I could sense an immediate rising tension in the official.

A statesman's worry

Mr Lee had shared with me, on several occasions, how one needed to go through crises — and be tested — to gain respect. He explained how he got to be recognised as a statesman by world leaders, how he had earned their regard through his analyses and projections of world events and crises, such as the Cold War, the Vietnam War and the emergent growth of China. He believed that crises test the true strength of a people.

He spoke what he believed was right and acted on what was right. He had the courage to hold a different point of view and make the hard decisions — and he was proven right on many counts. Through this, he gained the respect of world leaders and his foreign counterparts. Many sought his views and tapped on his knowledge.

For a statesman who was unafraid of speaking his mind and giving his point of view on world matters, he would get all animated and lively whenever the conversation touched on Singapore. He was passionate about Singapore and Singaporeans.

It was from Mr Lee that I first heard that no city-state in history has prospered beyond 50 years. That was a sobering thought that has stayed with me ever since and has, in some ways, influenced the way I manage threats and opportunities in business.

He worried constantly about Singapore — our survival and our relevance — in this highly competitive world. Singapore has to be successful, indeed, very successful, in order to survive; for if not, none in the world would give heed to us. So, can we survive the next 50 years? How do we remain successful with our limited talent pool? What are the foundational values and philosophies that we have that must never be compromised?

Drilling down to the details

My meetings with Mr Lee began when I returned from trips to China in the late 1980s and early '90s. He wanted to know my impressions of the country's development. To every answer I gave to his relentless questioning, he would persistently probe deeper until he was satisfied and had a thorough understanding of the subject.

That was his style. He was a keen learner. He asked everyone questions. Once, during dinner, he observed the server. Sensing that he was a foreigner, Mr Lee asked where he was from. Upon learning that he had come from China, he wanted to know more about his background, including his reasons for coming to Singapore. Then Mr Lee got even more interested and wanted to know how the server had managed to work while on a student visa. It was like a cross-examination! The questioning continued and you could see the server getting nervous. He must have been shivering and thinking, "Is this an immigration check or what?" Mr Lee was intrigued and fascinated by everything and drilled down to the details.

I recall in past Pyramid Club[1] dinners, Mr Lee would be asking all sorts of questions at the dinner table, and you could feel the tense atmosphere among the civil servants present. An ex-CEO of the Port of Singapore Authority was once asked about shipping matters and how the agency was run. Soon, he was grilled on technical details. Mr Lee wanted to know why shipping containers were measured in TEUs (Twenty-foot Equivalent Units, the standard unit for describing a ship's cargo carrying capacity) and why it had to be a 20-foot unit.

Thankfully, Mrs Lee was present and she put a stop to it by reminding the inquisitive mind that other people needed to eat. She was such a positive influence, and we were always happy and more relaxed whenever she was around.

But not everybody was nervous with Mr Lee. There were three gentlemen who were at ease with him.

One was the late Mr Lim Kim San, the first chairman of the Housing and Development Board, who would engage him in debates and discussions. When they held different points of view, they would discuss the topic at length and consider each other's views seriously. The other was prominent hotelier and businessman Mr Ong Beng Seng, who had a wealth of knowledge of developments in the world

CHENG WAI KEUNG | 289

and Southeast Asia. He would often pose provocative questions to Mr Lee, prompting reactions and counter opinions. These gave rise to many occasions of learning for me, as Mr Lee would generously share his perspectives and offer precise analyses on the topics being discussed. Yet another was Mr Stephen Lee, former President of the Singapore National Employers Federation and current Chairman of SIA, who was often humorous and even cracked jokes with him. These men seemed very relaxed around him.

Doing things right

Such was Mr Lee's singularity of focus, in wanting to understand and get things right, that he was highly demanding of himself and imposed on himself a high degree of discipline and perseverance in everything he pursued.

Mr Lee used to be a single handicapper in golf. He told me that he gained distance by practising long hitters — he would hang up a rubber tyre and hit his driver against it. When in China, he was often served beer which he enjoyed. Once, he asked for a foamless pour. The nervous waiter's hands shook so much that he could not manage the task. So Mr Lee took over and showed him how to do it skilfully. You see, he liked his beer without foam.

His exacting discipline extended to his daily living. He exercised daily, on the treadmill and in the pool. He kept up with his Chinese lessons every day. He was also careful with food. He ate more Japanese because it is healthy, and he took more vegetables and fruits. However, much as he would always eat healthily, he enjoyed ice cream. When Mrs Lee was around, he would limit himself to one scoop. Later on, when Mrs Lee could not accompany him at dinners, he would have more, telling us that even he should have an occasional indulgence.

290 | UP CLOSE WITH LEE KUAN YEW

His abiding passion, his legacy

Mr Lee was a man dedicated to his life's work that was Singapore. He often said this to me: "时势造英雄" (the times produce their heroes). And he would recount how he was able to assemble talented men and women, and rally a good team to help him accomplish and achieve our national goals.

At a private dinner held in January 2015 to kick-start SG50, he was asked what he thought of Singapore surviving the next 50 years. He replied that given what we have achieved and the foundation that we have built in the last five decades, he was confident that we could endure for the next 50 years; this was possible because we have built a solid foundation for good government.

Mr Lee often had a serious countenance and appeared stern, but the more I interacted with him, the more I got to see the warm and genuine side of him. His dedication to Singapore and her people was singular, equal to his love for his wife and family. He was an exceptional man.

Notes

[1] The Pyramid Club was formed in early 1963 and its first president was Dr Goh Keng Swee. The Club's aims were to provide opportunities and amenities for members to engage in a regular exchange of ideas and information on matters of public interest.

LEE SEOW HIANG
Principal Private Secretary, 2004–2008

❝Of the two, whom should I believe?❞
– Lee Kuan Yew

The first time I met Mr Lee was when he interviewed me for the position of principal private secretary (PPS). He was Minister Mentor then. I didn't know what to expect; but I just told myself that I would be honest with him. That was about the only rule I had in my mind.

The one perfunctory statement from him was, "Have a seat." After that, it was like a two-hour grilling session. Maybe "grilling" is the wrong word, but it was a relentless barrage of questions. I felt like I was being interrogated by a prosecuting attorney. I cannot quite recall the questions that came my way, except that the process took a good two hours. Trust me, there was no lull in those two hours!

Questions about my language skills came up quite early in the interview process as language was an important consideration for Mr Lee. It was later that I discovered from Andrew Tan, the PPS before me, that previous candidates had to write an impromptu essay in Chinese. I was glad he didn't require that of me.

As I was then serving with the Republic of Singapore Air Force, many of his other questions revolved around defence and geopolitics. His questions seemed almost trivial at first, but the manner in which he asked them told you there was nothing flippant about them. Every question had a purpose that only he, with his experience and ability to size up people, could fathom. It was just as well I did not attempt to second-guess him.

At the end of the interview, he just stood up and, for the first time, broke into a smile. He said he would have a word with Teo Chee Hean, then the Defence Minister. The two hours felt almost clinical, but also surreal for me. I felt like I had touched History.

A few months later, on 1 October 2004, I became his PPS. In my four years working for him, I felt like family. I didn't feel like he kept me at arm's length. There was no barrier or constraints that restricted me to see him at certain hours. At least, I assumed there was none, and he never once asked me to do otherwise. I took that to be a clear signal of trust and I honoured it. That privilege also taught me a precious lesson of leadership. He was truly authentic. He was not operating in one mode in public and in another in private. He was true to himself and had nothing to hide. It was a deep privilege to work for him.

Mr and Mrs Lee

During my time as PPS, Mrs Lee had just recovered from her stroke. She wasn't as mobile as before but she could still move quite well and keep up with her swimming. Clearly, Mr Lee had a deep desire to keep her engaged mentally and physically. Mr Lee travelled a lot and made sure that Mrs Lee went along with him.

I saw how they interacted with each other. There was deep love. I could see it in the way they looked at each other and the way they spoke to each other. Sometimes he would end up walking a bit ahead of her and she would call out, "Harry, wait for me!" and he would quickly turn back to make sure she was with him.

I am convinced that one of Mr Lee's secrets to work-life balance was the deep love he shared with Mrs Lee. It was evident to me that on trips where he had Mrs Lee by his side, he would remain energised even if the schedule was hectic and the itinerary long. On trips where Mrs Lee had to stay behind, often because Mr Lee did not want to tire her, I noticed he would invariably look more exhausted, even if the trips were short.

Mr Lee's dedication to Singapore

As Minister Mentor, he was very active. One of his priorities during the four years I was with him was working out how the world had changed after September 11. He was very keen to build bridges to extend our space internationally. There were many trips to countries like the US, Europe, and much of Asia where he had deep personal ties. But he also paid special attention to the Middle East and Russia with whom he was convinced Singapore could benefit from deepening ties.

Domestically, of course, he was always looking out for ideas that could improve Singapore. These ranged from supporting the acceleration of a fibre-optic network in Singapore to exploring upstream energy sources, and being engaged with projects such as Gardens By The Bay. Even though he was not Prime Minister, he was regularly kept updated on the progress of the new downtown gardens at Marina Bay. However, as with all other state matters, he left it to the decision makers to make the final call.

Everything he did was with a view to Singapore's development. He saw things with a very pragmatic eye and he learnt a lot from culture and architecture, and from how people live. He approached everything with a primary view to understanding. And from that understanding, he would always ask, how can it be relevant? Can it be of use?

His appreciation of art, for example, would probably not be for art's sake — it would be for understanding the bigger picture. I am not saying that he didn't like art; I can't affirm this. But I could see that what he observed and studied was driven deeply by his passion for Singapore.

Much has been said about his vision for a green Singapore and Gardens By The Bay. Did this stem from an innate love of plants? I don't know. Mrs Lee definitely loved plants. But Mr Lee clearly saw it as a strategic way of improving the lives of Singaporeans. It's all part of a vision that he never wavered from.

Mr Lee and his late hours

Mr Lee operated best at night, particularly after his evening swim. I suspect that, beyond spending time with Mrs Lee, the other thing that relaxed him was swimming. I know it because some of his best ideas would emerge after he had had his swim. Of course, ideas would come to him throughout the day. But after his daily swim, at about 10 p.m., he would come back to the office and record his ideas or dictate them on tape. So I think he probably regarded the swim not only as a discipline for keeping healthy but also as a form of relaxation that allowed him to think and be creative. The belief that he never stopped thinking about Singapore is true!

Even after he left the office, he would still communicate by email. Being from the military, I wasn't into counting hours; it wasn't something I was conscious of. Moreover, everything he did was purposeful and meaningful, and you knew it would lead to something of importance. As such, when you were with him, you were simply drawn into the issues; you weren't looking at the clock.

He was also extremely clear with his verbal instructions, which perhaps stemmed from his oratorical skills. Often his instructions to me would be recorded on tape, and sent to the office in the red box where Wong Lin Hoe, his private secretary, would transcribe the tapes — and that's how my day would start. This way, he didn't need to come into the office in the mornings.

Initially, I found this process of dictation and transcription a little puzzling and antiquated. Then, I chanced upon a BBC TV documentary which showed an exchange between Roosevelt and Churchill on a train as they strategised their next moves during the Second World War. The two men were thinking and talking, and their secretaries were busy transcribing notes as they spoke. They thought by speaking aloud. Sometimes, I feel our world has been invaded by computers and Microsoft Word. In school, we learn to think by writing (or typing). That is how we are tested. We start generating our ideas by writing, and then we change what we write.

I am amazed that people of Mr Lee's generation started thinking by speaking. Perhaps that is one reason why his speeches were so naturally powerful. I believe if you think by speaking aloud, you learn to develop a natural sense of storytelling in your conversations which, in turn, forms a fundamental building block for building relationships, at home and at work.

A great man with humility

Coming from the military, I am fascinated by the concept of leadership. When I was training with the Americans, the military academics at their Command and War Colleges often debunked the Great Man Theory as outdated. Now, they have new theories such as transformative leadership and distributed leadership.

I thought to myself, these people have not seen a great man! But having said that, Mr Lee, while a great man, also demonstrated the modern theories of distributed leadership. Maybe the problem lies in the theory itself. Maybe it is too reductionist. The Great Man Theory is not just about one man. Mr Lee was certainly the epitome of the Great Man Theory, but not in its idealised form, which is the problem of the myth. The theory is that the great man knows it all. But Mr Lee wasn't like that. He was aware when a shift had happened and there was a need to fill the gaps. He was a great man, one who was willing to learn from others.

He learnt by engaging people. He had this ability to almost charm you. One of my roles as PPS was to calm visitors down before they met him. Some foreign visitors — even world leaders — would be nervous. You could tell by their body language. But once you sat with him for one or two hours, he had this ability to make you feel you could share your life story with him.

Post-September 11, he met experts in Thailand to talk about the issues in the southern Thai provinces. When he went to the Middle East, he spoke to a lot of people to understand what was happening and how the United States was engaged. In one hour, he could update himself on the latest situation. It is hard to learn by reading alone because a book takes two to three years to publish and codifies knowledge that is often behind the curve. He read voraciously of course. But I suspect he learnt much more through meeting people and building a very high level of trust with them. His ability to instil trust in others emanated not from clever talk or manipulation, but from his own integrity, and a reputation that suggested to his guests that he demanded the same integrity of his interlocutors as they shared their views.

He was careful who he listened to. I remember my first overseas trip with him as his PPS. I was probably two weeks into the job. The very night before we flew, when I thought I had everything in control and the itinerary fixed, the phone rang. It was 10 p.m. His voice came across clearly and strongly over the line. Something was brewing in the security situation in the country we were visiting, and he wanted to be briefed in the afternoon after we touched down. End of instruction. Thankfully, I was familiar with — and knew people in — the security sector and within an hour secured two experts who could meet him the next day; one was from academia and the other a security professional from that country.

The meeting took place as planned when we arrived the next day. An hour into the briefing, Mr Lee asked for a break. As he was unfamiliar with the building, I ushered him to the restroom which was some distance away. A few minutes later, he emerged from the restroom. Instead of walking straight back to the briefing room where the experts were waiting, he turned and walked towards me. He looked at me and asked, "Of the two, whom should I believe?" It was a question I least expected then. Off the cuff, I answered him and gave my reasons. But I could tell in his eyes when he asked that he had decided the answer for himself. It was probably a test and, more importantly, a lesson for me — that we should listen and listen DEEPLY.

He was a great man, one who had deep convictions, which many people know, and the humility to match, which many don't. He would challenge your views, but in doing so he was reaching out. Some people say he didn't listen, but I don't agree with that. Of course, you had to have your own convictions when you spoke with him. If you disagreed with him, he would still listen to you if you were able to explain your position. He may not agree or shift his position easily but he would listen. And often in private, he would mull over the differing positions in his mind and test out those positions with others.

Mr Lee's acute sense of people, place and history

He was very sharp in his thinking and extracted a lot of information from mundane things that we often gloss over — CVs, for example. He could tell a lot about a person just from his CV. That's probably one reason why the civil service has this tradition of keeping CVs on file. He would pick out things like your life history, the country you are from, the languages you speak, the schools you went to, the era you grew up in, and the cities you have visited. In all probability, he had been to all those cities and studied how places and time shape a person. So, before you come in to see him, he has already placed you in your context. This also served as a base for him to build a relationship with you.

That he could size up people well was a trait well known. In addition, he could also size up whole communities and nations, often in a week! I saw that gift in him on our overseas trips. He had the advantage of history because he had been to these places over a long span of time, and could spot patterns and anomalies easily. Another factor was his deep relationships with key players. When he met world leaders, he often already knew not just the leader, but the leader's mentor and, in some cases, the mentor's mentor! For younger leaders like Rahul Gandhi, Mr Lee knew his father, grandmother and great grandfather. He had much to offer them, and they knew that. As a result, he created value that made him and Singapore relevant to all these people — and they reciprocated. Much of these interactions were not transactional but the result of deep friendships built over the years.

He would also analyse a country's culture. Culture doesn't change that rapidly, so that gave him another mapping tool. Not many analysts pay enough attention to cultural and social dynamics. And even when they do, too many fall prey to politically correct interpretations of culture, ethnicity, language and religion. What helped Mr Lee immensely was his ability to call the implications of culture and social dynamics as they were. And when he visited a place every year, straightaway he could see what had changed and what had not. And with each visit, he added another layer of knowledge.

I was amazed to see him reading maps. He read maps like a general! I remember him asking for satellite photos of Singapore. I got them from the air force and saw how he read satellite maps and the way he looked at terrain. From the photos, he analysed the potential of the Southern Islands.[1] Mr Lee just knew how to sense a place. Collectively, it added up to a sense of the nation. Because he could do this, he could continue making Singapore relevant.

Mr Lee's sense of humour

He had a sweet tooth and he loved ice cream. Now, all the overseas offices of the Ministry of Foreign Affairs (MFA) had guidelines on his likes and dislikes. On one occasion, he noticed he was not served ice cream. He asked why. Someone from MFA said they had been advised not to do so. He was somewhat annoyed and replied, "Is that so?" and promptly looked at me and asked to look at the guidelines. I did so after the trip. True enough, it was in there. He took the document, and at the part where it said "Do not serve ice cream" he simply added to the line: "…to Mrs Lee only". In that single stroke, he revealed to me his love for Mrs Lee and his wry sense of humour.

Late in 2014, in a light-hearted moment at one of his dinners with business leaders, Mr Ong Beng Seng was going on about how all the top lawyers in Singapore were Indians and how there were very few top Chinese advocates. Mr Lee, who had been quiet all this time, suddenly looked up at him and said, "I never noticed." He was 91 years old and still at his best.

Simplicity of his leadership

Was he a workaholic? By any measure in hours, he would have qualified. I am fortunate to be a late-night person, because that was exactly how he operated. Yet, in a strange way, I had observed such a balance in MM's life that I have learnt the richest lessons of simplicity in leadership while working for him.

For all the vagaries and complexities Mr Lee had to wrestle with, he kept a "simple" life. The simplicity came from the uncluttering of his office to the spartan nature of his home. But it came even more from his uncluttered focus of his life — his single and unceasing focus on making Singapore better. His work was his passion, and his passion became his mission in life.

The simplicity of his leadership was also a result of who he was. One thing that made him great was his ability to lead especially under public scrutiny for over 60 years. In order to do so, one had to be authentic. And he was. After all, one can only put up a show for a while. But with people sizing you up on the national and global stage, if you have not reconciled your public and private personas, I don't believe you can put up a show and be operating at the highest level, and making such an influence for so many years.

The success of his leadership was also found in the small things in life. He was very disciplined, not only in big things but also in the small things that one often overlooks. It was this that gave him strength and a natural endurance. It begins with how he organised his time. How he looked after his health is another mark of discipline and a source of balance. After a big event, when everyone would be winding down for the night, he would go back and exercise, either on the treadmill or in the pool. This discipline can also be seen in how he took it upon himself to learn new things. If something was worth doing, he was determined to work at it. Every week, he kept up with Chinese lessons. The Chinese language was not his natural strength but he was humble enough to want to master it. During my time with him, he asked if an iPad could be devised to display Chinese proverbs, so that he could attach it to the treadmill and memorise a few more words while he was exercising. He was always on the lookout for ways to improve himself until he reached perfection.

Above all, his enduring love for Mrs Lee, and her love for him, provided him with all the replenishing of energy he needed each day. I suspect for all the hours and years that he had put into his "work", MM enjoyed a work-life balance that few of us would ever achieve.

Mr Lee, the boss whom I will miss dearly

I treasure every moment I've had with him. I hesitated greatly when Liew Mun Leong asked me to write for this book. I cherish the access I had to MM and wanted to honour the privacy of that relationship. In any case, words can never do justice to Mr Lee as a man or as a founding father of this nation. But I agreed when Mun Leong convinced me that others should have the privilege of knowing who MM was at a personal level — even if it was only a glimpse. It was a privilege that would be selfish if I had kept it totally private.

My relationship with MM began with the most clinical interview I would probably ever experience in my life. By the time I left my official position as his PPS in 2008, I felt like I was taking care of my own grandfather, a fact that was even more poignant, I guess, because my own father passed away during the time I served Mr Lee.

I last met Mr Lee on 5 January 2015, at a private dinner arranged by his niece Kwa Kim Li. It was a small gathering to celebrate SG50. During the dinner, someone around the table commented that it would be great to have MM witness the National Day Parade in our Jubilee year.

Mr Lee smiled and said, "What for?" He was not being flippant with the remark. I looked at his eyes and could not help feeling that he was totally at peace knowing that he had done all that he had wanted to, and was quietly confident that the Singapore he had helped build was ready for even the era beyond him. Even then, I would miss him dearly.

Notes

[1] The Southern Islands consist of eight major islands off the southern coast of Singapore — Kusu Island, Lazarus Island, Pulau Seringat, Pulau Tekukor, St John's Island, Sentosa and the two Sisters' Islands.

CHEE HONG TAT
Principal Private Secretary, 2008–2011

❝I have not decided to pick you.❞
– Lee Kuan Yew

I was a student when I first met Mr Lee Kuan Yew in 1990, at the Prime Minister's Book Prize award ceremony. I remember he had a special aura about him as he entered the hall. It is hard to describe in words but you knew immediately from his body language, the way he walked, and his mannerisms, that this was a strong leader.

Years later, a friend shared an account about Mr Lee who was attending the funeral of a former Member of Parliament. When he arrived, everyone, including the children, stopped what they were doing and kept a respectful silence. I was told, most likely with some humorous exaggeration, that even the dogs stopped barking!

Learning from the Jedi master
My next meeting with Mr Lee was in 2007 when he interviewed me for the position of principal private secretary (PPS). He was then Minister Mentor. When I walked into his office, he was seated behind his desk. The air-conditioning in the room felt cold, and my nerves probably made it seem even colder. Mr Lee looked rather stern and serious, just as I remembered him from our first encounter in 1990. He pointed to the row of three chairs in front of his desk and said, "Sit down, in the middle seat."

I had expected him to grill me on some policy issue so his opening question threw me off. "What language do you speak at home with your children?" he asked, while glancing at my CV.

At that time, my children were aged seven, four and one. I replied, "Mostly English, although I try to speak some Mandarin to them too. My wife is more comfortable with English and she spends more time with the kids."

He continued with his pointed questions. "What language do you use with your parents, and what language do your children use with your parents?"

Mr Lee always had a keen interest in bilingual education and he wanted to understand how a child's dominant home language could help or hinder one's progress to being effectively bilingual. He did not appear very pleased with my answers when I told him that I use mainly English with my children even though I was fluent in Mandarin and grew up speaking Mandarin with my parents.

We did not discuss policy matters that afternoon, except for a brief exchange on preschool education. He allowed me to express my thoughts even though he disagreed with some of them.

Before the interview ended, Mr Lee asked if I knew what the PPS job entailed. "No," I said, "but I will try to learn as quickly as I can."

He shot back, "I have not decided to pick you."

The interview was over in less than 30 minutes, although it felt much longer than that. A few days later, the Public Service Division informed me that I had been selected.

Looking back, I believe Mr Lee wanted to get a better understanding of me as a person beyond the facts presented in my CV. It was his way of sizing someone up and assessing how the person would respond under pressure.

Mr Lee, the demanding taskmaster

My three years as Mr Lee's PPS from May 2008 to May 2011 offered me the most valuable learning in my career. Working with Mr Lee was certainly no walk in the park. He was a hard taskmaster with exacting standards and little patience for mediocrity. The reward for doing your job well was to be given more work. At times, he put me through difficult situations to see how I would perform under stress and whether I had the resilience to take punches. It was a very demanding and challenging job, but it was also the best job I ever had. A key reason was the chance to observe, work with and learn from Mr Lee at close proximity.

Mr Lee, the generous teacher

He was a generous teacher who gave his disciples ample opportunities to learn as much as possible. One of my memorable experiences was joining Mr Lee for a private lunch at Dr Henry Kissinger's residence in Connecticut, USA. It was very enlightening to hear two intellectual giants discussing geopolitics and debating vigorously on how these developments affected different regions and countries. As the Chinese saying goes, "听君一席话, 胜读十年书" (listening to a wise man is better than studying for ten years). One of my key takeaways was that, for a small country like Singapore to survive and thrive in an increasingly globalised environment, we have no alternative but to stay connected with the world and to have competent leaders who can navigate the international system skilfully and effectively.

Mr Lee was also an excellent communicator. He would use different methods to get his messages across to other world leaders. During a 2009 meeting with then US Secretary of State Hillary Clinton in Washington, D.C., Mr Lee asked me to bring along a copy of Rudyard

Kipling's poem, "The Young British Soldier". He recited the last few lines to Mrs Clinton to reinforce his point on why the US would not succeed in its nation-building efforts in Afghanistan.

"When you're wounded and left on Afghanistan's plains,
And the women come out to cut up what remains,
Just roll to your rifle and blow out your brains
And go to your God like a soldier."

I believe Mr Lee's comments had made an impact on the US government's subsequent decision to withdraw its troops from Afghanistan, and to focus more resources on the Asia Pacific region.

I learnt many other useful things during my time as PPS. Some lessons were picked up indirectly. For instance, just by watching Mr Lee in action, I saw how he tackled tough issues, how he made decisions and how he dealt with different types of people. Other lessons came from direct interactions with Mr Lee while at work, including getting reprimanded and receiving candid feedback from him on areas for improvement. These were part and parcel of the training I received, and I am grateful for the opportunities to improve myself. In the school of hard knocks, one cannot really learn if the skin is too thin or afraid of getting bruised. Just bear with the pain, rub some medicated oil and go back into the boxing ring. Mr Lee allowed his staff to make mistakes, as long as we learn from them and do better next time.

Mr Lee, the supportive and caring boss

Another reason why I enjoyed working with Mr Lee is simply because he was a great boss to work for. While many people are familiar with Mr Lee's reputation as a strong leader, what is less commonly known is that he was also someone who cared for his staff and showed genuine concern for their well-being. This included the team of dedicated officers from Police Security Command, of whom some had served Mr Lee for many years and continued to take good care of him until he passed away.

In addition, Mr Lee was decisive and set clear directions. Once you have gained his trust, he would back you up to get the job done. As PPS, I was willing to take calculated risks and go the extra mile because I knew I could count on his support as long as I did what was right for Singapore.

Mr Lee's commitment to Singapore

One constant that underpinned many of Mr Lee's decisions and actions was his single-minded focus on doing what was good for Singapore. In so doing, he was always putting the country's interests above his personal interests. This was the quality which I admired most in Mr Lee, above all the other attributes which made him an excellent leader. During the battle with the communists in 1961, Mr Lee said:

> "We have learnt one important thing during the last decade: that only those count and matter, who have the strength and courage of their convictions to stick up and stand up for what they believe in, for their people, for their country, regardless of what happens to themselves."[1]

If we did not have leaders like Mr Lee Kuan Yew during those critical periods of our history, Singapore today would be a very different place. While the current and future challenges for Singapore are different, they are no less difficult from what our pioneers faced. We will continue to need leaders who are willing to stand up for what they believe in and do what is right for the country and our people.

On 13 September 2008, Mr Lee was hospitalised for atrial flutter, or abnormal heart rhythm. He had originally been scheduled to have a dialogue that evening with the participants of the Global Philanthropy Forum organised by UBS, the Swiss financial services company. To honour his commitment to UBS and the participants, Mr Lee arranged for then Minister for Foreign Affairs George Yeo to take his place at the dialogue. As he wanted to keep his word and also encourage more successful Singaporeans to give back to society through philanthropy and volunteerism, he went one step further and asked me to set up a video-link from his hospital room to the actual venue, so that he could address the forum before handing over to Mr Yeo. His concern and dedication was greatly appreciated by the organisers and participants.

Two months later, Mr Lee underwent surgery to insert a pacemaker for his atrial flutter. The next day, against the advice of his doctors, he got on a plane to Hong Kong to keep his appointment with former US President Bill Clinton to speak at the inaugural Clinton Global Initiative Asia meeting. Needless to say, it was a very stressful trip for the doctors and me; we later joked that there were a few times we probably experienced some form of atrial flutter ourselves!

However, all the effort was worth it when we saw how Mr Lee projected Singapore internationally with great skill and finesse, and how he effectively engaged different world leaders to increase Singapore's influence and stature even more on the global stage. For a small nation, we have been able to punch way above our weight because we had a capable leader in Mr Lee who was fully committed to Singapore and commanded respect from other leaders, including those from much larger countries.

Even though Mr Lee is no longer with us, he continues to be a role model to me, as I am sure he has been for many others. He inspires me to push myself harder, to go further for Singapore, to focus on doing what is good for the country and to never give up in the face of adversity and danger.

Reflecting on what Singapore has gone through over the past 50 years and the challenges ahead, I feel it is important, especially in the current environment, to have enough committed people who are willing to put national interests above personal interests, and have the courage and conviction to step forward and serve. How well we can do this as a society will be a key factor in determining our collective future for the next 50 years and beyond.

Notes

[1] Lee Kuan Yew, "Realities of revolution" in *Battle for Merger*, Straits Times Press, 2014.

ANTHONY TAN

Principal Private Secretary & Special Assistant, 2011–2014

"Mr Lee's favourite question was 'So?'"

– Anthony Tan

I first met Mr Lee Kuan Yew in early 2011 when he interviewed me for the position of principal private secretary (PPS). Since he retired from Cabinet as Minister Mentor in 2011, the PPS position became known as Special Assistant. I was his last PPS and first Special Assistant.

The prospect of meeting Mr Lee one-on-one was daunting. From the time I was notified of the interview, I started mentally rehearsing answers to questions I thought he might ask me. What do you think of Singapore's bilingual language education policy? What do you make of the current state of Sino-US relations? Why aren't Singaporeans having more children? But it soon dawned on me that the interview wasn't an examination with a set syllabus, because Mr Lee could really ask about anything under the sun! How would he react if I gave silly answers to his questions? It was the biggest interview of my life and I was fast turning into a nervous wreck.

On the big day, I arrived at the Istana ahead of time and in my best suit. I was escorted to a holding area outside his office, where I was told to wait. It must have been the longest 15 minutes of my life, and I felt as anxious as a child on his first visit to the dentist. Before long, Ms Wong Lin Hoe, Mr Lee's long-time private secretary, told me he was ready to see me.

It was a long, lonely walk from his office door to his desk, and I could see him watching me from his seat. I felt he was already assessing me as I moved towards him. I thought to myself: *How many people in this world can say they have personally met the founding father of their nation, the man who made their country what it is today?*

I felt privileged to be there, but it was also a nerve-racking experience. I was worried I would say the wrong thing. I didn't know how to respond to him, or whether it was even appropriate for me to smile. Those who knew Mr Lee later told me it was normal to get the jitters when meeting him for the first time. But, they said, over time I would discover he was as human as the next person. They were right.

Mr Lee interviewed me twice. After the first interview in early 2011, Mr Lee had actually selected another candidate, Ms Sim Ann. But when the general election was called in May 2011, she decided to serve Singapore in a different capacity, not as a civil servant but as a politician.[1] I was then called for a second interview, after which Mr Lee decided that I would replace his incumbent PPS, Chee Hong Tat, who was going to take over the Energy Market Authority.

Mr Lee as talent-spotter

During the first interview, Mr Lee looked at my CV and started off by explaining that whilst he felt both Ann and I were strong candidates, Ann was the better fit. I cannot recall what exactly went through my mind then, but I probably responded with something along the lines of "I understand". I recognised that he had already made a choice, and I was not the selected one. I don't recall being disappointed, given that I had known Ann personally for some years and agreed with his assessment. Ann's command of the Chinese language and her understanding of the Chinese culture was certainly ahead of mine. She had also spent some years working in China, which would certainly be of help to Mr Lee as he continued to build up Singapore-China relations as Minister Mentor.

From this I found him to be an astute judge of character and ability. He had a knack for picking out talent and had a better hit rate than anyone else I know personally in judging who would turn out to be a good fit for the task at hand. Contrary to the general perception that he was elitist and looked only at academic credentials, he actually picked people whom he felt had the mettle and the wherewithal to shape Singapore in their own way. For instance, Mr Sim Kee Boon and Mr J.Y. Pillay who built up Changi Airport and Singapore Airlines respectively from scratch, despite the odds they faced when they were given their tasks. Many of Mr Lee's former PPSs — for example, Minister for Finance Heng Swee Keat, GIC Group President Lim Siong Guan, SPH CEO Alan Chan and Permanent Secretary (Home Affairs) Leo Yip, all of whom were talent-spotted by Mr Lee — have become successful people in their own right and in their respective fields.

Mr Lee, the exacting taskmaster

I started work for Mr Lee on 1 April 2011. As a boss, he had very high standards. His staff was expected to think things through carefully, considering all details and perspectives. As Minister Heng once mentioned, Mr Lee's favourite question was "So?" Such questioning forced me to consider what the key points of an issue were and to think twice about whether my recommendation would address the issue at hand.

At first, I was afraid to ask him questions to make sure I understood his instructions correctly. I was secretly afraid that I would look incompetent in front of him and receive a shelling from the man who was known not to suffer fools. But in not checking with him, I misinterpreted his instructions and had to redo the work. Things got smoother over time as we adjusted to each other. Sometimes, Mr Lee's security officers would help to confirm his instructions as they were by his side when he spoke to me over the phone.

Early on, I learnt that Mr Lee valued the integrity of his staff above all else. When you made a mistake, it was best to be totally honest and come clean, rather than try to fudge the truth. To Mr Lee, to fudge was to be lacking in integrity — a grave charge in his books. I think this had to do with his belief that good governance required leaders with the right values, since they were stewards of the nation and its resources. So, despite knowing he would be disappointed with my mistake, I would admit it, apologise, and try my very best not to repeat it.

Mr Lee also expected his staff to be absolutely punctual. As his former PPSs, we had not realised how much Mr Lee had rubbed off on us until we got together to celebrate his 91st birthday in September 2014. Dinner was at 8 p.m., but by 7.45 p.m., all seven of us who had served him over a span of three decades had already gathered outside the dinner venue, waiting for him to arrive. One of us remarked that Mr Lee had trained us so well that we had all become hyper-punctual. It had nothing to do with us having a fear of repercussions. To Mr Lee, being punctual was a matter of discipline.

Mr Lee, a man of conviction and vision

One of the key lessons I learnt from Mr Lee was the importance of being decisive. While consultation is important, a leader must be the ultimate decision-maker. I also learnt that every leader must always begin with a clear vision of the end game. Every part of Singapore life today came out of his vision of what Singapore could, and should, be.

For example, Mr Lee envisioned a Singapore where the majority of its people would be proficient in at least two languages, for example English and Mandarin, in order to be economically relevant to both the United States and a rising China. Many of our language policies, both in schools and in the mass media, were formulated with this goal in mind.

It is a little-known fact that, for four short months in 1975, Mr Lee was Acting Minister for Education. He believed firmly in the bilingual language education policy and practised what he preached. During my time with him, he took conversational Mandarin lessons daily from a group of teachers, who took turns to meet with him. He would even go back to the office on weekends for lessons. There was no defined syllabus and sometimes he would begin the lesson by discussing current affairs or asking about his teacher's experiences. He would also practise his Mandarin with his security officers, doctors and anyone whom he thought he could practise with.

Mr Lee did not let the fact that he picked up Mandarin relatively late in life stop him from mastering the language. He made up for lost time by working doubly hard at it. When he started using the iPad in 2011 (I think he was one of the first people in Singapore to own one) he quickly learnt how to use tools such as Google Translate and the search engine Baidu. He would also type out new words, ask his teachers for the correct pronunciation and revise them in his free time. In fact, I understand that right up to the day before Mr Lee was admitted to hospital in February 2015, weeks before he died on 23 March, he continued to take Mandarin lessons. He was a real exemplar of the Chinese term "活到老，学到老" (one is never too old to learn).

In 2011, Mr Lee was intrigued by new research that children absorbed language best at the preschool age. He decided to start the

Lee Kuan Yew Fund for Bilingualism[2] to promote bilingualism, with a focus on the young. The aim was to expose children to both English and their mother tongue languages at a young age through new methods at home and in school, to stimulate their interest in two languages. It was a tiring yet rewarding experience to start a greenfield project like this. As his Special Assistant, I had to help him with the fund-raising.

The establishment of the fund was announced at the launch of his book, *My Lifelong Journey: Singapore's Bilingual Journey*, which outlined his 50-year struggle to transform Singapore from a polyglot ex-colony to a united nation where everyone spoke a common language — English — in addition to their mother tongue. The target was an ambitious S$100 million, with S$50 million from donations and S$50 million to be matched by the Singapore government. Besides personally donating S$12 million, Mr Lee actively sought donations from corporations and individuals from all walks of life. He wrote tirelessly to potential donors and hosted thank-you dinners for major donors when the fund-raising activities ended. At Mr Lee's suggestion, I also worked with the People's Association to make it possible for all Singaporeans to donate towards the cause, regardless of the amount. This stemmed from his belief that all Singaporeans could and would support worthy causes, regardless of the amount they contributed. This was important to him. In the end, everyone's hard work paid off and more than S$112 million was raised.

I was also tasked to set up the fund and its governance structure. For this, I received tremendous support from the Ministry of Education. We worked closely with educators and industry players to ensure the money was channelled to the bilingualism cause. One of the initial recipients of the grant was *Thumbs Up! Junior*, a new bilingual newspaper targeted at preschoolers in July 2013. Educators and, most importantly, the young children, responded positively to the paper. Even today, my face lights up when I hear my friends with young children sing its praises.

Over the years, Mr Lee remained invested in the progress of the fund. I regularly requested updates from the fund secretariat and kept Mr Lee apprised of developments. His persistence in seeing a project through, from conception to implementation, to even monitoring its progress, was a real-life lesson on the importance of having a visionary leader who could see the end game from the very beginning.

Many of the things that we take for granted in Singapore today, such as our clean streets and smoke-free environment, are the result of the government's tough stance on littering and smoking, policies which were based on Mr Lee's vision of what Singapore should (and should not) be. When we became independent from the British in 1959 and later separated from Malaysia in 1965, we had to eke out a living for ourselves. Unwilling to allow Singapore to be perpetually reliant on Malaysia for imported water, Mr Lee threw the gauntlet at PUB[3] officials in our early years of independence to find ways for Singapore to become self-sufficient in water. Today, Singapore is on track to become self-sufficient by 2061, when our existing water agreement with Malaysia expires. In fact, the technology we have developed to reclaim used and sea water has even become an export for Singapore.

Mr Lee, the teacher

Perhaps because I joined Mr Lee at a later stage in his career, I was struck by his interest in connecting with the people who accompanied him on his overseas trips. Whenever there was time, he would invite a few of us, including his doctors, to his room, where he would chat with us for an hour or so over a plate of fruits. From these casual sessions, we got to hear his observations of the places he had visited and people he had met on the trip. He was also interested to hear our thoughts about the trip. Behind closed doors and away from the public eye, these were precious moments with our country's founding father, and I was among the lucky few who sat in on these conversations.

I also drew lessons from Mr Lee's conversations with his old friends, many of them international personalities and global leaders. Over three days in May 2012, Mr Lee had an intense and wide-ranging discussion about international affairs with former West Germany Chancellor Helmut Schmidt. This rather unique gathering of two old friends was arranged at the request of Chancellor Schmidt, who wanted to catch up with Mr Lee "for the last time". Key highlights of their conversation were eventually published in Chancellor Schmidt's book, *Ein letzter Besuch: Begegnungen mit der Weltmacht China von Helmut Schmidt*, (*One Last Visit: Encounters with China as a World Power*). Excerpts of the interview were also published as a chapter in Mr Lee's last book, *One Man's View of the World*.

As his Special Assistant, I had the privilege of sitting in the discussions, which were held at the Shangri-la Hotel. Mr Lee had suggested holding the meetings at the hotel, where Chancellor Schmidt was staying, so that it would be more convenient for the latter to get around in his wheelchair. There I was, listening to the views of these two elder statesmen live — in person! Their views on Europe, which was deep in economic crisis in 2012, were insightful and perceptive. Many of Mr Lee's projections of how the Eurozone crisis would pan out continue to play out today.

I have also had the opportunity to sit in on his meetings with other leading personalities. These included his friends such as former US Secretaries of State Dr Henry Kissinger and Mr George Shultz; world leaders like Chinese President Xi Jinping, US Vice President Joe Biden; and business leaders such as Mr Li Ka-shing and Mr Robert Kuok. Mr Lee's strong personal ties with these global leaders was a key reason why Singapore enjoys political and economic linkages to many countries today. He saw the importance of building up a network of fans and friends for a small city-state like Singapore, and did so by developing enduring friendships based on mutual admiration, trust and respect. Mr Lee was Singapore's first, and most successful, global statesman.

Mr Lee's humility

When Singapore Press Holdings was preparing to publish Mr Lee's book on global affairs in mid-2013, the editorial team proposed titling it "Lee Kuan Yew: My View of the World". But he quickly insisted that he could not profess to know everything about world matters and that he did not want to portray himself as having the only definitive view. He changed the title to "Lee Kuan Yew: One Man's View of the World".

To me, this showed Mr Lee's humility and awareness of his own limitations. Mr Lee, humble? Hardly, some people would say. But I think Mr Lee was successful precisely because he had the humility to listen to those he thought he could learn from, weave in his own perspective gleaned from years of experience, and then use those lessons to Singapore's advantage.

Mr Lee and his active lifestyle

In his later years, Mr Lee's typical day started off with breakfast at home, usually past 10 a.m. He was known to work late into the night and was therefore a late riser. After breakfast, he would read the newspapers in his study and then take a brisk walk on the treadmill in his exercise room for about 15 minutes. Then he read some more before taking a break. In the afternoon, he would go to his office at the Istana, where he would respond to emails and letters. Some of these were from Singaporeans and foreigners living in or visiting Singapore who had written to thank Mr Lee for his contributions to building the country. The volume of such mail usually peaked in the months of August (National Day) and September (his birthday) each year. Late afternoons were set aside for his Mandarin lessons. Occasionally, family, friends or acquaintances would arrange to meet him for dinner.

My day, however, started before he stepped into the office. In fact, it began the moment his famous red box arrived at the office in the morning; this is the official document bag containing his instructions, from the night before, on what he wanted us to look into that day. Often, it was an instruction to check some facts for a speech or article he was writing, or a matter that required the attention of the National Parks Board or some other government agency. I always acted upon his instructions immediately so that I could update him when he arrived in the office later in the day. I did not think that he expected less from his Special Assistant in this regard.

Although he was no longer in Cabinet and did not actively comment on local or global affairs, Mr Lee regularly contributed articles to *Forbes* to share his views — and to keep his mind active. He was also Senior Advisor to sovereign wealth fund GIC, a job he took seriously. On occasion, he would ask to meet young analysts to get a pulse of the organisation and a sense of staff morale. In November 2011, when he travelled to Washington to receive the Ford's Theatre Lincoln Medal,[4] he made it a point to visit the GIC New York office and interact with the staff. These young GIC staff were all thrilled to have the opporturnity to meet with Mr Lee, and those who had the chance to sit in the dialogues with him always came away delighted that they had learnt something in the process.

Much has been said about Mr Lee's commitment to greening Singapore. In his later years, I think he enjoyed seeing the fruits of his labour. Once in a while, he would take walks in various parks, from those in housing estates like the new Punggol Waterway Park to landmarks such as Gardens By The Bay and the Botanic Gardens. He continued to take an interest in the government's greening plans, often asking for updates from the National Parks Board, and giving his views — usually a word of praise. Right until the last few months of my term as Mr Lee's Special Assistant, which ended in October 2014, he would ask why a certain tree had been chopped down or tell me of a specific tree he had spotted that did not look healthy and that needed attention to ensure it did not wither away.

Like many Singaporeans, Mr Lee enjoyed nature, food and reading. He also loved his late wife of 63 years, Madam Kwa Geok Choo, deeply. I never met her, but even in her death she continued to be present in his life. He displayed photographs of her in his office and dedicated the books he wrote to her.

Mr Lee and letting go

Gradually, as Mr Lee approached his late eighties and entered his nineties, he kept a lower profile as he had become physically weaker. However, if he made a commitment, he would muster all his strength to keep his word.

The annual National Day Parade was one such commitment. It was an event when Singaporeans looked forward to seeing their country's founding father. The loudest cheers were always reserved for him when he made his appearance at Singapore's biggest birthday party. He did his utmost not to disappoint them, even staying behind to mingle with those invited to the post-parade reception.

I remember the two-and-a-half-week trip we made together at the end of 2011 to Turkey and France, and Washington, D.C. and New York in the United States. We had been travelling for almost two weeks when we arrived in Washington, D.C., where Mr Lee was to receive the Lincoln Medal. It was a tiring trip for a 30-something-year-old like me, what more for an 88-year-old! But at the awards ceremony, Mr Lee persevered. He psyched himself up and was fully engaged throughout the evening where he gave an address and socialised with guests. It was mind over matter.

But Mr Lee had always accepted that age had caught up with him. This he dealt with in a pragmatic fashion. Eventually, he stopped travelling and held on only to those duties that were necessary for Singapore. He left the running of the country to its present leaders.

Mr Lee and me

I was one of few who had regular access to Mr Lee after he stepped down from Cabinet. Over the three years I worked for him, he transformed from a towering presence and an intimidating boss to a person I deeply respected and admired. I could relate to him, for in him I saw my ageing parents who also continued to worry about their family despite their own growing frailty. What was different was that Mr Lee continued to worry over one big child — Singapore.

I think what set Mr Lee apart from the rest of us was his self-discipline, his ability to stay the course, his sheer resilience and his love for his country. He was driven by a mission to build a successful Singapore, and in this he never wavered.

Of course, history is always debated by people with different worldviews. Some people would say Mr Lee was lucky. But in reality his actions and decisions were always very consistent. I have seen this with my own eyes. Mr Lee's children have said that he was not a demonstrative father. He was the same as a boss, sparing in his praise whilst being very exacting in his expectations of his staff. But he took very good care of his staff, regardless of their rank. If he should learn of someone in his staff facing problems, he would try to help them to the best of his ability. This is the most significant lesson I learnt from him. It is something that I have been endeavouring to emulate with my colleagues. This is also how I will remember him — a dedicated father, a caring boss and an unwavering patriot.

Notes

1 Ms Sim Ann was previously Senior Parliamentary Secretary at the Ministry of Education and Ministry of Law. She is currently Senior Minister of State at the Ministry of Finance and Ministry of Culture, Community and Youth, as well as Deputy Government Whip.

2 The Lee Kuan Yew Fund for Bilingualism was set up on 28 November 2011 to supplement efforts by the Ministry of Education in the teaching and learning of English and the mother tongue languages.

3 Public Utilities Board.

4 The Lincoln Medal recognises "individuals who, through their body of work, accomplishments or personal attributes, exemplify the lasting legacy and mettle of character embodied by ... President Abraham Lincoln". Source: www.fordstheatre.org

LIM TECK KIAT

Special Assistant to Mr Lee, 2014–2015

❝I have been busy all my life and will leave it to others to be busy with the [SG50] celebrations instead.**❞**

– Lee Kuan Yew

I first met Mr Lee up close in April 2009 when he was Minister Mentor. I was seated next to Mr Lee, staffing a meeting between him and an elderly Chinese businessman. They were old friends and they discussed a variety of topics in Chinese. At one point, Mr Lee said that his focus was to consolidate Singapore's position in the world so that Singaporeans would have a better future. He said he had been criticised for being authoritarian but he wasn't bothered about such criticisms and would stick to his convictions. Later in the meeting, the businessman asked Mr Lee about his formula for active ageing. Mr Lee replied that one needed to exercise regularly, eat in moderation and sleep well. My first encounter with Mr Lee was brief. But what he said was thought-provoking and left a deep impression on me.

I never expected that, some five years later, I would have the privilege to directly serve Mr Lee and witness firsthand how he lived out what he said at that meeting. Mr Lee interviewed me for his special assistant position in August 2014. He asked for my views on China and the US, immediately impressing upon me the importance of geopolitics and their implications for Singapore. He asked me how proficient I was in English and Chinese, underscoring the value he placed on being bilingual.

Working with Mr Lee, I saw clearly how his thoughts constantly centred on making Singapore better. In his meetings with foreign dignitaries, he would get their perspectives on international developments, ask very pointed questions and subsequently process what all that information meant for Singapore.

Mr Lee was equally passionate about domestic issues. For example, it was common knowledge that one of his preoccupations was the development of Singapore into a garden city. What many people do not know was that he asked to receive regular updates from NParks and other agencies on their latest developments in greening Singapore. Whenever he saw trees dying along the route he travelled, he would want to know why. Mr Lee never missed the annual Tanjong Pagar tree planting ceremony even when he was not feeling well, again demonstrating his unwavering commitment to green developments in Singapore.

Mr Lee, the ceaseless learner

Mr Lee's work ethic was instructive too. I saw firsthand how he worked hard even though he was 91 years old. Mr Lee would read his papers and clear his emails on a daily basis.

When he came across interesting articles that he did not fully understand, he would make it a point to find out more. I recall answering his queries on green energy and oil dependency and details like where the town of Vinalhaven was located.

He embodied continuous learning and took Chinese lessons six days a week. In fact, one of Mr Lee's last appointments before he was admitted to hospital in February 2015 was with his Chinese tutor. When Mr Lee came across new Chinese words and idioms, he would take the effort to clarify with his staff what those words and idioms meant, increasing his vocabulary bank in the process and subsequently surprising us when he used the new words.

Mr Lee sometimes burnt his weekends to complete his work. On one of the last weekends before he was hospitalised, he was still running through every single word of a new chapter to his book, making thoughtful edits to improve it.

I believe it was because of Mr Lee's inquisitive mind and his breadth of knowledge that *Forbes* magazine continued to ask him to contribute articles on a quarterly basis. Indeed, Mr Lee wrote wide-ranging yet incisive articles, covering topics from politics to transport accidents to Ebola.

The softer Mr Lee

Outside of work, I saw a softer side of Mr Lee that he was not publicly known for. In the few months that I served him, he asked me about my children and how they were coping with their schoolwork. He also often reminded me how fortunate I was to live in stable and affluent times, leaving me with the message not to take things for granted but to continue to work hard and strive for even better days ahead.

He also smiled and shared jokes in our conversations. He himself would tell a few jokes! I recall a particular exchange where a friend said to Mr Lee that he must be very busy with the SG50 celebrations. Mr Lee quipped, "I have been busy all my life and will leave it to others to be busy with the celebrations instead."

Mr Lee kept to a daily treadmill exercise routine. He was most considerate; he said that he would want to keep healthy, lest his poor health became a burden to others.

If I were to summarise my thoughts about Mr Lee and what he stood for, it would be his immense and steadfast dedication to Singapore and the virtues of diligence and care-for-others that he embodied. Mr Lee's devotion to Singapore has inspired me and my colleagues to always put in our best to serve Singapore and Singaporeans. Mr Lee's legacy shall live on in a successful, cohesive and vibrant Singapore.